JESUS AND THE SON OF MAN

JESUS
AND THE
SON OF MAN

By
A. J. B. HIGGINS, Ph.D.

*Senior Lecturer in New Testament Language
and Literature,
University of Leeds, England*

FORTRESS PRESS
PHILADELPHIA

First published 1964

© 1964 A. J. B. HIGGINS

Library of Congress Catalog Card Number 65-21083

PRINTED IN GREAT BRITAIN

Contents

τίς ἐστιν οὗτος ὁ υἱὸς τοῦ ἀνθρώπου; (John 12: 34)

PREFACE

IF IT IS important to understand early Christian beliefs about Jesus as recorded in the New Testament, it is even more important to attempt to discover how far these beliefs may have been derived from Jesus' own teaching, and consequently to what extent they were justified. It is not enough to accept the fact that the New Testament writings, including the gospels, reveal the beliefs about Jesus of the first generations of Christians, so that we can be united with them in common faith. The gospels also profess to record the teaching of Jesus himself and the claims that he made.

Within its own limits the present work is an attempt to trace the connection between early Christian belief about Jesus and Jesus' own teaching. Nowhere is this problem more difficult than in regard to the title and concept "Son of man". Despite all that has been written, and continues to be written, on the subject,[1] there is room for a re-examination of the problem of the connection between the primitive Son of man Christology and the use and meaning of the title in Jesus' own teaching. The present study is therefore both exegetical and theological. The significance of Jesus' use of the Son of man concept lies in the soteriological connection he saw between his life of humiliation and final rejection, degradation and sacrificial death, and his future activity characterized as that of the "Son of man". The development of the Son of man Christology in the early church may be described as "retrogressive"—in the sense that, beginning with the adaptation of current Jewish eschatological beliefs, it came retrospectively to interpret first the passion and resurrection, and then the life and ministry of Jesus, in terms of the Son of man.

My contribution, "Son of Man-*Forschung* since 'The Teaching of Jesus' ", to the memorial volume for Professor T. W. Manson edited by me (*New Testament Essays*, 1959), gives some idea of the wide variety of views on different aspects of the question.

[1] F. Hahn, *Christologische Hoheitstitel (Forschungen zur Religion und Literatur des Alten und Neuen Testamentes* 83, 1963) appeared too late for me to use.

Since that paper may serve as *prolegomena* to the present work, much of the literature referred to there is not mentioned here.

Chapters 6 and 7 contain (with some modifications) the material of my Franz Delitzsch Lectures for 1961 given in the University of Münster and to be published in Germany under the title *Menschensohn-Studien*. I am grateful to Professor K. H. Rengstorf, Director of the Institutum Judaicum Delitzschianum, and to Dr. Cecil Northcott, editorial secretary of the Lutterworth Press, for kindly agreeing to the inclusion of this material.

For the text and (with a few exceptions) the critical apparatus of the Greek New Testament I have used the excellent edition prepared by Professor G. D. Kilpatrick to mark the 150th anniversary of the British and Foreign Bible Society (1958).

Biblical quotations are based on the *Revised Standard Version of the Bible* copyrighted in 1946 and 1952 by the Division of Christian Education of the National Council of the Churches of Christ in the U.S.A., but with my own numerous modifications as occasion required.

I am indebted to my wife and daughter for assistance in compiling the indexes.

December 1963

A. J. B. HIGGINS

ABBREVIATIONS (I)

BARRETT, *John*	C. K. Barrett, *The Gospel according to St John* (1955).
BLACK, *Aramaic Approach*	M. Black, *An Aramaic Approach to the Gospels and Acts*[2] (1954).
BULTMANN, *Tradition*	R. Bultmann, *Die Geschichte der synoptischen Tradition*[4] (1958)
BULTMANN, *Theology*	R. Bultmann, *Theology of the New Testament*, i (1952), ii (1955).
CULLMANN, *Christology*	O. Cullmann, *The Christology of the New Testament* (1959).
DODD, *Scriptures*	C. H. Dodd, *According to the Scriptures* (1952).
DODD, *Interpretation*	C. H. Dodd, *The Interpretation of the Fourth Gospel* (1953).
FULLER	R. H. Fuller, *The Mission and Achievement of Jesus* (1954).
KÜMMEL	W. G. Kümmel, *Promise and Fulfilment* (1957).
MANSON, *Teaching*	T. W. Manson, *The Teaching of Jesus*[2] (1935).
MANSON, *Sayings*	T. W. Manson, *The Sayings of Jesus* (1949).
MANSON, *Son of Man*	T. W. Manson, "The Son of Man in Daniel, Enoch and the Gospels", *Studies in the Gospels and Epistles*, ed. M. Black (1962), 123–45.
MOWINCKEL	S. Mowinckel, *He That Cometh* (1956).
PERCY	E. Percy, *Die Botschaft Jesu* (1953).
SCHULZ	S. Schulz, *Untersuchungen zur Menschensohn-Christologie im Johannesevangelium* (1957).
SCHWEIZER, *Menschensohn*	E. Schweizer, "Der Menschensohn", ZNW 50 (1959), 185–209.
SCHWEIZER, *Lordship*	E. Schweizer, *Lordship and Discipleship* (1960).
SJÖBERG	E. Sjöberg, *Der verborgene Menschensohn in den Evangelien* (1955).

TAYLOR, *Mark*	V. Taylor, *The Gospel according to St. Mark* (1952).
THÜSING	W. Thüsing, *Die Erhöhung und Verherrlichung Jesu im Johannesevangelium* (1960).
TÖDT	H. E. Tödt, *Der Menschensohn in der synoptischen Überlieferung* (1959).
VIELHAUER	P. Vielhauer, "Gottesreich und Menschensohn in der Verkündigung Jesu", *Festschrift für Günther Dehn*, ed. W. Schneemelcher (1957), 51–79.

ABBREVIATIONS (II)

NTE	*New Testament Essays: studies in memory of T. W. Manson*, ed. A. J. B. Higgins (1959).
RGG³	*Die Religion in Geschichte und Gegenwart³* (1957ff.).
SB	H. L. Strack and P. Billerbeck, *Kommentar zum Neuen Testament aus Talmud und Midrasch* (1922–28).
TWNT	*Theologisches Wörterbuch zum Neuen Testament*, ed.† G. Kittel and G. Friedrich (1933ff.).

CJT	*Canadian Journal of Theology* 6 (1960), 200–210: A. J. B. Higgins, "The Old Testament and Some Aspects of New Testament Christology".
ET	*Expository Times.*
JBL	*Journal of Biblical Literature.*
JR	*Journal of Religion.*
JTS	*Journal of Theological Studies.*
NTS	*New Testament Studies.*
TLZ	*Theologische Literaturzeitung.*
ZNW	*Zeitschrift für die neutestamentliche Wissenschaft.*

LXX	Septuagint
NEB	The New English Bible
RSV	Revised Standard Version

Chapter 1

INTRODUCTION

1. Preliminary Considerations

It is not necessary to salvation to believe that Jesus called himself the Son of man. This belief has never been a criterion of orthodoxy. It is otherwise with his Sonship. The divine Sonship of Jesus is an established article of belief in the New Testament period, and since. "I believe . . . in one Lord Jesus Christ, the only-begotten Son of God." The author of 1 John regards as the very mark of Antichrist the denial of Jesus Christ as the incarnate Son of God. The question whether Jesus explicitly and in so many words called himself the Son or the Son of God has received different answers. But his references to the Father are of such a kind as to prove that he believed himself to be God's Son in a special and unique way. His sense of Sonship is the presupposition of his teaching. That teaching, therefore, contains an implicit Son of God Christology. The same thing applies to the Servant concept. Despite his reluctance to apply to himself names and titles, the ideal of the vicarious suffering of the Servant of the Lord seems to have formed the conscious background of his life on earth. The problem confronting the early believers was that of finding a connection between the humble life, rejection, and death of Jesus, and the glory of the exalted Son of man of which he had spoken. They solved this problem by making the Son of man concept the chain which linked together in a logical sequence the Lord's life among men of humiliation and renunciation, his shameful death on the cross and his resurrection, and his subsequent exaltation to incomparable majesty at the right hand of God.

Yet the Son of man Christology, no less than the Christologies of the Son of God and the Servant, though with important differences, is ultimately rooted in the teaching of Jesus himself. It seems to me quite certain that Jesus did speak about the Son

13

of man. We learn from the gospels that after his resurrection the early church soon came to think of Jesus as the Son of man in all three aspects, in his earthly life, in his death and resurrection, and in his heavenly glory. It is the purpose of this book to re-examine the relationship between Jesus' own teaching about the Son of man and the reinterpretation of this aspect of his teaching on the part of the early communities.

All this obviously involves acceptance of the quest of the historical Jesus as a feasible and rational undertaking. If it is not, we might as well give up the pretence of regarding the gospels as providing us with anything more than information about the beliefs of the first Christian generation or so. There is, however, a marked inclination to renew the quest, with the advantage that it is now realized that "the Jesus of history" is not a figure to be discovered by the removal of the encrustments of Christian doctrine, but is the same Jesus who is proclaimed in the New Testament. The Jesus who preached the good news of the kingdom of God and the Jesus who became the subject of the post-resurrection church's own proclamation are identical.

This having been said, the fact remains that scholars of equal distinction and sharing the same devotion to Jesus Christ as Lord and Saviour have reached divergent conclusions from the study of the same sacred text. The explanation is partly the inevitable element of subjectivity involved in making exegetical distinctions between the authentic and the secondary, especially in regard to the sayings attributed to Jesus. Nowhere is this more evident than in the Son of man sayings studied in this book. I make no claim myself to complete emancipation from subjectivity in this matter. But, for what they are worth, the conclusions have been reached by an independent and, I hope, unprejudiced study of the available materials. The suggestions in section 4 of this chapter are no exception. They do not form part of a preconceived hypothesis, but are prompted by the findings in the following chapters. At a deeper level the explanation is that the words of Jesus indirectly reflect rather than directly describe his convictions about himself and his mission. This is the basis of the often noticed but not always properly understood secrecy or hiddenness which appears to pervade the synoptic presentations of his Messiahship.

It is not to be expected that the suggestions put forward in the following pages and chapters will be any more successful in winning acceptance than previous studies of this complex and fascinating subject. The mystery of Jesus is so profound that full comprehension will ever elude us.

2. *Jewish Antecedents*

I do not propose to spend time discussing the Son of man concept in Judaism[1] except in so far as it is strictly relevant to the New Testament problem.

It is also possible to state quite summarily my views on Dan. 7 and the Similitudes of Enoch (1 En. 37–71), reserving details for the exegesis of the relevant New Testament texts. I follow E. Sjöberg[2] and Mowinckel in accepting the Son of man passages in the Similitudes as Jewish, and as valuable evidence for belief in certain circles in the time of Jesus in the Son of man as a messianic heavenly judge and ruler, and deliverer of the righteous from their oppressors. That this belief is much older is shown by Dan. 7, which presents a corporate interpretation ("the saints of the Most High") of the "one like a son of man".[3] It is this idea of the apocalyptic Son of man which Jesus adapted in his teaching.

Another view, represented earlier by E. A. Abbott[4] and D. Völter,[5] and still not without supporters, is that the primary source of Jesus' use of the term is the book of Ezekiel, in which the prophet is very frequently addressed by God as "son of man" (*ben-'ādhām*). This means that the title is taken to be Jesus' own self-designation, and to be mainly prophetic in

---

[1] See now especially Mowinckel 346–444. For some views on the origin of the concept see my paper "Son of Man-*Forschung* since 'The Teaching of Jesus'" in NTE 121f. Cf. also J. A. Emerton, "The Origin of the Son of Man Imagery", JTS, n.s. 9 (1958), 225–42; J. Muilenburg, "The Son of Man in Daniel and the Ethiopic Apocalypse of Enoch", JBL 79 (1960), 197–209; O. Moe, "Der Menschensohn und der Urmensch", *Studia Theologica* 14 (1960), 119–29; J. Morgenstern, "The 'Son of Man' of Daniel 7: 13f. A new interpretation", JBL 80 (1961), 65–77; J. Coppens and L. Dequeker, *Le Fils de l'homme et les Saints du Très-Haut en Daniel, VII, dans les Apocryphes et dans le Nouveau Testament*[2] (*Analecta Lovaniensia Biblica et Orientalia*, ser. III, fasc. 23, 1961).

[2] *Der Menschensohn im äthiopischen Henochbuch* (1946).

[3] In 2 Esdras 13 the Man who rises from the sea and flies with the clouds of heaven is another form of the same idea.

[4] *The Son of Man* (1910).

[5] *Die Menschensohn-Frage neu untersucht* (1916).

content.[1] Our studies will show that this is an impossible view. In any case the Ezekielic hypothesis cannot explain the necessity of suffering in the predictions of the Son of man's passion even unto death, nor the august dignity of the Son of man in sayings portraying him as the heavenly witness or judge to whom Jesus appeared to point as if to a figure distinct from himself.[2]

3. The Philological Question[3]

It is established that in the older Palestinian Aramaic *bar nāš* means "a man" and *bar nāšâ* "the man".[4] Indeed, we do not have to look further for a first proof of this than Dan. 7: 13, "one like a son of man" (*kᵉbhar 'ᵉnāš*). This, however, is not perhaps the common everyday expression, but is reserved for some kind of emphasis.[5] This could conceivably account for Jesus' use of the phrase *bar nāšâ*, the Man, as a sort of title.

The language of the Similitudes of Enoch is still disputed. Even if they were originally written not in Aramaic but in Hebrew,[6] this would not mean that Jesus did not employ the

---

[1] Cf. Pierson Parker, "The Meaning of 'Son of Man'", JBL 60 (1941), 151–57; W. A. Curtis, *Jesus Christ the Teacher* (1943); G. S. Duncan, *Jesus, Son of Man* (1947); W. Eichrodt, "Zum Problem des Menschensohnes", *Evangelische Theologie* 19 (1959), 1–3.

[2] Ezekiel's sufferings (cf. Eichrodt, op. cit.) are on a totally different plane; cf. Fuller 99–102; Manson, *Son of Man* 124f.; Percy 256f. C. S. C. Williams, *The Acts of the Apostles* (1957), 112, wrote: "There can be little doubt that Jesus used this title 'Son of Man' of Himself in the Psalmist's sense of the phrase and Ezekiel's and in the apocalyptic sense of Daniel vii, and even perhaps in the sense in which it is found in the *Similitudes of Enoch*." But it is very difficult to imagine how Jesus could have combined all these ideas in a unitary conception of the Son of man. The reference to the Psalmist is presumably to Pss. 8: 4 and 80: 17. But Jesus does not use these Psalms. Cf. Dodd, *Scriptures* 32–34, 108, 117. Ps. 8 is quoted as a testimony in Heb. 2: 6–8. Ps. 80, although nowhere quoted in the New Testament, may be, Dodd suggests, the source of the vine metaphor in John 15, which implies the Son of man concept, since in the Psalm the vine (verse 14) is the son of man and the man of God's right hand (Dodd, ibid., 102; *Interpretation* 411). But none of this is to be found in Jesus' recorded sayings, and I doubt, with C. F. D. Moule (*Novum Testamentum* 5 (1962), 183, n. 1), whether the Son of man is present in John 15 at all.

[3] Cf. G. Dalman, *The Words of Jesus* (1902), 234–41; Sjöberg, op. cit., 40ff.; M. Goguel, *Jésus* (1950), 246f.; Mowinckel 346f.; Cullmann, *Christology* 138f.; Coppens, op. cit., 100f.

[4] Cf. J. Bowman, ET 59 (1948), 286.

[5] Mowinckel 347; but cf. Black, *Aramaic Approach* 250, n. 2.

[6] So R. H. Charles, *The Book of Enoch translated*, etc.[2] (1912), lxiff.

Aramaic expression, for it is much more likely that he drew upon current Son of man beliefs in the common Aramaic speech than that he had direct recourse to the Similitudes, assuming that they had been written by his time. If he did borrow from current ideas there is again no obstacle in the way of supposing that he used "Son of man" as a title.

Theoretically Jesus could have used the first person singular pronoun in the sayings of groups A or B, but hardly in those of group C.[1] It has often been suggested, especially in regard to sayings in the first category, that Jesus used "I", and that this was replaced by "Son of man". Alternatively, ὁ υἱὸς τοῦ ἀνθρώπου has been taken to be a mistranslation of bar nāšâ', which could mean not only Son of man, but also in its indeterminate form "a man" in the sense of "I", of a speaker referring to himself. M. Black[2] adduces an example from *Bereshith Rabbah* 7 of the use of the Aramaic bar nāš by a speaker referring to himself, and with the force of "I". "A man (bar-nash) who has spoken a word according to Torah to be punished. Strange, indeed!..." But this seems as natural a mode of speech as in Greek (2 Cor. 12: 2, "I know a man", i.e., "myself"), and even in English. This occasional Aramaic usage is rather slight support for Jesus' reported frequent employment of the expression. Where else do we hear of anyone applying it to himself as often as he is recorded as having done? Of course, allowance must be made for Jesus' originality in the use of what he borrowed. But in addition, the Greek ὁ υἱὸς τοῦ ἀνθρώπου would seem to presuppose the definite Aramaic form bar nāšâ', *the* Son of man or the Man.[3]

The most likely explanation, therefore, is that Jesus employed the definite form as a title.

4. The improbability of Jesus having called himself the Son of man

(a) His avoidance of titles

According to the synoptics Jesus avoided the use of titles and discouraged their application to himself.[4]

---

[1] For this classification of the sayings see the beginning of chapter 2.
[2] ET 60 (1948), 35, n. 1; *Aramaic Approach* 250, n. 2.
[3] Cf. Manson, *Teaching* 212f., 217f.
[4] Cf. E. Schweizer, *Church Order in the New Testament* (1961), 2c.

Son of David

That Jesus was of Davidic descent is a conviction firmly embedded in the tradition from a very early date.[1] There seems no good reason to deny either the fact of his Davidic lineage or the authenticity of his reference to the Messiah as a descendant of David.

"And Jesus answered and said, as he taught in the temple, How do the scribes say that the Messiah is the son of David? David himself said in the Holy Spirit,

> The Lord said to my Lord, Sit at my right hand
> Until I put thine enemies under thy feet.

David himself calls him Lord, and how is he his son?"[2]

Jesus points out the inadequacy of current views about Messiahship, which depends on higher considerations than Davidic ancestry. Although he does not openly claim such ancestry for himself, neither does he repudiate or deny it. It is a secondary matter.

Messiah

The predominant belief was that the Messiah would be a Davidic ruler.[3] The political associations of the term account for Jesus' reserve when it was applied to him by Peter at Caesarea Philippi, even amounting to prohibition of its use.[4]

Son of God

The Son of God Christology arose not from Jesus' use of the titles Son of God or the Son as a self-designation, but from his consciousness of a unique filial relationship to God as Father. Jesus never used either of these titles.[5]

Jesus' non-use of these titles is *prima facie* a strong argument

---

[1] Mark 10: 47f. (parr. Matt. 20: 30f.; Luke 18: 38f.); Matt. 1: 1; 9: 27; 12: 23; 15: 22; 21: 9, 15; Acts 13: 22f.; Rom. 1: 3; 2 Tim. 2: 8; Rev. 3: 7; 5: 5; 22: 15.

[2] On the authenticity of Jesus' quotation of Ps. 110: 1, widely used in the early church, see my remarks in CJT.

[3] Cf. Pss. Sol. 17: 23; John 7: 42 (Mic. 5: 2).

[4] Mark 8: 29 parr. That immediately afterwards Jesus foretold the fate that awaited him we may well believe, but the form of the prediction is widely held to be secondary.

[5] See below, p. 196 n. 2.

against his having called himself the Son of man, but needs the support of other considerations.

(b) *Son of man sayings and I-sayings*

If the title Son of man was so important to Jesus, why did he not use it consistently in reference to his ministry instead of using the first person singular pronoun like other men, as he is in fact reported to have done in the overwhelming majority of cases? In this respect I believe the form of his teaching has been correctly transmitted. The exceptions (the sayings in group A) are not haphazard exceptions to accurate transmission caused by mistranslation by "Son of man" of the Aramaic *bar nāšâ* used as an equivalent of "I", but are special cases to be quite differently explained.

(c) *The psychological question*[1]

The evidence of the synoptics does not exclude the possibility that Jesus believed himself to be the Messiah. But if Mark 14: 62 is an authentic utterance of his, two conclusions follow. Firstly, it was only when finally pressed for a reply by the high priest's demand, "Are you the Messiah?" that he admitted it, or at least did not deny it.[2] Secondly, he affirmed that it was not by his being the (Davidic) Messiah of popular expectation that the scripture (Ps. 110: 1) would be fulfilled, but by the session and coming of the Son of man.[3] This enormously increases the psychological difficulties involved in supposing that he thought himself to be the Son of man. How could a sane man have entertained such thoughts of himself? In fact, it seems most probable that Jesus neither referred to the Son of man *as an objective existent being* distinct from himself, nor therefore identified himself with such a figure. Nevertheless, I believe that he did see some kind of connection between himself and the Son of man *concept*—an interpretation which is more credible than

---

[1] See the treatment by J. Knox, *The Death of Christ* (1959), 52–77.

[2] Mark 14: 62, σὺ εἶπας ὅτι Θ f13 *pc* Or.

[3] Cf. Knox, op. cit., 57: "His conception of God's agent in the coming crisis, if he had a conception of this kind at all, was not the traditional one of the human being whom God would choose, endow, and exalt to the office of Messiah, whether conceived of in kingly, priestly, or prophetic terms, or in terms of some combination of these conceptions, but rather took the form of a supernatural being who at the appointed time would appear on the clouds of heaven."

19

any other known to me, and which removes the psychological difficulties to which reference has been made.

5. Some recent views[1]

I confine myself to brief statements of the more outstanding recent contributions to the debate. Detailed criticism is not necessary here because the conclusions to be drawn from our study, if correct, render all these solutions untenable.

(a) The collective interpretation of the Son of Man

The leading name here is that of T. W. Manson.[2] Although he came to allow more weight to the Hebrew idea of oscillation between the individual and the group which often results in "a tendency to see the corporate personality as embodied in a person",[3] this did not affect his main thesis that, as in Dan. 7, so in the gospels the Son of man is a corporate conception. The difficulties of this interpretation seem to me insuperable. No Son of man saying requires this collective meaning, and it is hard to see how the disciples could have understood their Master if he had applied this apocalyptic term in the corporate sense to themselves with him as leader here upon earth.[4]

(b) The suffering Son of man

The protagonists of the view that Jesus created a new synthesis of the Suffering Servant in Deutero-Isaiah and the apocalyptic Son of man are too numerous to mention. There are others, however, who maintain that this synthesis had already previously been made, either in the Old Testament itself,[5] or

---

[1] On various aspects of the problem and for fuller details of some of the material mentioned in what follows, see my paper in NTE 119–35.

[2] *Teaching* 211ff., 263ff.; *Son of Man; The Servant-Messiah* (1953), 72–74; cf. also C. J. Cadoux, *The Historic Mission of Jesus* (1941), especially 90–103.

[3] *Son of Man* 142.

[4] Cf. F. W. Beare, JBL 79 (1960), 131: "It is to me utterly inconceivable that Jesus should have used the term in any such sense, or that anyone should have understood him if he had done so."

[5] According to W. D. Davies, *Paul and Rabbinic Judaism* (1948), 280, n. 1, Dan. 7: 21, 25 implies that the Son of man figure represents the persecuted saints of the Most High; cf. also Dodd, *Scriptures* 117, n. 2; C. F. D. Moule, *Studiorum Novi Testamenti Societas Bulletin* 3 (1952), 40ff. But H. H. Rowley, *The Servant of the Lord* (1952), 62, n. 2, points out that the Son of man imagery is applied to the saints only after their investiture with power.

in the Similitudes of Enoch.[1] I agree with those who are not convinced either that the evidence of the gospels suggests that Jesus thought of the Son of man as a figure of suffering, or that the figure was so understood in pre-Christian Judaism.

(c) (i) *E. Sjöberg, "Der verborgene Menschensohn in den Evangelien"* (1955).

To Sjöberg the belief in the pre-existent heavenly messianic Son of man, cherished by certain apocalyptic circles, and reflected in the Similitudes of Enoch, is the presupposition for the understanding of the New Testament problem with which we are concerned. Basic to Sjöberg's thesis is the idea of the concealment of this pre-existent figure until the arrival of the time for his revelation to the world and his activity. Meanwhile he remains both hidden and inactive, although he is partially known to the elect. Correspondingly the synoptics contain sayings about the earthly life and sufferings of the Son of man, and the prophecies of his parousia in full power and glory. The Son of man title serves both to conceal and to indicate the mystery of the person of Jesus. These ideas, firmly rooted in current Jewish thought, owe their Christian form to Jesus himself.

It must be urged, however, that the synoptic sayings contain neither the conception of the Son of man's pre-existence[2] nor that of his concealment, and offer no proof for the theory that Jesus must have claimed to be the *hidden* Son of man because he appeared on earth in advance of the Son of man's proper time, the *Endzeit*.

(ii) *O. Cullmann, "Christology" 137ff.*

Cullmann's whole approach is vitiated by an uncritical and unexamined acceptance of the opinion that Jesus employed the Son of man title as a self-designation, and included in it the

---

[1] J. Jeremias, *The Servant of God* (1957), 58ff. (= TWNT V. 686f.); cf. *Aux Sources de la Tradition chrétienne* [M. Goguel Festschrift] (1950), 113ff. This view is decisively rejected by Sjöberg, op. cit., 116ff.; *Der verborgene Menschensohn in den Evangelien* (1955), 70f., 257, and Mowinckel 410ff.

[2] Cf. H. Conzelmann in RGG[3]3 (1959), 631: "Es ist zu beachten, dass die synoptische Tradition keine andere himmlische Präexistenz des Menschensohnes kennt als den Zeitraum zwischen Erhöhung und Parusie." On Sjöberg see also T. A. Burkill, ZNW 52 (1961), 206ff.

idea of the Suffering Servant. For Cullmann the unique element in Jesus' teaching in this respect is that the Son of man, a figure of heavenly glory, must suffer, and has come in his own person along with the transference of the *Endzeit* into the present. He brushes aside Bultmann's conclusion,[1] widely shared by others, that the Son of man passion predictions are *vaticinia ex eventu*. Failing to appreciate that the three categories of Son of man sayings represent different stages of development, he treats the idea of the Son of man as if it were everywhere uniform.[2]

(iii) P. Vielhauer[3]

Vielhauer rejects as unauthentic both the sayings about the earthly work of the Son of man, where the term is a title (and not equivalent to "man" or "I"), but a secondary intrusion into the tradition, and the sayings about suffering which he takes to have been proved to be community formations by Wrede, Wellhausen, Bultmann, Dibelius, and Bornkamm.[4] The real problem is that of the coming Son of man, and the question to be answered is, Why in the oldest part of the synoptic tradition are the Son of man and the kingdom of God not combined?[5] Briefly Vielhauer's findings are these. The kingdom of God and the Son of man have nothing to do with one another in origin and are unconnected in late Judaism, as in the teaching of Jesus. Since it is undeniable that Jesus proclaimed the kingdom of God, he could not have referred either to himself or to another figure as the Son of man. In fact, he never used the title at all. The unconnected coexistence in the synoptic tradition of the kingdom of God and the Son of man is to be explained as the result of the replacement in the early church of the expectation of the near arrival of the

[1] Bultmann, *Theology* i. 29; Cullmann, *Christology* 156, n. 4.

[2] Cf. in Tödt's critique of Cullmann's methodology and theorizing (Tödt 288–97) the observation (297) that he "behandelt den Menschensohngedanken, als wäre er durch alle neutestamentlichen Texte hindurch eine geschlossene und eindeutige Grösse".

[3] See the long discussion in Tödt 298–316. Vielhauer is followed by H. Conzelmann, *Zeitschrift für Theologie und Kirche* 54 (1957), 277ff., and RGG[3] 3 (1959), 630f.

[4] Vielhauer 56.

[5] H. B. Sharman, *Son of Man and Kingdom of God* (1944) found no association of these two ideas in the teaching of Jesus: "the Son of Man has no kingdom and the Kingdom of God has no Son of Man" (89); cf. H. A. Guy, *The New Testament Doctrine of the "Last Things"* (1948), 81.

kingdom as proclaimed by Jesus, by that of the return of Jesus as the Son of man.

The phenomenon, however, can be explained more satisfactorily than by the excision from Jesus' teaching of all allusions to the Son of man. Even if we do not attach too much importance to Dan. 7 as the background of the thought of Jesus, I do not see how the ideas of the kingdom of God and the Son of man could have been kept completely isolated in his teaching.

(iv) *E. Schweizer*[1]

Schweizer gives a different answer from that of Vielhauer to the problem of the non-association of Son of man and kingdom, because he thinks that Jesus did use the term Son of man. It is probably correct that the large number of occurrences of the expression in words attributed to Jesus[2] can hardly be explained otherwise than on the assumption that he did so. Regarding some at least of the sayings describing the Son of man's life of humility on earth as certainly traceable to Jesus, and in any case as belonging to the most important category, Schweizer does not think it likely that he ever spoke of the parousia of the Son of man, even in Mark 14: 62, the original form of which he believes referred to exaltation and vindication. This theme of the exaltation and vindication of the Son of man after his humiliation and rejection on earth is central to Schweizer's thesis, and underlies also the predictions of the passion and resurrection in their present elaborated form. The reason for the non-association of Son of man and kingdom of God is that in the teaching of Jesus the eschatological role of the Son of man is not that of the bringer of the kingdom, but that of the witness at the last judgement. It is certainly correct that in the teaching of Jesus the Son of man will play this role,[3] but the view that Jesus referred to himself as the exalted and vindicated Son of man is vulnerable from two sides.

In the synoptics exaltation as a *process* is not connected with the Son of man sayings. Further, only Luke (9: 51; 24: 26)

---

[1] *Menschensohn;* "The Son of Man", JBL 79 (1960), 119–29; *Lordship* 39–41; *Erniedrigung und Erhöhung bei Jesus und seinen Nachfolgern*[2] (1962), 33–52, 65–71, with references to the most recent literature; also "The Son of Man again", NTS 9 (1963), 256–61.

[2] Some forty-one times in the synoptics alone, excluding parallel passages.

[3] Or that of the judge.

speaks directly of exaltation at all. But the really important texts for early Christian belief in the exaltation of Jesus occur in Acts.[1] However valuable these may be for early belief about him, these texts can tell us nothing of any teaching of Jesus himself about his exaltation.[2]

Schweizer tries to find in the Fourth Gospel confirmation of his thesis that the idea of the exaltation and vindication of (himself as) the Son of man goes back to Jesus.[3] I do not think this can be proved. My chapter on the Fourth Gospel shows how these very important texts should be understood as witnessing to a very early Palestinian tradition interpreting Jesus' references to the Son of man in the light of the post-resurrection identification of him with the glorified and exalted Son of man.[4]

(v) *H. E. Tödt*[5]

Tödt holds, with others (e.g., Bultmann, Knox), that Jesus did not identify himself with the Son of man, but that the church did this. But in doing so the church preserved the distinction between Jesus on earth and the future Son of man, in not endowing the earthly Jesus with the transcendent attributes proper to the Son of man. This is another way of saying that, since the church of course believed Jesus to be the Son of man, the distinction is a differentiation between two stages, the earthly and the heavenly, of Jesus' messianic activity. In the earthly sayings, however, Jesus is invested with divine authority. So far I should agree. Tödt further holds that

---

[1] Acts 2: 36; the word in Acts 2: 33 and 5: 31 is ὑψοῦν, so important in the Fourth Gospel.

[2] Cf. Tödt 26of., referring to the German original (*Erniedrigung*, etc. (1955)) of *Lordship*.

[3] *Menschensohn* 203–5.

[4] Cf. J. A. T. Robinson, *Jesus and His Coming* (1957), 162ff. Although rightly stressing the Fourth Gospel's independence of the synoptics (see my book, *The Historicity of the Fourth Gospel* (1960) in defence of this standpoint), he goes too far in trying to find in it evidence of Jesus' own "inaugurated eschatology" preserved by a tradition which had escaped the apocalyptic tendency manifest in the synoptics. In any case Robinson does not undertake a full and systematic examination of the Johannine Son of man.

[5] See the review by W. Grundmann, TLZ 86 (1961), 427–33. On the views of Tödt and Schweizer see also P. C. Hodgson, "The Son of Man and the Problem of Historical Knowledge", JR 41 (1961), 91–108.

the passion narrative reacted on an already existing Son of man tradition containing sayings of groups A and C, of which the latter includes some authentic sayings, but not the former, and led to the production of the passion sayings in group B. Probably, however, only the C category existed at the beginning of the process of development, because it alone includes authentic utterances of Jesus. The process may rather have been that Jesus, who was believed to have been exalted to power and glory as Son of man through having been raised by God from the dead, came to be regarded as having suffered death precisely as the Son of man, and so as having exercised his ministry on earth as the Son of man.[1]

Tödt covers a broader canvas than the present work. On the other hand, he does not deal with the Fourth Gospel. The Johannine Son of man tradition, however, is very important, and is fully treated in chapter 7.

[1] See further below, p. 192.

Chapter 2

THE SON OF MAN IN MARK

The Son of man sayings, both in the synoptics and in the Fourth Gospel, may be grouped in the following categories:[1]

A. *Earthly activity of the Son of man.*
B. *Sufferings of the Son of man.*
C. *Glory of the Son of man.*

The following sayings occur in Mark:

A. 2: 10; 2: 27f.
B. 8: 31; 9: 12; 9: 31; 10: 33f.; 10: 45; 14: 21; 14: 41.
C. 9: 9; 8: 38; 13: 26; 14: 62.

A

Mark 2: 10. "But that you may know that the Son of man has authority on earth to forgive sins . . ." (parr. Matt. 9: 6; Luke 5: 24).

It is unlikely that Mark, with which alone we are at present concerned, uses the expression Son of man with more than one meaning. It can safely be asserted that primarily, and perhaps even solely, the phrase has an individual meaning. There is no support in the other Markan occurrences, except possibly 2: 28, for taking the phrase to denote "man" in general,[2] and as a misunderstanding of the Aramaic *bar nāšá*.[3] There are examples of men pronouncing forgiveness in the name of God,[4] but more

---

[1] For similar groupings of the synoptic sayings see, e.g., *The Beginnings of Christianity*, ed. F. J. Foakes Jackson and Kirsopp Lake, i (1920), 375f.; Bultmann, *Theology* i (1952), 30; Sjöberg 234–36; Fuller 96f.; J. Héring, *Le royaume de Dieu et sa venue*[2] (1959), 90ff.; J. Knox, *The Death of Christ* (1959), 88ff.

[2] The idea of man having authority on earth to forgive sins "is alien to the mind of Judaism and of early Christianity", Taylor, *Mark* 199.

[3] Manson, *Teaching* 214.

[4] E.g. Nathan (2 Sam. 12: 13); the priests act as intermediaries between God and the people by offering sacrifices.

than that is involved here. No reference is made by Jesus to God's forgiveness, although of course this is implied by the passive verb. He announces the forgiveness, which is tantamount in the eyes of his opponents to claiming to forgive sins on his own authority. But this is the prerogative of God alone.

It is conceivable that Jesus is speaking of the Son of man as another figure, the Son of man in heaven who, he declares, forgives sins on earth through himself as his representative.[1] This, however, can only be maintained if all the Son of man sayings other than those in category C are judged unauthentic. Suspicion is aroused by the awkward construction of the passage, especially verse 10, " 'But that you may know that the Son of man has authority on earth to forgive sins'—he says to the paralytic—'I say to you . . .' ". The words "he says to the paralytic" are a repetition from verse 5, and if everything in between is omitted the story becomes a healing miracle with no mention of the forgiveness of sins. There can be little doubt, however, that not the evangelist but the tradition he has incorporated is responsible for the composite nature of the pericope, a combination of a miracle story and a pronouncement story. To what is the combination due? Has the pronouncement story (verses 5b–10a) as strong claims to substantial historicity as the remainder of the pericope? Opinions are sharply divided. The only other place in the synoptics where Jesus forgives sins is Luke 7: 36–50, which has difficulties of its own which need not concern us here.

But two points should be noticed. In both passages the declaration of forgiveness is in identical terms, "Your sins are (have been) forgiven"; in both the pronouncement of forgiveness is criticized by Jewish religious leaders—in Mark by the scribes, in Luke by "those who were at table with" Simon the Pharisee, presumably other Pharisees—as at best an irresponsible presumption, at worst as sheer blasphemy. It is surprising that the gospel record of this topic is so meagre if it played, shall we say, as prominent a part in the ministry of Jesus as the problem of sabbath observance. In Mark the Son

---

[1] Cf. R. P. Casey in *The Background of the New Testament and its Eschatology: Studies in honour of C. H. Dodd*, ed. W. D. Davies and D. Daube (1956), 60, and JTS, n.s. 9 (1958), 265.

of man, in Luke Jesus forgives sins. We see here the earlier[1] and the later forms of the church's justification for pronouncing forgiveness. The Lord himself had done so. Later still this power is attributed to a direct commission from the risen Christ. "Receive the Holy Spirit. If you forgive the sins of any, they are forgiven" (John 20: 22, 23).[2] Matthew's conclusion to our narrative reflects the same conviction. "They glorified God, who had given such authority to men" (Matt. 9: 8).

There is no need to deny that the question of forgiveness of sins may well have been a point at issue between Jesus and his religious opponents, and that this narrative is evidence of the fact. But in the story of the paralytic (as well as in that in Luke 7) the words "Your sins are forgiven" have come to be regarded as an ecclesiastical formula of absolution, and the association of the pronouncement story in Mark 2 ("the Son of man has authority on earth to forgive sins") with the healing narrative was made in order to combat Jewish objections to the church's claim to pronounce forgiveness, by appealing to the authority of Jesus as the Son of man.

It follows that this Son of man saying must be put on one side when we are considering the meaning the term had on the lips of Jesus. Here it is the church which is speaking.

Mark 2: 27f. "The sabbath was made for man, and not man for the sabbath; so the Son of man is lord even of the sabbath" (parr. Matt. 12: 8; Luke 6: 5).

The first question to be settled is that of the correct text. Matthew and Luke do not reproduce verse 27, which is also omitted in Mark by D it. W sys omit the words "and not man for the sabbath". Despite these facts there is no real reason to question the originality of verse 27.[3]

What is the connection between the two verses in Mark?

---

[1] E. Lohmeyer, *Das Evangelium des Markus* (1954), 54, points out that only here in the gospels is forgiveness of sins associated with the name Son of man.

[2] Cf. the power of binding and loosing conferred upon Peter (Matt. 16: 19) and upon all the disciples (Matt. 18: 18); A. E. J. Rawlinson, *The Gospel according to St Mark*[7] (1953), 24.

[3] As is done by E. Meyer, *Ursprung und Anfänge des Christentums* i (1921), 106, n. 1.

On the most satisfactory answer to this question depends the decision as to whether Jesus uttered the whole saying or either of its two parts. It may be added that the reason for the omission of verse 27 by the Western text of Mark and by Matthew and Luke may be the same difficulty as is felt by modern critics in finding a satisfactory connection with verse 28.

One way is to take "man" in verse 27 and "Son of man" in verse 28 as having the same meaning in the underlying Aramaic, *bar nāšā'* having been misunderstood in one of its two occurrences. Manson formerly held that the misunderstanding arose in verse 28, where *bar nāšā'* meant man in general, as in the preceding verse.[1] But this is unlikely, since it is difficult to imagine either Jesus or the early church claiming man's lordship over the sabbath.

Another way, later adopted by Manson in place of his earlier view, is to find the misunderstanding of *bar nāšā'* in verse 27, and to translate, "The sabbath was made for the Son of man, and not the Son of man for the sabbath".[2] Like his earlier suggestion, this does provide a good connection of thought between the two verses. The starting point is Rabbinic teaching about the sabbath as summed up by R. Simeon b. Menasya (c. A.D. 180) in the pronouncement, "The sabbath is delivered to you [the Jewish nation], not you to the sabbath". The saying of Jesus, as interpreted by Manson, is a kind of Christian counterpart to this, the Son of man being Jesus and his disciples. This is a further application of the collective view of the term Son of man which, in Manson's opinion, Jesus derived from the figure "like a son of man" in Dan. 7: 13, where it is equivalent to "the people of the saints of the Most High". But it is for this very reason that I do not believe this explanation to be the correct one. There is no compelling evidence in the gospels for the collective meaning of the Son of man.

The solution lies elsewhere than in attempts to preserve a tolerable sequence of thought between the two verses by postulating a misunderstanding of *bar nāšā'* in one or other of them. It may be that verse 27 records a genuine saying of

[1] *Teaching* 214; cf. also C. C. Torrey, *The Four Gospels*, 73.
[2] *Coniectanea Neotestamentica* 11 (1947), 138–46.

Jesus. This is not certain, although its presence provides the pronouncement characteristic of stories such as this. The saying in verse 28 is a creation of the early community, which saw in the story about David a messianic meaning. If David, in eating the shewbread, showed himself as it were lord of the sabbath, how much more is this true of David's descendant, the Messiah. The saying, "The Son of man is lord even of the sabbath" is, therefore, a Christological affirmation like Mark 2: 10, and was perhaps provoked by Pharisaic criticism of inadequate sabbath observance on the part of the Palestinian community.[1] If this is right, the absence of a fully satisfying connection of thought between the two verses is readily explicable.

B

Mark 8: 31. "The Son of man *must suffer many things, and be rejected* by the elders and the chief priests and the scribes, *and be killed,* and after three days *rise again*" (parr. Matt. 16: 21; Luke 9: 22).

Mark 9: 12. "And how is it written of the Son of man, that he *should suffer many things* and be treated with contempt?" (par. Matt. 17: 12).

The un-italicized words after "rejected" are attributable to the influence of the passion and resurrection narrative.

It is a remarkable fact that, with hardly any exception, the synoptics do not represent Jesus as referring to his sufferings and death in the first person singular except in metaphorical language. Besides the obvious allusions to his death in the words spoken over the bread and wine at the Last Supper, he asks James and John if they can drink the cup he must drink or undergo the baptism which will be his (Mark 10: 38, par. Matt. 20: 22), he speaks of the baptism which awaits him (Luke 12: 50), and alludes to his death as a "going" (Luke

---

[1] Since this was written F. W. Beare has made a similar suggestion ("The sabbath was made for man?" JBL 79 (1960), 130–36). But I do not find convincing his view that verses 23–26 were written as a setting for the affirmation in verse 28.

13: 32f.).[1] The exceptions turn out on examination to be sayings which cannot be accepted as authentic utterances. Moreover, they all three occur in Luke. The most important one stands in Luke 22: 15, "I have earnestly desired to eat this passover with you before I suffer". This is the sole instance in the gospels where Jesus uses the word "suffer" in the first person singular. The saying, therefore, can hardly be in its original form, but has been influenced by the language of the church in the Lukan tradition of the Last Supper.[2] The second instance is in Luke 22: 37, "For I tell you that this scripture must be fulfilled in me, 'And he was reckoned with transgressors'". This is a quotation of Isa. 53: 12 in language almost identical with the LXX,[3] and is therefore to be attributed to the church or to the evangelist. The third example consists of words attributed to the risen Christ, and so is to be regarded in the same way. "These are my words which I spoke to you, while I was still with you, that everything written about me in the law of Moses and the prophets and the psalms must be fulfilled" (Luke 24: 44).

Twice in Luke 24 the risen Jesus speaks of the necessity, based on scripture, of the sufferings of *the Christ*. "Was it not necessary that the Christ should suffer these things and enter into his glory? And beginning with Moses and all the prophets, he interpreted to them in all the scriptures the things concerning himself" (Luke 24: 26f.). The form of expression of the idea of scriptural warrant for the Christ's sufferings, ἔδει παθεῖν τὸν Χριστόν, recurs only in Acts 17: 3.[4] While the verb "suffer" is of course found outside the Lukan writings in reference to Christ,

---

[1] On the perhaps originally shorter form of this saying see Fuller 62f.; but cf. Black, *Aramaic Approach* 152f. The word πορεύεσθαι occurs in Luke's version (22: 22) of Mark 14: 21 (ὑπάγει). Cf. also more veiled allusions in Mark 2: 19(20); 12: 1–9; 14: 8, 27. E. Stauffer, *Jesus and His Story* (1960), 139f., regards Luke 12: 49f. and Mark 10: 38 as sayings of the *mashal* type, to which belong also the eucharistic words (185, n. 28; John 12: 24 is also included by him among the authentic utterances of this type). He is even prepared (141) to accept the substantial genuineness of Mark 8: 31; 9: 31; 10: 33f., except for the mention of resurrection which was reshaped later by the church from words "probably cast originally in the form of a *mashal*".

[2] Cf. my book, *The Lord's Supper in the New Testament* (1952), 47: "The word 'suffer' without any object may well be due to this cause"; cf. Luke 24: 46; Acts 1: 3; 3: 18; Heb. 2: 18; 13: 12; 1 Pet. 2: 21, 23; 3: 18 (v. l.); 4: 1; G. Dalman, *Jesus-Jeshua* (1929), 127f.

[3] καὶ μετὰ ἀνόμων (LXX ἐν τοῖς ἀνόμοις) ἐλογίσθη.

[4] But cf. Acts 26: 23, παθητὸς ὁ Χριστός.

the subject is never ὁ Χριστός.[1] The second passage in Luke 24 reads, "Thus it is written, that the Christ should suffer and on the third day rise from the dead" (verse 46). The expression παθεῖν τὸν Χριστόν recurs only in Acts 3: 18 and 17: 3. What is said about the necessity of the suffering of the Christ in the two passages in Luke 24 has very close parallels to what is said in Mark about the necessity of the suffering of *the Son of man*.

a {
Luke 24: 26, οὐχὶ ταῦτα ἔδει παθεῖν τὸν Χριστόν . . .
Mark 8: 31, δεῖ τὸν υἱὸν τοῦ ἀνθρώπου πολλὰ παθεῖν.[2]
}

b {
Luke 24: 46, οὕτως γέγραπται παθεῖν τὸν Χριστόν.
Mark 9: 12, καὶ πῶς γέγραπται ἐπὶ τὸν υἱὸν τοῦ ἀνθρώπου, ἵνα πολλὰ πάθῃ καὶ ἐξουδενηθῇ;[3]
}

Only in Mark 9: 12 is it said in so many words that scripture prophesies the sufferings of the Son of man. Yet it is obvious that δεῖ in Mark 8: 31 means scriptural necessity, as Luke 24: 25–27 and Acts 17: 2f. clearly bring out.[4]

We have, therefore, in Luke and in Mark, two pairs of very similar sayings relating (a) to the necessity (δεῖ) of the sufferings of the Christ and of the Son of man respectively, and (b) to the scriptural warrant for this (γέγραπται). In the traditional form the distinction has been expressed thus: "'The Son of Man must suffer', said Jesus as he taught his disciples: 'the Christ must suffer', said the Christian preachers as they proclaimed the scriptural doctrine of the Messiah, now fulfilled in Jesus' death and resurrection."[5]

[1] Except by implication in Heb. 5: 8, from verse 5; cf. 2 Cor. 1: 5, τὰ παθήματα τοῦ Χριστοῦ.

[2] Cf. Luke 17: 25.

[3] Since these words break the continuity of the preceding and following statements, with which they have no necessary connection, they may be an isolated logion (cf. their omission in par. Matt. 17: 11 which is, however, compensated for in verse 12b). The same thing applies to Mark 14: 21, which resembles this logion. J. Wellhausen, *Das Evangelium Marci* (1903), 76, accepts the variant in D, εἰ Ἠλείας instead of Ἐλείας μέν. With verse 13 the meaning then is that Elijah (John the Baptist) also died in accordance with scripture instead of removing the difficulties in the way of the Messiah, as the scribes mistakenly thought the scriptures foretold that he would; cf. Sjöberg 129, n. 2.

[4] Cf. Matt. 26: 54, πῶς οὖν πληρωθῶσιν αἱ γραφαὶ ὅτι οὕτως δεῖ γενέσθαι; On this meaning of δεῖ see W. Grundmann, TWNT ii. 22ff.; E. Fascher, "Theologische Beobachtungen zu δεῖ", *Neutestamentliche Studien für Rudolf Bultmann*, Beiheft 21 zur ZNW (1954), 228–54.

[5] A. Richardson, *An Introduction to the Theology of the New Testament* (1958), 134.

Whether Luke's use of the title Christ, and especially of "the Christ" (Acts 2: 31; 3: 18, 20; 4: 26; 5: 42; 8: 5; 9: 22; 18: 5) is derived from primitive usage or is Lukan,[1] it is certainly true that it is retrospective. This is shown by the fact that it is the *risen* Jesus who in Luke 24 speaks of the scriptural necessity for the sufferings of the Christ. The first part of the quotation above will need drastic modification in the light of what has been said about the correspondences between the two Lukan sayings and Mark 8: 31 and 9: 12. These Son of man sayings also must be regarded as expressions of Christian belief rather than as words of Jesus. They must be very early, perhaps earlier than or at least contemporaneous with their counterparts about "the Christ" (if these are not purely Lukan). This is because of the actual term Son of man, an expression which Jesus certainly employed, though not, as we shall see, and as already we begin to see, as regards his passion.

Mark 9: 31. "The Son of man *will be delivered into the hands of men, and they will kill him,* and when he is killed, *he will rise* after three days" (parr. Matt. 17: 22f.; Luke 9: 44).

It seems reasonable to assign the three predictions of the passion of the Son of man in Mark 8: 31; 9: 31; and 10: 33f. to the creativity of the primitive community.[2] But does this involve "carrying back the Hellenistic kerygma [of Jesus' death and resurrection] into the preaching of Jesus" himself?[3] The difficulty here is the very term Son of man itself. Why should the *Hellenistic* community have perpetuated the use of this almost unintelligible Greek equivalent of the Aramaic *bar nāšāʾ*? Was it simply in order to lend verisimilitude to its creations by employing a title which, according to the old Palestinian tradition, Jesus had used in other connections, even though it had become, so to speak, out of date and fundamentally unsuitable in a Hellenistic milieu?[4]

[1] H. Conzelmann, *The Theology of Saint Luke* (1960), 171, n. 2. J. C. O'Neill, *The Theology of Acts in its Historical Setting* (1961), 118ff., explains the Lukan usage in the light of second-century Christian and Jewish disputes about the identity of the Messiah.

[2] "sekundäre Gemeindebildungen", Bultmann, *Tradition* 163; "*vaticinia ex eventu*", Bultmann, *Theology* i. 29.

[3] Bultmann, *Theology* i. 83.

[4] Such a process would be the fabrication of "Aramaic 'antiques' ", in the pointed phrase of Richardson, op. cit., 133. Nevertheless, this process did exist, though only to a limited extent.

If we exclude those parts of Mark 8: 31 which appear to reflect details in the passion narrative, and also exclude from present discussion the reference there to resurrection, we have in that passage, along with 9: 12, the statements that the Son of man will suffer, be rejected, be treated with contempt, and be killed. Mark 9: 31 thus stands out as distinctive. It may be that these three prophecies are merely variant forms of one saying. At any rate the evangelist intends them to be three separate utterances. The setting of each is different, as was bound to be the case with sayings arranged in a progressive narrative framework. It is, of course, inherently probable that Jesus foretold his passion to his closest followers on more than one occasion. But the predictions in Mark 8: 31; 9: 12; and 10: 33f. have been affected either by details drawn from the passion narrative (8: 31; 10: 33f.), or by the theology of the early church (the Son of man will "suffer" in accordance with scripture, 8: 31; 9: 12), or by both (8: 31). Mark 9: 31 is not only free from the influence of details drawn from the passion narrative, and thus superior especially to the detailed prediction in 10: 33f., but also, because of its non-use of the verb "suffer", freer from liturgical-theological influence. Yet despite these advantages its general resemblance to the other sayings about the Son of man puts it also into the category of church formulations. It is a summary statement of the passion story: the handing over of the Son of man to his enemies, and his death at their hands followed by resurrection.

Mark 10: 33f. "The Son of man *will be delivered* to the chief priests and the scribes, and they will condemn him to death, and deliver him to the Gentiles; and they will mock him, and spit upon him, and scourge him, and *kill him*; and after three days *he will rise*" (parr. Matt. 20: 18f.; Luke 18: 31–33).

While the description in verse 32 of the circumstances in which this last of the three predictions of the passion was uttered is more graphic than the introductions to the other two, and may rest on good tradition, the prediction itself is so detailed that it must be regarded in its present form as a *vaticinium ex eventu*.

I venture to reproduce a table in which V. Taylor[1] brings

---

[1] *Mark* 436.

out the relationships between the three predictions and the passion narrative.

	First Prophecy	Second Prophecy	Third Prophecy	Passion Narrative
1. Handing over to the Chief Priests	—	(9: 31)	10: 33	14: 53
2. Condemnation by the Chief Priests	(8: 31)	—	10: 33	14: 64
3. Handing over to the Romans	—	—	10: 33	15: 1
4. Mocking, Spitting, and Scourging	—	—	10: 34	14: 65, 15: 15, 16–20
5. Execution	8: 31	9: 31	10: 34	15: 24, 37
6. Resurrection	8: 31	9: 31	10: 34	16: 1–8

This comparison throws into bold relief the superiority of the predictions in 8: 31 and 9: 31, especially the latter. In 8: 31 the mention of the elders, chief priests, and scribes comes from the passion narrative. It may be added that the word "rejected" (ἀποδοκιμασθῆναι) in Mark 8: 31, although intended to refer, in the saying in its present form, to the condemnation of Jesus to death (14: 64, echoed in 10: 33), represents the Hebrew $h^a dhal$ of Isa. 53: 3,[1] and so is independent of the passion narrative. 9: 31 is distinctive. As Taylor remarks of 8: 31 and 9: 31, "Only in respect of the death and the resurrection is the agreement precise."[2]

All three prophecies say that the Son of man will be killed and rise again after three days. If we regard the third prophecy, apart from its special features derived from the incidents of the passion, as constructed on the basis of the first two, it is perhaps surprising that it is much more akin to 9: 31 than to 8: 31. Not only does it share with the former the references to the Son of man's deliverance (handing over), being killed, and resurrection, but it also agrees with it, against 8: 31, in not using the verb "suffer". Therefore, although 10: 33f., in regard to the many details it has attracted to itself from incidents in the passion narrative, is inferior to the two earlier predictions, when shorn of these features it is remarkably similar not to 8: 31, but to 9: 31 which, as we have seen, is freer from external influences. Whether 10: 33f. is actually an expanded form of

---

[1] Cf. Fuller 56f.   [2] Op. cit., 437.

35

9: 31 constructed by the evangelist or comes from a separate source, cannot be decided. At any rate these two of the four sayings about the passion of the Son of man are free from the theological term "suffer".

Mark 10: 45. (a) "For the Son of man also came not to be served but to serve, (b) and to give his life as a ransom for many" (par. Matt. 20: 28).

With this saying a new element seems to be introduced. In the earlier Markan sayings the sufferings of the Son of man are foretold in scripture as necessary because they are the will of God, or are predicted as about to take place. Here the Son of man comes for the express purpose of serving and of surrendering his life. Yet this element is a difference of emphasis rather than an altogether radical departure, for the express and deliberate purpose for which the Son of man came is the working out of the divine plan that he should suffer. So far, therefore, this saying is not alien to the four predictions of the Son of man's passion already examined. But it poses a number of difficult problems.

1. Is (a) prior in time to (b), i.e., does (a) concern the earthly ministry of Jesus, and (b) his passion regarded as the predestined culmination of (a)? Or are (a) and (b) different descriptions of the same thing?

2. Is Mark 10: 45 dependent, as some have thought, on Luke 22: 27, or is the dependence the other way round? Or are the two sayings independent?

3. Above all, how far is Mark 10: 45 dependent on the servant conception of Isa. 53?

1. Formally (a) is prior in time to (b). The verse is a couplet in synthetic parallelism; the two preceding verses form a synonymous couplet:

"Whoever would be great among you must be your servant,

And whoever would be first among you must be slave of all";

but combinations of different kinds of parallelism are a feature of Semitic poetry.[1]

In this verse, then, we have a saying of which only the second part belongs strictly to the category "sufferings of the Son of man". Yet I have deliberately refrained from including the

---

[1] C. F. Burney, *The Poetry of Our Lord* (1925), 63f.

first part among sayings about the Son of man's earthly activity, because the saying as a whole envisages the Son of man's passion, of which the prelude, "serving", is an integral part. In essence, therefore, if not merely formally, there is much truth in the second alternative view of the verse or, more exactly, the second part defines the nature of the service the Son of man performs.

2. Despite important linguistic differences the sayings leading up to both Mark 10: 45 and Luke 22: 27 are essentially the same. Luke 22: 27 lacks any direct allusion to death, but this is compensated for by the setting at the Last Supper. A significant difference is that in Luke Jesus does not refer to the service performed by the Son of man, but to himself in the first person singular as the one who serves.

If, as has been widely held, the Lukan saying, "For which is the greater, one who sits at table, or one who serves? Is it not the one who sits at table? But I am among you as one who serves", is the more original, then the Markan version dependent on it, is a rewriting of it in the interests of a ransom theology.[1] Mark or his source shows by the link καὶ γάρ (Matt. 20: 28, ὥσπερ) that the saying was subsequently appended to the preceding verses. Moreover, the thought in verses 43b, 44 has a close parallel in Mark 9: 35 (=Luke 9: 48b; cf. also Matt. 23: 11), which is introduced by a dispute about priority among the disciples (and not only between James and John, as in Mark 10: 35ff.), as is the Lukan counterpart (22: 24–27) to our present passage. The point is that, when compared with the other synoptic instances of the theme of dispute about priority, the addition of Mark 10: 45 is an unexpectedly strong climax. The conclusion of Luke's corresponding section, on the other hand, with verse 27b, "But I am among you as one who serves", seems much more in keeping with what precedes than the introduction in Mark of the fresh thought of death as a ransom.

But there are difficulties. Firstly, while the omission of Mark's reference to Christ's death as a ransom for sin would be in accord with Luke's reduced theology, it is difficult to avoid the impression that Luke or his source has constructed verse 27 in order to fit the setting of the Last Supper. The word "serve" in the preceding verse may have suggested its meaning of

---

[1] Bultmann, *Tradition* 97, 154.

serving at table, and so verse 27 provides a special instance of the principle just enunciated.[1] But as J. M. Creed pointed out,[2] verse 27 does not really fit the picture, for Jesus is not waiting at table but is presiding, a difficulty which would disappear if Luke had related the feet-washing of John 13.

Leaving aside for the moment the suggestion that the ransom idea in Mark is secondary and Pauline, it is to be observed, secondly, that the whole section Luke 22: 25-27 is almost exactly parallel in thought, though with notable differences in language, to Mark 10: 42b-45. Apart from the last verse in each passage the differences occur in the antitheses:

Mark	Luke
μέγας—διάκονος	μείζων—νεώτερος
πρῶτος—δοῦλος	ἡγούμενος—διακονῶν.

It has rightly been suggested that the Lukan terms betray current church usage: νεώτερος ("youngest" or "younger") and ἡγούμενος ("leader") "reflect the concern of the Hellenistic Churches with the differentiation of the members in the local congregation",[3] for which see respectively 1 Tim. 5: 1, 2, 11, 14; Titus 2: 6; 1 Pet. 5: 5, and Heb. 13: 7, 17, 24 (cf. Acts 15: 22), although it is going too far to assert, with Fuller, that the original saying, as found by Luke in his source, "has been modified into a rule for church order".

Thirdly, and perhaps most decisive of all, why, if Luke is more original than Mark, does Jesus speak in the first person singular: "I am among you as one who serves", while in Mark it is the Son of man who has come to serve? It is much more likely, if one gospel must be supposed to depend on the other at this point, that it is Luke which is dependent. For if Mark 10: 45 were based on Luke 22: 27, it would be sheer archaizing fabrication of a saying about the Son of man out of an I-word from the *Greek*-speaking church. We have earlier noted the allusive and metaphorical nature of Jesus' references in the first person singular to his approaching passion. With this

---

[1] Verse 26b, ὁ ἡγούμενος ὡς ὁ διακονῶν, 27b, ἐγὼ . . . ὡς ὁ διακονῶν.

[2] *The Gospel according to St. Luke* (1930), 267.

[3] Fuller 57; cf. A. R. C. Leaney, *The Gospel according to St. Luke* (1958), 269.

would disagree Luke 22: 27b, "I am among you as one who serves". Even though, as we have seen, the mention of serving was probably suggested by the idea in the verse before, and even though the saying in itself does not necessarily suggest suffering, it was surely intended to do so by the evangelist, with the idea of the suffering Servant foremost in his mind. The word is spoken at the Last Supper, and is immediately followed by reference to the trials the disciples have shared which, although past, or rather still present, are but the prelude to the final trial (cf. verses 40 and 46), and by Peter's declaration of readiness to share death with his Master (verse 33). Moreover, in verse 37, "And he was reckoned with transgressors", Jesus quotes Isa. 53: 12 as to be fulfilled in himself (cf. 24: 44), which disposes of any doubts that ten verses earlier the evangelist is thinking of Jesus as the suffering Servant—cf. verse 15, "before I suffer". These I-words are not authentic, and that in verse 27 cannot be so either. It is too direct an allusion to the idea of the suffering Servant to have come from Jesus himself, when compared with the indirectness of his other references to his passion.

In comparison with Mark, therefore, Luke 22: 25–27, and not only the last saying, is secondary. But does this necessarily imply dependence on Mark?

In principle it might be thought quite natural for Luke to have omitted the ransom part of Mark 10: 45 (unless that part of it was a later addition subsequent even to Luke's writing). On the assumption of dependence, Luke verse 27b, "I am among you as one who serves", is a rewriting of the first part only of Mark 10: 45, "The Son of man came not to be served but to serve", designed to accommodate the saying to what precedes. We have already seen that Mark 10: 45 has probably been appended, but at a very early stage, to the section on true greatness. Luke 22: 27 has also been appended to the verses before it. Mark 10: 45 and Luke 22: 27 are not in a relation of dependence one way or the other, but are independent and provide climactic conclusions to the preceding sections Mark 10: 35–44 and Luke 22: 24–26 respectively, both sections belonging to independent traditions, the former Palestinian, the latter Hellenistic in origin, or perhaps a Hellenized recasting of a separate tradition. These appendages, if such they are, were added so early that it is impossible to be quite certain whether they were first made by the evangelists or had already been made in the materials as they came to them.

The result is that Mark 10: 45 must be examined more or less independently of its present context and on its own merits.

3. The problem of the Son of man as a figure of suffering becomes particularly acute in this saying. The use of the verb "serve", with the climax of the death of the Son of man in the second part of the verse, at once suggests the suffering Servant of Isa. 52: 13–53: 12 as the main background of thought. Since, however, this has been challenged, it may be appropriate to summarize at this point the position adopted by the majority of scholars, using the classic treatment of J. Jeremias as a basis.[1]

He shows that in post-Septuagintal Judaism a distinction must be drawn between Hellenistic and Palestinian interpretations of the Servant poems in Deutero-Isaiah. The former is collective, the latter individual and messianic, and in broad agreement with New Testament exegesis. The direct application to Jesus of the actual title Servant of God in Acts 3: 13, 26; 4: 27, 30 occurs in "a Palestinian stratum of tradition", and stems from the original Aramaic-speaking church.[2] It could, of course, be urged that there is nothing Christological in this usage, since late Judaism attributes the honorific title Servant of God to outstanding figures like Moses, and especially David, as also in Luke 1: 69; Acts 4: 25; Did. 9: 2. Jeremias supposes that in the New Testament there is a transition from this more general use to the special Christological sense in which the title was applied to Jesus, as exemplified especially by "thy *holy* servant Jesus" in Acts 4: 27, 30, perhaps with deliberate differentiation from its application to David (4: 25).

The relation between this predication of Jesus as God's Servant and the recognition of him as the embodiment of the Servant ideal in Deutero-Isaiah is a delicate but vital matter. Which, if either, is prior? Or is the question misleading when put in the following form?

". . . we must consider whether the use of the title 'Servant' suggested the idea of the Servant Songs, or whether the identi-

---

[1] Parts III and IV of *The Servant of God* (with W. Zimmerli, 1957) [translated from art. παῖς θεοῦ in TWNT v].

[2] Jeremias, op. cit., 80.

fication of Jesus with the Servant of the Songs led to the use of the title 'Servant'."[1]

That it is misleading is supported by the clear allusions (ἐδόξασεν, παρεδώκατε, δίκαιον) to the fourth Servant song (Isa. 52: 13–53: 12) in the first of the passages in Acts (3: 13f.), where Jesus is called God's Servant. The impression is that both processes, attribution to Jesus of the title Servant and Christological interpretation of the Servant songs, proceeded *pari passu*, once it was realized that the term Servant as applied to him must have a very much deeper content than in its application to other figures. That this was recognized from the start is shown by the virtual equation of Jesus as the Servant and as the Messiah in the application of Ps. 2: 2 in Acts 4: 26f.:

> "The kings of the earth set themselves in array,
> and the rulers were gathered together,
> against the Lord and against his Anointed (τοῦ Χριστοῦ αὐτοῦ)—

for truly in this city there were gathered together against thy holy servant Jesus, whom thou didst anoint (ὃν ἔχρισας) . . ."

This equation is not the result of adaptation of a Jewish use of "Servant" as a messianic name, which was non-existent,[2] but is due to the Christian belief in Jesus as the Messiah. Whether the idea of Jesus as the Servant actually originated with the primitive community, or was in some way indebted to his own teaching, we are not yet ready to say. But like the designation of Jesus as the Servant, Christological interpretation of the Servant songs, as illustrated both by quotations and by allusions, especially in Paul, the gospels, and Acts, is of the greatest antiquity.[3]

Let us now return in more detail to Mark 10: 45.

καὶ γὰρ ὁ υἱὸς τοῦ ἀνθρώπου οὐκ ἦλθεν διακονηθῆναι ἀλλὰ διακονῆσαι καὶ δοῦναι τὴν ψυχὴν αὐτοῦ λύτρον ἀντὶ πολλῶν.

διακονῆσαι. In the LXX the verb διακονεῖν does not occur at all, and the root ʿbd, from which comes the Hebrew word for

---

[1] Morna D. Hooker, *Jesus and the Servant* (1959), 110. Miss Hooker argues for the former alternative.

[2] Except in divine discourse, as "my servant", Jeremias, op. cit., 49f.

[3] Jeremias, op. cit., 88ff.

"servant", *'ebhedh*, is not rendered there anywhere by this verb, nor by any of its cognates. Linguistically, therefore, the connection of Mark 10: 45 at this point with Isa. 53 is non-existent. Nor do any of the Servant poems contain the Hebrew verb "to serve". We must beware, however, of being tied down too rigidly by purely linguistic considerations, for important though these are, in the final analysis it is congruity of thought which must be allowed to determine the existence or non-existence of real connections between such sayings as that in Mark 10: 45 and the Old Testament. But there is little doubt that the actual choice of διακονεῖν has been determined by διάκονος in verse 43,[1] just as ὁ διακονῶν in Luke 22: 27 was suggested by its presence in the previous verse. It seems, therefore, that this portion at least of the first part of Mark 10: 45 comes from the Greek-speaking church. Yet this first part of the verse is more primitive than Luke 22: 27, in that the subject is not "I" but the Son of man. Only here, however (and in the Matthaean parallel), is the Son of man said to serve. The *idea* of serving, as well as the word chosen to express it, was suggested, as in Luke, by what precedes. But in both gospels in different ways an already familiar belief that Jesus was the Servant of God comes to expression.

Isa. 53: 12		LXX
δοῦναι τὴν ψυχὴν αὐτοῦ.	*he⁺rāh lammāweth naphšô*, "he poured out his soul to death"; cf. also Isa. 53: 10, *tāśîm 'āšām naphšô*.	παρεδόθη εἰς θάνατον ἡ ψυχὴ αὐτοῦ.

Is the expression in Mark in fact dependent on Isa. 53: 12 at all, whether the Hebrew or the LXX, or is it a purely Greek expression which can quite well be totally free of influence from Isa. 53: 12?

C. K. Barrett,[2] on the basis of the post-biblical Jewish use of ψυχὴν διδόναι for the death of martyrs,[3] reaches the somewhat

---

[1] δοῦλος (Isa. 49: 3, 5 LXX = *'ebhedh*) in verse 44 would have produced the over-servile word δουλεύειν, which also does not form a passive.

[2] "The Background of Mark 10: 45", NTE 5.

[3] For examples see F. Büchsel in TWNT ii. 168, e.g., 1 Macc. 2: 50, δότε τὰς ψυχὰς ὑμῶν ὑπὲρ διαθήκης πατέρων ἡμῶν. The post-biblical Hebrew equivalent is *nāthan naphšô*, cf. A. Schlatter, *Der Evangelist Matthäus* (1948), 602.

vague conclusion that Mark's phrase, while not having "a background of its own other than Isa. 53", cannot be said either to point "unambiguously to that chapter". He also refers to the view that *lammāweth* metrically is an addition in Isa. 53: 12. This addition, if such it is, is retained in the LXX (and in the Targum), but its omission would in fact be an argument in favour of Mark's dependence on the presumed original Hebrew text. No emphasis, however, can be laid on this point. Barrett points out that "he poured out his soul" is an unexampled meaning of the Hebrew verb in the Old Testament. "To give" in Mark, we might add, seems a very weak and colourless rendering of a word which means "expose", "abandon", "surrender". According to Jeremias[1] the expression "he emptied himself" (ἑαυτὸν ἐκένωσεν) in Phil. 2: 7, "attested nowhere else in the Greek and grammatically extremely harsh, is an exact rendering" of the Hebrew for "he poured out his soul" in Isa. 53: 12. The occurrence both of δοῦλος (verse 7, corresponding to *'ebhedh* in Isa. 52: 13) and of μεχρὶ θανάτου (verse 8) establishes not merely the widely recognized connection of the whole passage Phil. 2: 6–11 with Isa. 52: 13–53: 12, but the view that Isa. 53: 12 is here actually translated. If it be asked why Paul, or an earlier translator whose work he is adapting, chose such an unusual translation as ἑαυτὸν ἐκένωσεν, the answer is partly because the unique Hebrew demanded a unique translation, partly because he may have known that sometimes the verb *'ārāh* is rendered in the LXX by ἐκκενοῦν,[2] and partly because he wanted a word far richer in content than the LXX παρεδόθη at this point, the object being to give not a bare attempt at a translation, but a theologically interpretative rendering. We thus arrive at the paradox that Phil. 2: 7 provides a translation of the Hebrew which is at one and the same time the most literal possible and of immense theological significance.[3]

Mark 10: 45 offers a much simpler translation of Isa. 53: 12, or rather not so much a translation as an adaptation of the passage (influenced perhaps, it may be conceded, by current

[1] Op. cit., 97; cf. Dodd, *Scriptures* 93.
[2] Gen. 24: 20; 2 Chron. 24: 11; Ps. 136 (137): 7.
[3] On Phil. 2: 6–11 as a pre-Pauline hymn see now V. Taylor, *The Person of Christ in New Testament Teaching* (1958), 62ff.

Greek expressions) to the following idea of the ransom. But before coming to the ransom idea in detail we may compare Mark 10: 45 with the Christological hymn in Phil. 2 and with a later passage very similar to Mark 10: 45.

Mark 10: 45. καὶ γὰρ ὁ υἱὸς τοῦ ἀνθρώπου οὐκ ἦλθεν διακονη-θῆναι ἀλλὰ διακονῆσαι καὶ δοῦναι τὴν ψυχὴν αὐτοῦ λύτρον ἀντὶ πολλῶν.

Phil. 2: 6–8. . . . ἐν Χριστῷ 'Ιησοῦ . . . ἑαυτὸν ἐκένωσεν (Isa. 53: 12) μορφὴν δούλου ('ebhedh, Isa. 52: 13) λαβών . . . καὶ σχήματι εὑρεθεὶς ὡς ἄνθρωπος . . . μεχρὶ θανάτου (Isa. 53: 12).

1 Tim. 2: 5f. εἷς γὰρ θεός, εἷς καὶ μεσίτης θεοῦ καὶ ἀνθρώπων, ἄνθρωπος Χριστὸς 'Ιησοῦς, ὁ δοὺς ἑαυτὸν ἀντίλυτρον ὑπὲρ πάντων (cf. Titus 2: 13f. . . . Χριστοῦ 'Ιησοῦ, ὃς ἔδωκεν ἑαυτὸν ὑπὲρ ἡμῶν ἵνα λυτρώσηται ἡμᾶς . . .).

1 Tim. 2: 5f. is a Hellenistic rewriting of the original Semitic form in Mark (Semitic are: the Son of man (= the man), to give his soul (= to give himself), for many (= for all)). The later passage reframes in Hellenistic language a logion concerning the Son of man, making explicit the idea of mediation by borrowing the word "mediator" from popular Greek speech. Very clear also is the series of renderings of the Hebrew *he'rāh naphšô* in Isa. 53: 12: the literal translation "emptied himself" in Phil. 2: 7, the simpler but still Semitic "to give his soul" in Mark 10: 45 (the Targum has the exact Aramaic equivalent, *m'sar naphšêh*), and the purely Greek equivalent "gave himself" in 1 Tim. 2: 6. Possibly not only 1 Tim. 2: 5f., but also the passage in Philippians is dependent in some way on the logion in Mark. If so, the great antiquity of this logion is guaranteed, especially if the passage in Philippians is not Paul's own composition but an adaptation of an older hymn. The case for the connection of the hymn with Mark 10: 45 is greatly strengthened if, with E. Lohmeyer,[1] "as a man" in Phil. 2: 7 is taken as rendering the Aramaic "as Son of man" (*k'bhar nāšâ*).

λύτρον ἀντὶ πολλῶν. Many difficulties would be avoided if we could suppose that originally λύτρον formed no part of Mark 10: 45, that this read ὑπὲρ πολλῶν, and that a later substitution

[1] *Der Brief an die Philipper* (1956), 95; see also below, p. 151, n. 1.

of ἀντί suggested λύτρον. But we have to take the saying as it stands.

An old argument in favour of the priority of Luke 22: 27 to our text has been that the latter is a recasting of it in the interests of Pauline ransom theology.[1] Paul, however, never uses the word λύτρον, which does not occur in the New Testament outside this passage and its parallel, Matt. 20: 28; and even the equivalent ἀντίλυτρον occurs only once, in 1 Tim. 2: 6 which, as we have seen, is directly dependent on Mark 10: 45. Paul's theology, while in line with the thought of this passage,[2] yet "reveals its distinctiveness".[3] Nor must it be forgotten that much of Paulinism is rooted in primitive Christian belief.[4]

It is widely held that λύτρον renders 'āšām in Isa. 53: 10, "when thou makest his soul an offering for sin", RSV margin (= Hebrew 'im tāśîm 'āšām naphšô; RSV text, "when he makes himself an offering for sin" follows the Vulgate, "si posuerit pro peccato animam suam"; LXX has ἐὰν δῶτε περὶ ἁμαρτίας). Thus Fuller regards it as "a perfectly adequate rendering" of the Hebrew word.[5] This view has been challenged, but on inadequate grounds. Thus Kümmel,[6] in opposing the whole idea that Jesus believed himself to be fulfilling the role of the suffering Servant, states that none of Jesus' sayings contains any clear allusion to Isa. 53, and that Mark 10: 45, "in which doubtless ideas of Isa. 53 are to be found, stands completely alone and cannot be explained with certainty". Barrett, in his study of Mark 10: 45 already referred to, attempts to disprove the equation in meaning of λύτρον and 'āšām. He emphasizes that in the LXX λύτρον never renders 'āšām, and that the fundamental meaning in 'āšām is guilt, while in λύτρον it is equivalence. Apart from the existence of a certain difference of opinion as to the extent to which the idea of compensation is proper to 'āšām,[7] and with due allowance for the inescapable necessity of

---

[1] Cf. e.g. B. H. Branscomb, *The Gospel of Mark* (1937), 190f.: influence of the Pauline view of Christianity as a religion of redemption.

[2] Rom. 3: 24–26; 1 Cor. 6: 20; 7: 23; Gal. 1: 4; 2: 20; 3: 13; 4: 5.

[3] Taylor, *Mark* 445.

[4] Taylor, ibid., 446; Fuller 57.

[5] Fuller 57; cf. G. Dalman, *Jesus-Jeshua* (1929), 119: "the expression [to give his life a ransom for many] has most probably its Biblical background in Isa. liii. 10f.".

[6] Kümmel 72–74.

[7] See Barrett's paper, p. 6 and n. 22.

the study of the exact meaning of words, the correctness of upholding, as regards Mark 10: 45, this hard and fast distinction between the Hebrew and Greek words is open to question.

In the first place, it is a tenable view that the ransom metaphor should not be unduly pressed, and that "the phrase [in Mark 10: 45] sums up the general thought of Is. liii, and expresses the idea of a vicarious and voluntary giving of life, with the thought also implied that the sacrifice was in some way mysteriously necessitated by sin".[1]

Should this be judged an insufficiently exact approach, there are other considerations. If Mark 10: 45 is substantially a translation of a Semitic original, the translator must have been aware that λύτρον is a not uncommon word in the LXX (e.g., for *kōpher*, Exod. 30: 12; for *pidhyōn*, Exod. 21: 30). The fact that λύτρον in the LXX never represents '*āšām* is not an absolutely decisive reason why it should not do so in Mark 10: 45. We cannot expect the New Testament writers always to be confined within the limits of Septuagintal usage, and they are not so confined.[2] λύτρον in Mark could be a variant translation of '*āšām*, which the LXX here renders by περὶ ἁμαρτίας.

There seems to me no compelling reason for abandoning the view that Mark 10: 45 has as its main background elements derived from Isa. 53. It is not a plain and straightforward Greek translation of any single verse. Its second part draws on key words and ideas in Isa. 53: δοῦναι τὴν ψυχὴν αὐτοῦ ("he poured out his soul", verse 12) λύτρον ('*āšām*, verse 10) ἀντὶ πολλῶν ("many", verses 11f.).

The first part of the verse is peculiar. On the one hand, the

---

[1] A. E. J. Rawlinson, *The Gospel according to St. Mark* (1953), 147f.

[2] For a striking example we need go no farther than the rendering of *he'erāh naphšô* in Isa. 53: 12 by ἑαυτὸν ἐκένωσεν in Phil. 2: 7.

Isa. 53: 12, root '*ārāh*.
LXX, παραδιδόναι.
Mark 10: 45, διδόναι.
Phil. 2: 7, κενοῦν.

The three Greek words are different attempts to render the same Hebrew word. It should, however, be mentioned that Jeremias (op. cit., 96) regards δοῦναι τὴν ψυχὴν αὐτοῦ in Mark rather as one of several translation variants of *śîm naphšô* in Isa. 53: 10. This would be supported by '*āšām* in that verse, corresponding to λύτρον in Mark. But in favour of the other view is the resemblance of "for many" in Mark to the "many" in Isa. 53: 12: "because he poured out his soul to death, and was numbered with the transgressors; yet he bore the sin of many".

use of διακονεῖν suggests, as we have seen, a Greek origin; on the other, the Semitic and therefore primitive parentage of its prototype is evident in the title Son of man and the idea of the Son of man as the Servant. Mark 10: 45 is, in fact, a unique composition. The expression "not . . . but" may be an addition, but this cannot be pressed because the contrast is intended to counter the notion in the preceding verses that to be a servant is inferior.

At this point we return to Barrett who, having tried to show, unsuccessfully in my opinion, that the language of Mark 10: 45 is no more closely related to Isa. 53 than to any other Old Testament passage, turns to the background of thought. He points out that the idea of service is to be found often elsewhere in the Old Testament, and suggests that the background of the saying is to be sought in the theology of martyrdom as a means of atonement familiar from the Maccabaean period onwards, the corporate understanding of which is epitomized in the Son of man figure in Dan. 7, whose role is regarded as "a mythological, eschatological expression of the deeds of the martyrs".[1] The figure in Daniel is indeed a corporate symbol for the saints of the Most High. But it is not a figure of suffering, for it represents the saints only after their reception of power and dominion.[2] If this is right, Barrett's thesis cannot be accepted.[3] He has, however, recognized that the crux of the whole problem of this very difficult saying lies precisely in its being a Son of man saying.

What are the conclusions to be drawn about it?

It is of great antiquity, with its roots stemming from the earliest period of the church.

It is basically Semitic and would mean, "the Son of man came to fulfil the role of the Servant of God in giving his life as a ransom for many". But is it a creation of the early church or an utterance of its founder? As so often in these matters, a

[1] Op. cit., 14.

[2] Cf. H. H. Rowley, *The Servant of the Lord* (1952), 62, n. 2, and my paper, "Son of Man-*Forschung* since 'The Teaching of Jesus' ", NTE 129.

[3] The treatment of Mark 10: 45 by Miss Hooker, op. cit., 74–79, exemplifies an almost totally negative approach to the traditional view of Jesus and the Servant conception. In an important review Jeremias (JTS n. s. 11 (1960), 140–44) disputes her conclusions, that Jesus did not regard himself as the Servant, and that the early church did not assign any special significance to the idea of vicarious suffering.

simple choice of one of two alternatives is not possible. The answer lies somewhere in between. Since nowhere else is it said that the Son of man serves, it is probable that the first part of the saying crystallizes early Christian thought about Jesus as the Servant of God rather than reports his actual words.[1] Neither is its second part, "(The Son of man came) to give his life as a ransom for many", to be accepted without more ado as the *ipsissima verba* of Jesus.

Attention has already been drawn to the fact that δοῦναι τὴν ψυχὴν αὐτοῦ is a form of expression used for the death of martyrs, but I have urged that, while there may have been some influence of this usage on the choice of this particular language in Mark 10: 45, it is in fact a rendering of the Hebrew of Isa. 53: 12. Behind Mark 10: 45 there probably lies a saying of Jesus in which he spoke in the first person singular of giving his life[2] as a ransom, just as elsewhere he refers to his sufferings and death in metaphorical language (drinking the cup, Mark 10: 38; undergoing a baptism, Mark 10: 38; Luke 12: 50; going, Luke 13: 32f.).

Though an original and unique composition, the saying is clearly not homogeneous. The reference to serving is probably a summary statement of early Christian application to Jesus of the Servant concept of Deutero-Isaiah, while in the words "to give his life as a ransom for many" a transposition has been made from the first person used by Jesus to the third person, in order to harmonize with the Son of man as subject. That the original utterance out of which Mark 10: 45 was constructed was something like, "I shall give my life as a ransom for many", is supported by the similarity of Jesus' word over the cup at the Last Supper, in the probable form, "This is my blood which is (to be) poured out for many", Mark 14: 24.[3] Like Mark 10: 45 this is strongly reminiscent of Isa. 53: 12. If Jesus' saying, as we have seen reason to suppose, contained no explicit

---

[1] This is strongly supported by the fact to which J. A. Emerton (JTS n. s. 11 (1960), 334f.) has called attention, that διακονηθῆναι (and therefore also διακονῆσαι) cannot be a translation of the Aramaic root *'bd*, because the passive (ithpe'el) would not mean "to be served", but "to be done, to be made, to become".

[2] Cf. John 10: 15, τὴν ψυχήν μου τίθημι ὑπὲρ τῶν προβάτων (also 10: 11, 17; 15: 13), and N. Johansson, *Parakletoi* (1940), 239; for more distant echoes cf. Gal. 1: 4; 2: 20; Eph. 5: 2, 25; Titus 2: 14.

[3] See my book, *The Lord's Supper in the New Testament* (1952), 29-34.

reference to serving, it is probable that already in the pericope as it reached the evangelist verse 45 had been expanded to its present form from an I-word of Jesus about giving his life as a ransom by the reference to serving suggested by the immediately preceding verses, but also because the allusion to Isa. 53: 10, 12 in the actual saying of Jesus was recognized.

There are thus three stages in the growth of the saying.

1. A saying of Jesus, "I shall give my life as a ransom for many".

2. "The Son of man came[1] to give his life as a ransom for many."

3. The present form of the saying, achieved by the insertion of the reference to serving which was suggested by the theme in verses 43f., that the truly great man is the servant of others, regarded as an apt context for the saying in which was recognized the Servant theme of Deutero-Isaiah.

Mark 10: 45 is not free from the influence of early beliefs about Jesus. For while, despite what may be urged to the contrary, Jesus referred by implication to Isa. 53 in the utterance which I have argued as being the kernel of the logion, the reference is made quite explicit in its final form by the introduction of the actual word "serve". Although linguistic considerations point to the Greek-speaking church as responsible for this detail, it expresses a belief inherited from the Palestinian church that Jesus fulfilled the Servant ideal.

There could be no more suitable setting for the word of Jesus than the Last Supper where, in words not dissimilar, he declared, "This is my blood which is (to be) poured out for many". Some support for this view is derived from the fact that, although independent of Mark, Luke 22: 27b, "I am among you as one who serves", concluding verses 24–27a, corresponds in meaning not only to Mark 10: 45a, "The Son

---

[1] Apart from this passage and its Matthaean parallel, the expression "the Son of man came" is confined to Luke 7: 34 = Matt. 11: 19; Luke 19: 10 (9: 56 v.l.; Matt. 18: 11 v.l.). This form of expression is attributed to Jesus himself by E. Ashby, "The Coming of the Son of Man", ET 72 (1961), 360–63. Only the last (three) has, like Mark 10: 45, the infinitive of purpose. The expression "the Son of man came to" is theological retrospect, but could be based on an I-word like "I came not to call the righteous but sinners" (Mark 2: 17, parr. Matt. 9: 13; Luke 5: 32); cf. also Matt. 5: 17; 10: 34f.; Luke 12: 49, 51. Jesus may, therefore, have said, "I came to give my life . . ."

of man came not to be served but to serve", concluding verses 35–44, but also, as intended in Luke as an indirect allusion to the suffering and death of Jesus as the Servant of God, to Mark 10: 45b as well. What the Lukan tradition preserves in a secondary form but in the authentic setting, Mark preserves in a form at any rate much closer to the words of Jesus, but in an artificial context.

Mark 14: 21. "For the Son of man goes as it is written of him, but woe to that man by whom the Son of man is betrayed. It would have been better for that man if he had not been born" (parr. Matt. 26: 24; Luke 22: 22).

This saying resembles 9: 12 in its reference to scriptural necessity for the Son of man's passion, and 9: 31 and 10: 33 in the use of παραδιδόναι, but with the introduction of the new feature of allusion to the traitor as the instrument of his deliverance to his enemies, who are not here mentioned. On the other hand it differs from 8: 31 and 9: 12 in the non-use of the term "suffer", from 8: 31 and 10: 33f. in lacking details drawn from the passion narrative, and from 8: 31, 9: 31 and 10: 34 in lacking reference to the resurrection. The saying as it stands can hardly be regarded as the *ipsissima verba* of Jesus.

In the first place, the ὅτι at the beginning is surprising. Of the two possible explanations, it seems more likely that the sentence in this particular context is an addition from a sayings source, either made by the evangelist or already found by him in its present position, than that the words "and he said", to introduce it, have fallen out.[1] The saying is not necessary to the context, which is quite complete without it.

But the main difficulty concerns ὑπάγει ("goes"). In the saying it is virtually equivalent to παραδίδοται at the end, and some Western texts actually have this word here.[2] Since ὑπάγει, apart from the Fourth Gospel, is unexampled in the sense it has here, of going to death, and in view of the occasional use of the Aramaic *'ᵃzal* with this meaning, an Aramaic original is to be postulated.[3]

---

[1] Cf. Taylor, *Mark* 542 for the textual evidence (omission of ὅτι or substitution by καί) indicative of a felt difficulty about the word.

[2] D a c i.

[3] Cf. A. Schlatter, *Der Evangelist Matthäus* (1948), 740; Black, *Aramaic Approach* 237f. J. Christensen in an article on Mark 14: 21 in *Studia Theo-*

In the Fourth Gospel Jesus speaks of his departure by death as ὑπάγω: 7: 33; 8: 14, 21, 22; 13: 33, 36; 14: 4, 28; 16: 5, 10, 17 (cf. 13: 3; 14: 5). Along with this must be taken the fact that only in Mark 14: 21 (and par. Matt. 26: 24. Luke 22: 22 has πορεύεται[1]) is it said that the *Son of man* "goes" (ὑπάγει). All the occurrences of "I go" (ὑπάγω) on the lips of Jesus in the Fourth Gospel are found in the setting of the Last Supper, like Mark 14: 21, except those in chapters 7 and 8; and these are anticipations, in very similar language, of what Jesus says to the disciples in 13: 33 about their inability to follow him, despite their searching.

In its present form the saying in Mark 14: 21 is a community creation.[2] But it is by no means a sheer invention. The Johannine evidence must be taken seriously,[3] for there is reason to suppose that the Fourth Gospel preserves, although usually in a more or less disguised form, genuine reminiscences of sayings of Jesus. Behind the Markan saying is possibly to be presumed an I-word like that in John 16: 5 (= 7: 33), "I go (ὑπάγω) to him that sent me". The theme of God's sending of Jesus his Son into the world is Johannine, but is not confined to John. Mark 9: 37, "Whoever receives me, receives not me but him who sent me" (par. Luke 9: 48); Matt. 10: 40, "He who receives me receives him who sent me"; Luke 10: 16, "He who rejects me rejects him who sent me". Jesus may well have spoken of his approaching passion as a "going", as John reports, using the Aramaic verb *ᵃzal* in the first person. Such a saying would be another example of the metaphorical allusions to his own death which we have already noted, including the "going" in Luke 13: 33. On the one hand the Fourth Gospel has used this as a basis for sayings illustrative of the theme of Jesus going back to the heavenly realm whence he came. On

---

logica 10 (1957), 28–39, points to contacts between ὑπάγει and the theme of "departure" of the son of man in Ezek. 12. But the influence of the prophet/son of man in Ezekiel on the gospel tradition is very questionable.

[1] Luke 22: 22 is a rewriting of Mark (cf. H. Conzelmann, *The Theology of Saint Luke* (1960), 158); cf. πορεύομαι in John 14: 2, (3), 12, 28; 16: (7), 28.

[2] Cf. C. G. Montefiore, *The Synoptic Gospels* i (1927), 325: "The verse bears all the marks of a later date than Jesus."

[3] Taylor, *Mark* 542, thinks that the expression ὑπάγει "is not compromised on the historical side" simply because it is typically Johannine, and "is better appraised as a mode of speech characteristic of Jesus".

the other, the Markan tradition, as in the case of Mark 10: 45, has transformed the original utterance into a Son of man saying, and has introduced the idea of scriptural necessity (cf. 9: 12).

Probably spoken at some time during the Last Supper, as in the Fourth Gospel, the saying (in its new form) has been given its present apt and dramatic position in the narrative for homiletical purposes, which come to light in the second part of the verse, "woe to that man by whom the Son of man is betrayed! It would have been better for that man if he had not been born." "The Son of man is betrayed", an already familiar theme (9: 31; 10: 33; 14: 41), is given special point here by its climactic allusion to the traitor.

Mark 14: 41. "The hour has come; behold, the Son of man is betrayed into the hands of sinners"[1] (par. Matt. 26: 45).

The use of ὥρα here is due to the gospel tradition, in which the word has a special meaning denoting the hour of death. Jesus "prayed that, if it were possible, the hour might pass from him" (Mark 14: 35); in Luke 22: 53 he declared to those who had come to arrest him, "This is your hour, and the power of darkness". The Johannine ring of the second utterance has often been noted. In the Fourth Gospel "the hour" refers to the death of Jesus viewed in the Johannine manner as his glorification: 2: 4; 7: 30; 8: 20; 12: 23, 27; 13: 1;[2] 17: 1. In every case except 12.27 ("I came to this hour") the hour has not yet come, or has come. That the Johannine tradition upon which the fourth evangelist drew is to some degree parallel to the synoptic tradition is shown by the resemblance between John 12: 27, πάτερ, σῶσόν με ἐκ τῆς ὥρας ταύτης, and Mark 14: 35, προσηύχετο ἵνα εἰ δυνατόν ἐστιν παρέλθῃ ἀπ' αὐτοῦ ἡ ὥρα...Ἀββα ὁ πατήρ, and still more strikingly by that between John 12: 23 and Mark 14: 41.

παραδίδοται, with the Son of man as subject, occurs also at Mark 9: 31; 10: 33 (future); 14: 21. This association receives an expansion in narrative in Luke 22: 48 (L), "Judas, do you

---

[1] J. Wellhausen, *Das Evangelium Marci* (1903), 128, omits these words, while E. Klostermann, *Das Markus-Evangelium*[4] (1950, ed. G. Bornkamm), 151, favours the view that they and the next verse are redactional. Neither of these suggestions is convincing.

[2] Cf. on Mark 14: 21 and the Johannine theme of "departure". In John 13.1 μεταβαίνειν is a synonym for ὑπάγειν.

betray the Son of man with a kiss?" All these Son of man sayings are church formulations, and Mark 14: 41 is no exception. It has a special importance of its own. It illuminates the earlier Markan associations of the Son of man and παραδιδόναι, and in fact establishes that they are church formulations. The close resemblance between Mark 14: 41 and John 12:23 has been mentioned above.

Mark 14: 41, ἦλθεν ἡ ὥρα, ἰδοὺ παραδίδοται ὁ υἱὸς τοῦ ἀνθρώπου εἰς τὰς χεῖρας τῶν ἁμαρτωλῶν.

John 12: 23, ἐλήλυθεν ἡ ὥρα ἵνα δοξασθῇ ὁ υἱὸς τοῦ ἀνθρώπου.

The coming of "the hour" and the Son of man title are common to both, while John's version is coloured by the introduction of his theme of glorification by death. The Markan saying is to be viewed as the dramatic climax to the earlier predictions of the Son of man's passion. This notion of undertones leading up to the climax of the arrival of the time for the Son of man to be delivered up is in some ways more dramatically presented in Mark than in John, who has anticipated the climax by his earlier chronological setting of 12: 23.

If, therefore, we seek anything approaching an authentic allusion of Jesus to his betrayal, we must look elsewhere than in Mark 14: 41. It is to be found in Mark 14: 18, "Truly I say to you that one of you shall betray me" (=Matt. 26: 21; cf. Luke 22: 21). The resemblance between this and John 13: 21 is very close.

Mark 14:18, Αμην λέγω ὑμῖν ὅτι εἷς ἐξ ὑμῶν παραδώσει με.

John 13: 21, Αμην αμην λέγω ὑμῖν ὅτι εἷς ἐξ ὑμῶν παραδώσει με.

Apart from the typical Johannine doubling of "amen", the saying in the Fourth Gospel is exactly the same as the Markan one. Mark 14: 18 is important because Jesus speaks of the betrayal not of the Son of man, but of himself. It is the ultimate basis not only of Mark 14: 41, but of the predictions of the betrayal of the Son of man in Mark 9: 31; 10: 33; 14: 21 (cf. 8: 31, rejection; 9: 12, contemptuous treatment), of which Mark 14: 41 is the dramatic fulfilment. In a similar way the almost exact Johannine counterpart to Mark 14: 18 in John 13: 21 may be regarded as the ultimate basis in the tradition of the Johannine saying about the glorification of the Son of man in John 12: 23 (cf. 13: 31), the counterpart to our present Markan saying about the Son of man's betrayal.

53

Although the subject is not the Son of man, as in the synoptics, but "the Lord Jesus", the use in traditional formulae of the passive of παραδιδόναι confirms this approach to the formulation of the synoptic saying, "the Son of man is betrayed". The formulae in question are:

Rom. 4: 25, ('Ιησοῦν τὸν κύριον ἡμῶν) ὃς παρεδόθη διὰ τὰ παραπτώματα ἡμῶν.

1 Cor. 11: 23, ὁ κύριος 'Ιησοῦς ἐν τῇ νυκτὶ ᾗ παρεδίδετο.

The Son of man sayings relating to betrayal (Mark 9: 31; 10: 33; 14: 21, 41) are just as much community creations as these are. Whereas the latter, even when, as in 1 Cor. 11: 23, a narrative is introduced, employ the confessional title of Jesus as Lord (Rom. 10: 9; 1 Cor. 12: 3; Phil. 2: 11), the former depict Jesus as referring to himself as the Son of man because he was known to have used the term, though not, it would seem, in contexts of this kind. In other words, the Markan passages speak of the Son of man ("the Son of man is betrayed") because of the narrative setting within the ministry of Jesus.

C

Mark 9: 9. "And as they were coming down from the mountain, he charged them to tell no one what they had seen, until the Son of man had risen from the dead" (par. Matt. 17: 9).

We may take this passage first because it is the only Son of man saying which deals solely with the resurrection; and it may be allotted to this category of sayings because it refers to the future of the Son of man after the passion is over. Since, however, it speaks not of the parousia but of the resurrection, it is associated with those passion sayings which include reference to the resurrection (8: 31; 9: 31; 10: 34). It also serves as a link between these and the three remaining passages in group C (Mark 8: 38; 13: 26; 14: 62). We thus approach the problem of the relation between the resurrection of Jesus and the parousia of the Son of man. The question is whether the conflict of views on this matter may not be rather beside the mark, because they commonly assume the possibility of knowing the thought of Jesus himself both about his resurrection and about *his* parousia as the Son of man. As with the passion sayings, it is necessary to distinguish between sayings in which Jesus refers to the resurrection of the Son of man and those in which he speaks in the first person.

In 8: 31, 9: 31 and 10: 34 the Son of man will rise "after three days". It may be noted that the saying in Mark 9: 9, although lacking this secondary time-reference, is in indirect speech.[1] At the outset, therefore, the case for the authenticity of this saying is weak; but its context must be taken into account.

Of the immediately preceding transfiguration narrative various views have been held: a displaced resurrection story[2], a foreshadowing of the parousia,[3] Petrine reminiscence of a vision during the life of Jesus,[4] application to Jesus of the theme of the enthronement of the Messiah.[5] Although the view which sees in the transfiguration an anticipation of the parousia would set our saying firmly among the parousia passages, the explanation that it is based on a resurrection narrative has perhaps most in its favour.[6] If this is accepted, Mark 9: 9 supplies no evidence for the thought of Jesus about his resurrection as the Son of man, and is to be regarded as a comment on the adapted resurrection story whose origin had now been forgotten. Even if, as many would prefer, the story relates a vision during Jesus' lifetime, the verse may be a later explanation of why the transfiguration was not known in the community until after the resurrection.[7] The term Son of man is used because, as in 8: 31, 9: 31 and 10: 33f., it became customary in narrative to represent Jesus during his lifetime as referring to his passion and resurrection as the Son of man.

It follows that if the saying is so regarded, nowhere in Mark is there evidence that Jesus spoke of his resurrection any more than of his suffering and death *as the Son of man*. In deciding the question whether or not Jesus distinguished between resurrection and parousia, and envisaged an interval of time between them, the Markan sayings about the Son of man's resurrection

[1] Changed to direct speech in par. Matt. 17: 9.
[2] Bultmann, *Tradition* 278–81, and Erganzungsheft 36f.
[3] G. H. Boobyer, *St. Mark and the Transfiguration Story* (1942).
[4] Meyer, op. cit. (above p. 28, n. 3), i. 154–56.
[5] H. Riesenfeld, *Jésus Transfiguré* (1947).
[6] Moses and Elijah were introduced when the narrative was remoulded to its present form.
[7] Cf. Kümmel 67: "Mark 9: 9 is undoubtedly an ending formulated by the evangelist and not part of the old tradition."

can play no part. It is therefore necessary to discover what evidence, if any, Mark has to offer that Jesus alluded specifically in the first person to his resurrection.

In Mark 14: 28 alone does Jesus speak directly of his resurrection.

"But after I am raised up, I will go before you into Galilee" (par. Matt. 26: 32. Luke, following a tradition of non-Galilean appearances, omits). With this goes Mark 16: 7, "But go, tell his disciples and Peter that he is going before you into Galilee; there you will see him, as he told you" (par. Matt. 28: 7). 16: 7 may look back to 14: 28, or 14: 28 may be a later insertion made with the object of anticipating the outcome in 16: 7. The Fayyum papyrus fragment[1] omits 14: 28, but perhaps only for the same reason which has led some critics to reject it as an insertion suggested by 16: 7, namely, that it interrupts the connection between verses 27 and 29.[2] Elsewhere in the synoptics there is hardly any evidence that Jesus referred to his resurrection. A possible exception is Luke 13: 32, in which the mention of the third day may point to the resurrection as well as to death.[3] Possibly also, although not in the first person, Luke 16: 31, "If they do not hear Moses and the prophets, neither will they be convinced if some one should rise from the dead", may rest on an authentic allusion by Jesus to his own death and resurrection. Its indirectness would in that case resemble his other allusive references to his death. Matt. 27: 63 (" . . . that impostor said, while he was still alive, After three days I will rise again"), does not call for consideration because it belongs to the latest and least trustworthy of the synoptic traditions.

In trying to solve the problem whether Jesus foresaw an interval between his resurrection and the parousia of the Son of man, and therefore distinguished the one from the other,

[1] See *The Beginnings of Christianity* v (1933), 12. The fragment, however, may not be a quotation from a gospel at all; cf. R. H. Lightfoot, *Locality and Doctrine in the Gospels* (1938), 52, n.1.
[2] Cf. H. J. Holtzmann, *Die Synoptiker*[3] (1901), 174; Lightfoot, op. cit., 52; Klostermann, op. cit., 148f.; Lohmeyer, op. cit. (above, p. 28, n. 1), 311f.: the saying gives the impression of being "der losgerissene Schluss einer Verkündung von Tod und Auferstehung", and is not in its original form or context.
[3] But "on the third day I am perfected" may be an interpolation, cf. Fuller 62f.

the Markan predictions of the Son of man's (passion and) resurrection afford no help, while the synoptic evidence that he spoke in the first person about his resurrection is extremely slight. Even, however, if these meagre and uncertain hints are thought to be inadmissible as evidence, it is almost inconceivable that as a Jew Jesus did not expect resurrection to follow his death.

It is therefore quite possible that Mark 14: 28, although perhaps an insertion in its present context, is an isolated logion with some claim to acceptance. That in its present form it is at least early is shown by the choice of the verb ἐγείρεσθαι, which is used in the resurrection narratives in all four gospels (Mark 16: 6 (14); Matt. 28: 6, 7; Luke 24: 34; John 21: 14), and in the traditional formulae of the preaching of the resurrection (1 Cor. 15: 4; Rom. 4: 25; also Rom. 6: 4; 7: 4; 8: 34; 2 Cor. 5: 15; 2 Tim. 2: 8 (credal)). As A. Oepke points out,[1] the New Testament prefers this word to the intransitive ἀναστῆναι, "rise up", because it expresses the conviction that it was God who raised up Jesus from the dead. Nevertheless, ἀναστῆναι became a customary term, but it is secondary to the other verb.[2]

These linguistic data can admittedly not be pressed as evidence for the actual authenticity of Mark 14: 28. But if the words are those of Jesus, as I believe, he clearly expected his resurrection within a very short period after his death. There is no other evidence on this matter to which to appeal, since the predictions of the passion and resurrection of the Son of man, including Mark 9: 9, are excluded as community formulations. The conclusion, therefore, is that Jesus did distinguish between his resurrection from death and the parousia of the Son of man. What this parousia is, and who the Son of man is, we begin to see in the next three sayings to be discussed.

Mark 8: 38. "For whoever is ashamed of me and of my words in this adulterous and sinful generation, of him will the Son of

---

[1] Art. ἐγείρω, TWNT ii. 334.

[2] In no gospel passage is the older word ἐγείρεσθαι employed in referring to the *Son of man* except in parallels to the Markan predictions of the passion and resurrection: Luke 9: 22 (par. Mark 8: 31); Matt. 17: 23 (par. Mark 9: 31); Matt. 20: 19 (par. Mark 10: 34); Matt. 17: 9 (par. Mark 9: 9). See further on Luke 24: 7 (p. 82).

man also be ashamed, when he comes in the glory of his Father with the holy angels" (parr. Matt. 16: 27; Luke 9: 26).

This saying is reproduced substantially by Luke 9: 26. The Matthaean parallel, however, is not nearly so close, and is the evangelist's remoulding of Mark: "For the Son of man will come in the glory of his Father with his angels, and then he will repay each man according to his conduct." The change is due to the desire to represent the Son of man as the eschatological judge of men according to their deeds, and any distinction between him and Jesus is completely removed.

The Markan saying cannot be isolated from the corresponding one in Q, recorded in variant forms in Luke 12: 8f. and Matt. 10: 32f.

(a) Luke 12: 8, "Everyone who acknowledges (ὁμολογήσῃ) me before men, the Son of man also will acknowledge (ὁμολογήσει) before the angels of God";

(b) Luke 12: 9, "but he who denies (ἀρνησάμενος) me before men will be denied (ἀπαρνηθήσεται) before the angels of God."

"Will be denied"—by whom? The parallel with (a) puts it beyond doubt that it is by the Son of man that the disloyal follower of Jesus will be denied. Hence in Mark and Q the Son of man will speak against those who have been "ashamed of" or have "denied" Jesus. These two verbs are virtually synonyms in these contexts, with the nuance that the second one denotes the outward and public manifestation, in barefaced denial, of the attitude to Jesus engendered by persecution.[1]

(a) Matt. 10: 32, "So every one who acknowledges me before men, I also will acknowledge before my Father who is in heaven";

(b) Matt. 10: 33, "but whoever denies me before men, I also will deny before my Father who is in heaven".

The substitution of "I" for Son of man in (a) and its introduction in (b), together with the replacement twice of "the angels of God" as a circumlocution for God by "my Father in heaven", shows that in Matthew we have a secondary form of the Q logion which is much more accurately preserved in Luke. With (a) in Matthew should be compared Rev. 3: 5, ὁμολογήσω τὸ ὄνομα αὐτοῦ ἐνώπιον τοῦ πατρός μου καὶ ἐνώπιον

---

[1] Mark 8: 34-37; Luke 12: 4-7, 11f.; Matt. 10: 17ff., 28-31.

τῶν ἀγγέλων αὐτοῦ. In view of "his angels" in parallelism with "my Father", this is another more formalized variation of the original Q saying. With (b) is to be compared 2 Tim. 2: 12, εἰ ἀρνησόμεθα, κἀκεῖνος ἀρνήσεται ἡμᾶς. Here the idea of punishment in kind for denial of Jesus is stylized within a hymn.

It is therefore with Luke 12: 8f. that Mark 8: 38 has to be compared. Three salient points are at once apparent. Mark 8: 38 (down to αὐτόν) has as a parallel only the *second* member of the Q saying; the Son of man is not actually mentioned in Luke 12: 9, but is to be assumed from the preceding verse; the main difficulty is that Q has nothing apocalyptic about it and no trace of the parousia, while Mark (in the usual view) has both. For this reason Mark is commonly regarded as giving a secondary version as compared with Q.[1] Yet Mark, like Luke, preserves the mystery of the relation between Jesus and the Son of man. The second part of Mark 8: 38 resembles 13: 26 and 14: 62, but with the addition of the reference to angels, a feature shared with Luke 12: 8f. In Luke, however, the angels are a periphrasis for God, before whom the Son of man will appear as a witness or counsel for the defence or the prosecution, as the case may be. This is the more original form of the saying, transformed in Mark under the influence of the parousia expectation of the early church (cf. 1 Thess. 4: 15–17; 2 Thess. 1: 7).

The parousia or descent of the Son of man from heaven may, however, not be present in Mark 8: 38. The Son of man may be described as taking up his place in the presence of God, and the angels are his entourage. This would have some support in its reproduction in essentials in Luke 9: 26, with but slight changes. Luke can hardly be accused of predilection for parousia ideas, as his omission in 22: 69 of the second part of Mark 14: 62 clearly shows. Perhaps Luke did not see in Mark 8: 38, which he leaves in essentials untouched, the parousia doctrine which he did see in Mark 14: 62, and accordingly omitted. The background is Dan. 7, but is less distinct than in 13: 26 and 14: 62. The angels are mentioned because they were a feature of the original tradition[2] preserved more exactly

[1] E.g., T. F. Glasson, *The Second Advent* (1945), 74f.; Taylor, *Mark* 384.
[2] The original association of angelic beings is with God, Dan. 7: 10; 1 En. 61: 10 (along with the Elect One, usually equated with the Son of man). Angels are associated with the Son of man also in Matt. 13: 41; 25: 31; John 1: 51, but elsewhere in Mark only at 13: 27.

in Q (Luke 12: 8f.). But this non-parousia understanding of Mark 8: 38 cannot be pressed.

If a choice has to be made, the preference should be given to Q, in which the twofold form of the logion (acknowledging and denying) is more likely to approximate to an original utterance than the Markan form with its omission of the first part. In both cases the context is secondary: in Mark the words are addressed to the crowd "with his disciples" (8: 34), in Q to the disciples alone.

The relation between Jesus and the Son of man in this passage falls short of absolute identity, but the connection is extremely close because the Son of man stands on the same side as Jesus over against those who in this life have been ashamed of Jesus. The expression "his Father" in relation to the Son of man is unparalleled, of course, in Jewish apocalyptic. It is probably attributable to early Christian identification of Jesus and the Son of man. Or it may conceivably reflect a hint by Jesus himself at the relation between himself and the Son of man—the Son of man/Jesus replaces Jesus—Jesus achieves the status of that figure. In Matt. 10: 32f. this enigma of the relation between Jesus and the Son of man, also present in Q (Luke 12: 8f.), is resolved by making the identification so explicit that the Son of man is not mentioned at all. The precise nature of the association of Jesus and the Son of man cannot be decided on the basis of Mark 8: 38 (and the Q parallel) alone. But our conclusion on this logion would be that its Markan form, although inferior to Luke 12: 8f., is of sufficient value to warrant its being regarded as preserving in essentials an utterance of Jesus concerning the future activity and glory of the Son of man. The distinction between Jesus and the Son of man in both Mark and Luke can hardly be due to the community, but must have formed part of the original utterance from which the different forms are derived. In fact, the connection between Jesus and the Son of man is one both of distinction and of some kind of future association.

Mark 13: 26. "And then they will see the Son of man coming in clouds with great power and glory" (parr. Matt. 24: 30;[1] Luke 21: 27).

[1] See the discussion of this text in chapter 4.

In comparison with 8: 38 one difficulty at least is absent from this saying: the problem of the relationship between Jesus and the Son of man simply does not arise. But the very absence of this difficulty raises in its turn even greater problems which do not apply even to 14: 62, the most enigmatic of the so-called Markan "parousia sayings" and the one whose relationship to Dan. 7: 13 and its meaning are hotly disputed.

Even if the saying now under discussion stood in some other position than the one it occupies in Mark 13 which is, on any view, of composite origin, the difficulty would remain that Jesus is represented as referring to the Son of man as another figure without the slightest hint that that figure is in any way related to himself. It stands in a section of Mark which has been analysed in different ways,[1] but of which verses 24–27 are usually agreed to be the most suspect element,[2] consisting as they do of little more than a string of Old Testament quotations unexampled elsewhere in the teaching of Jesus.

If first we leave out of account the setting of Mark 13: 26 as if it might be a word of Jesus originally preserved in isolation and only later given its present position by being linked by καὶ τότε to the preceding Old Testament quotations, what is the result? A comparison with 8: 38 and 14: 62 is necessary.

8: 38, ὅταν (ὁ υἱὸς τοῦ ἀνθρώπου) ἔλθῃ ἐν τῇ δόξῃ τοῦ πατρὸς αὐτοῦ μετὰ τῶν ἀγγέλων τῶν ἁγίων.

13: 26, καὶ τότε ὄψονται τὸν υἱὸν τοῦ ἀνθρώπου ἐρχόμενον ἐν νεφέλαις μετὰ δυνάμεως πολλῆς καὶ δόξης.

14: 62, καὶ ὄψεσθε τὸν υἱὸν τοῦ ἀνθρώπου ἐκ δεξιῶν καθήμενον τῆς δυνάμεως καὶ ἐρχόμενον μετὰ τῶν νεφελῶν τοῦ οὐρανοῦ.

8: 38 has little direct contact with the other two passages, this being confined to "come" in all three and to "glory" in 13: 26. In addition, however, the angels figure in 13: 27 as the Son of man's emissaries to gather in the elect, as in 8: 38 they serve as his entourage. In contrast with 14: 62 the understanding of the present passage is not complicated by the problem of determining the priority of the session of the Son of man at the right hand of God or of his coming with the clouds, and the

---

[1] See especially G. R. Beasley-Murray's two thorough books, *Jesus and the Future* (1954), and *A Commentary on Mark Thirteen* (1957).
[2] Cf. Glasson, op. cit., 187.

meaning of the latter idea. The coming alone is mentioned. This fact, and the absence of any suggestion of some kind of connection between the Son of man and Jesus such as is present in the other two passages (14: 61f., "I am (the Messiah), and you shall see the Son of man. . . ."), in themselves suggest that 13: 26 is secondary.

The contrast between ὄψονται in 13: 26 and ὄψεσθε in 14: 62 cannot be fortuitous, in view of Rev. 1: 7, ἰδοὺ ἔρχεται μετὰ τῶν νεφελῶν, καὶ ὄψεται αὐτὸν πᾶς ὀφθαλμός. The third person plural in Mark 13: 26 is another form of the expression in Rev. 1: 7, "every eye shall see him". This similarity indicates that, as in the latter passage, we have also in the former the language of the church. "You shall see" in Mark 14: 62 is, therefore, further removed from church usage, being the probable basis, in a word of Jesus himself, of the employment of Dan. 7: 13 as a testimony passage in the early church.

Mark 14: 62 has *"with* the clouds", 13: 26 "in clouds". In Dan. 7: 13 the Aramaic "with the clouds of heaven" is translated in Theodotion's version (Θ) by μετὰ τῶν νεφελῶν τοῦ οὐρανοῦ, the exact language of Mark 14: 62. The LXX, however, has ἐπὶ τῶν νεφελῶν τοῦ οὐρανοῦ, and so has the Peshitta Syriac. It has been suggested that, because only God moves upon the clouds (cf. Ps. 104: 3; Isa. 19: 1), the ἐπί of the LXX represents an original *'al* ("upon") which was subsequently altered to *'im* ("with") in order "to minimise the divine manifestation in the one like to a son of man".[1] The agreement of the Peshitta, if Jewish in origin, might be held to support this view. Of course, if the following statement of Dalman is correct: "The words ἐν νεφέλαις, Mark 13[26], ἐν νεφέλῃ, Luke 21[27], similarly imply accompaniment, and presuppose μετά = ‎עם‎" (ibid.), there is nothing to discuss in the variants ἐν in 13: 26 and μετά in

---

[1] G. Dalman, *The Words of Jesus* (1902), 242; cf. R. H. Charles, *A Critical and Exegetical Commentary on the Book of Daniel* (1929), cxvii, 165, 186, who thought the corruption took place "perhaps not earlier than the beginning of the Christian era" (186). R. B. Y. Scott in an article entitled "Behold, he cometh with clouds", NTS 5 (1959), 127–32, regards Dalman's suggestion as unnecessary, because *'im* could be translated either by ἐπί or μετά, and is also interchangeable with *bᵉ* in Daniel (128). But the statement "that all [New Testament] variants are possible translations of ‎עם‎ as used in Daniel" (128, n. 4) is rendered less certain by closer scrutiny of their relationships.

14: 62. The identical meaning of these two Greek prepositions, however, is not as certain as Dalman supposed.

ἐν νεφέλαις in Mark 13: 26 in the parallel passage Matt. 24: 30 becomes ἐπὶ τῶν νεφελῶν τοῦ οὐρανοῦ (= LXX). The implication is that to Matthew ἐν did not denote accompaniment, but "upon" or "in", but he adopted the ἐπί of the LXX to render more clearly this meaning. Further, when this same form is used in Matt. 26: 64, which is the parallel to Mark 14: 62 (μετά), ἐπί and μετά are clearly not synonyms. Matthew in both cases follows the LXX, Mark 14: 62 follows Θ. The difficulty of Mark 13: 26 remains. The textual position may be tabulated thus.

Dan. 7: 13
"with (μετά) the clouds
of heaven", Aramaic, Θ, Vulgate   = Mark 14: 62; Rev. 1: 7
                                     ("with the clouds").

"on (ἐπί) the clouds of heaven",
LXX, Peshitta   = Matt. 24: 30 (par. Mark
                                     13: 26, ἐν); 26: 64 (par.
                                     Mark 14: 62, μετά); Rev.
                                     14: 15, 16 (ἐπὶ τῆς νεφέλης);
                                     Rev. 14: 14 (ἐπὶ τὴν
                                     νεφέλην).

In the LXX ἐν νεφέλη renders the Hebrew expression be'ānān (Gen. 9: 13, 14, 16; Exod. 16: 10; 34: 5; Lev. 16: 2; Num. 11: 25; Deut. 1: 33; Ps. 77 (78): 14), and both the Hebrew and the Greek prepositions mean "in" rather than "with" in the sense of *accompaniment*. The *absolute* equation, therefore, of ἐν νεφέλαις in Mark 13: 26 with μετά in 14: 62, proposed by Dalman, is not very likely; but ἐν is closer to ἐπί.

Matthew's adoption of the ἐπί of the LXX of Dan. 7: 13 in his parallels to both the Markan passages points to church usage. Bousset suggested that, despite the Aramaic word for "with" in Dan. 7: 13, the LXX preferred and was responsible for the introduction of ἐπί in the interests of messianic interpretation of the passage.[1] The important thing is that ἐπί was felt to be the more suitable word not only by Matthew but

---

[1] W. Bousset, *Die Religion des Judentums im späthellenistischen Zeitalter*, ed. H. Gressmann (1926), 265, n. 1.

also by the author of Revelation, and it may be assumed that this preference is a reflection of current understanding of the Danielic passage as referring to Jesus the Messiah in his eschatological role as the divine Son of man from heaven. While it is true enough that "whatever the preposition [with, upon, or in the clouds], the idea would necessarily connote divinity, or at least a close relation with the Deity",[1] the degrees of emphasis implied by the different prepositions should not be overlooked. The expression "with the clouds" in Mark 14: 62, it is suggested, is due to the fact that we have here a substantially authentic utterance of Jesus faithfully translated from the Aramaic in which he quoted from Dan. 7: 13 as holy scripture and therefore without any modifications.[2] Rev. 1: 7 presents us with a distinct echo of this logion.[3] From this Mark 14: 62 appears as clearly superior to the Matthaean parallel. Mark 13: 26, ἐν νεφέλαις (cf. par. Luke 21: 27, ἐν νεφέλῃ, the singular perhaps being reminiscent of Acts 1: 9, 11) is peculiar. LXX usage shows that the phrase usually means "*in* clouds". If a distinct nuance is to be sought, it is probably to be found in the desire to stress, even more than by ἐπὶ, the divinity of the Son of man who, like God in the Jewish scriptures, comes *in* the clouds. It is reasonable to expect this tendency in specifically apocalyptic circles, and that is exactly where we do find it, within the pericope Mark 13: 24–27.

There are three other marks of the secondary nature of the present saying.

"Power" is used differently in 13: 26 and 14: 62. In the second passage it is a Jewish periphrasis for God,[4] and does not belong to that part of the saying which refers to the coming with clouds, while in 13: 26 the Son of man comes in clouds "with great power and glory".

"Glory" is not mentioned in 14: 62, as it is in Mark 8: 38, which is inferior to Luke 12: 8f.

---

[1] G. R. Beasley-Murray, *A Commentary on Mark Thirteen* (1957), 92.

[2] However, the agreement of Mark 14: 62 with Θ may be due to the existence of a pre-Theodotionic translation of Daniel.

[3] Cf. C. C. Torrey, *The Apocalypse of John* (1958), 46, who sees in Rev. 1: 7, "with the clouds", an echo of the Aramaic preposition '*im* in Dan. 7: 13.

[4] On the rarity of this periphrasis see Lohmeyer, op. cit. (above, p. 28, n. 1), 328.

The only places in Mark where angels are associated with the Son of man are 8: 38 and 13: 27. The role of the angels in 8: 38 is that of the entourage of the Son of man, described in apocalyptic terms which are secondary to Luke 12: 8f. (Q), where the angels are a periphrasis for God. But in 13: 27 the angels are emissaries sent out to assemble the elect.[1] That verses 26 and 27 belong together is shown by their correspondence with Matt. 25: 31f.: coming of the Son of man, angels, gathering together of the elect (in Matthew, "all the nations" for judgement; the role of the angels is implied in the passive συναχθήσονται).

To return to the whole section, verses 24–27. The literature on Mark 13 is immense, and no attempt is called for to deal with it here. However, amidst the welter of analyses and views of the chapter three main standpoints are distinguishable. The first (that of T. Colani and his followers) regards the chapter as of Jewish or Jewish-Christian[2] origin, the basis being an apocalypse, and as containing little that can be attributed to Jesus. The second view is that the discourse goes back, at least in essentials, to the teaching of Jesus. The leading contemporary exponent of this view is Beasley-Murray who is, however, at pains to deny the belief that Mark 13 was spoken by Jesus precisely in its extant form. "I wrote [*Jesus and the Future*] to show that the contents of the discourse have high claim to authenticity, which is a different matter. I pointed out that the discourse must either be an expansion of what Jesus spoke in explanation of Mk. 13: 2 or was spoken on one occasion and reproduced in a fragmentary condition through casual quotation (hence its disjointedness). 'Between these alternatives no fine decision seems possible', I stated, but expressed the hope

[1] The beginning of verse 27 with καί τότε, identical with that of verse 26, betrays the patchwork character of this section. The words "from the four winds, from the end of the earth to the end of heaven" are an artificial combination of the LXX text of Zech. 2: 6 and Deut. 30: 4 (cf. Klostermann, op. cit., 137). For the gathering together of scattered Israelites see Isa. 52: 7ff.; 60: 4ff.; Baruch 5; Pss. Sol. 11; 17: 2; 2 Esdras 13; and of other nations, Isa. 2: 2f.; 60: 3; Zeph. 3: 9. The role of angels as emissaries of the Son of man to gather the elect has no precise Jewish parallel. Dan. 7: 10 and 1 En. 61: 1–5, 10 are not true parallels. One can but conclude that the association of angels with the Son of man is another form, in Son of man language, of the early hope in the appearance of the Lord Jesus "from heaven with his mighty angels" (2 Thess. 1: 7).

[2] Cf. W. L. Knox, *The Sources of the Synoptic Gospels* i (1953), 103–14.

that the latter alternative would not be dismissed as impossible".[1]
The third view, represented by V. Taylor, sees in Mark 13
an editorial combination of different groups of sayings. The
first of his four main groups[2] consists of sayings relating to signs
preceding the parousia, verses 5–8, 24–27. It is a merit of
Taylor's approach that he draws attention to the "disparate
tradition" which lies behind the difficulties of the chapter. The
section verses 24–27 he calls "secondary and derivative", "an
apocalyptic writing rather than a spoken discourse. It is
highly doubtful therefore if 26 can be regarded as an actual
saying of Jesus", though it "may be a distorted echo of His
words. The same interpretation accounts equally well for
24f. and 27".[3] Some such decision seems unavoidable. I would
urge, however, that it is not its resemblances (in apocalyptic
colouring) to 8: 38 and 14: 62 which point to the secondary
nature of 13: 26, so much as its differences from them.

The conclusion to which we are led is that Mark 13: 26
cannot be regarded as an utterance of Jesus; at the most, as
Taylor says, it "may be a distorted echo of His words". It
cannot, therefore, be included in any attempt to understand
his teaching upon the future role of the Son of man. In this respect
it is radically different from 8: 38 and, as we shall see, still
more so from 14: 62. It concerns solely the parousia of the
Son of man, and gives no hint, as do these other two sayings,
of some sort of relationship between this figure and Jesus.
Since there is no mention of the Son of man's session in the
presence of God, explicit in 14: 62 and implicit in 8: 38 and in
the Q form (Luke 12: 8f.), no question arises as to the chronological priority of the session or of the coming with clouds.

Mark 14: 62. "I am; and you will see the Son of man sitting
at the right hand of Power, and coming with the clouds of
heaven" (parr. Matt. 26: 64; Luke 22: 69).

This saying occupies a unique position among the Markan
Son of man words. It is the most important and the most crucial
of them, and is the only one of which it can be and has been
urged that the audience which is reported to have heard it

[1] *A Commentary on Mark Thirteen*, 11, n.
[2] *Mark* 636–44.
[3] Ibid., 519.

was not of a kind which could be expected to be a source of information for Christians. The first question, therefore, which demands some answer before the saying itself can be discussed, is whether this declaration of Jesus, if he made it, could have been known to his followers. The alternative would be that it is the product of early Christological application of Ps. 110: 1 and Dan. 7: 13; for what occasion could have been more apt than that of his arraignment before the Jewish religious leaders for Jesus to have made known his beliefs about the session and parousia of the Son of man?

Lietzmann rejected as unhistorical and as Christian fiction the whole section Mark 14: 55–65 concerning the hearing before the sanhedrin,[1] although later he conceded the possibility of the preservation of at least a faint reminiscence of what took place.[2] While it is likely that the nocturnal setting of the meeting of the sanhedrin in Mark is secondary, and that this really took place in the morning, as in Luke 22: 66–71,[3] there is the problem of whether Luke is using Mark or another source,[4] a problem whose chief importance for our purpose lies in Luke's variant version of Jesus' reply to the questioning about his claims. It is not inherently incredible that the Christian community made it its business to find out as far as possible the crucial question addressed to Jesus before the sanhedrin and his reply to it. We may, therefore, proceed with some confidence that behind the report in Mark there lie an actual question and an actual answer which were known to the earliest gospel tradition. How accurately they have been recorded, and in which of the synoptics, is a matter upon which there is wide divergence of view. In any case Mark 14: 62 cannot be examined without prior reference to the high priest's question.

"Are you the Christ, the Son of the Blessed?" Matt. 26: 63 is all but identical: "the Son of God".[5] This is not the place to examine the superiority or inferiority of the two questions of

[1] H. Lietzmann, *Der Prozess Jesu* (*Sitzungsberichte der Preussischen Akademie der Wissenschaften zu Berlin*, 1931), 313–22.
[2] *The Beginnings of the Christian Church* (1949), 60.
[3] Cf. my book, *The Historicity of the Fourth Gospel* (1960), 51–53.
[4] Cf. J. Blinzler, *The Trial of Jesus* (1959), 115–17.
[5] On "the Blessed" as a substitute for "God" see Dalman, op. cit., 200; SB ii. 51.

the whole sanhedrin in Luke (22: 67–70): "If you are the Christ, tell us", separated from "Are you the Son of God, then?" The net result is the same. Jesus is asked if he is the Messiah, the Son of God. Is such a question, equating Son of God with Messiah, likely on Jewish lips at that period? Despite the virtual absence in pre-Christian Jewish usage of Son of God as a messianic title,[1] such an equation can scarcely be dismissed as quite impossible, because the king could be so called (Ps. 2: 7), and the expectation of a Messiah sprang from the as yet unrealized ideals of kingship.[2] So much for the question reported as having been addressed to Jesus. It is perfectly possible, and may legitimately be regarded as belonging to accurate information concerning the appearance of Jesus before the sanhedrin, which in some way was acquired by contemporary followers of Jesus and passed into the tradition.[3]

For the direct acceptance of Messiahship by Jesus, "I am", there is an important variant, "You said that I am",[4] favoured by some scholars.[5] This, it is maintained, would account for σὺ εἶπας in Matt. 26: 64, and even for ὑμεῖς λέγετε ὅτι ἐγώ εἰμι in Luke 22: 70. The differences, however, are not of vital importance, for in any case Jesus admits in some sense, directly or indirectly, the status of Messiah, and moreover implies some kind of relationship between himself and the Son of man, as in Mark 8: 38 and its Q equivalent, Luke 12: 8f. This latter point favours the authenticity of at least the basis of the present saying which was understood by the hearers as blasphemy.[6]

In the discussion of Mark 13: 26 it was suggested that by contrast the language of Mark 14: 62 may point to an utter-

[1] Dalman, op. cit., 272, 275; Dodd, *Interpretation* 253; Mowinckel 293f., 368; Cullmann, *Christology* 274.

[2] Cf. Blinzler, op. cit., 102, n. 30.

[3] H. Conzelmann, *The Theology of Saint Luke* (1960), 84, considers the pericope Luke 22: 67–70 as "meant to set out explicitly the fundamental identity of the current Christological titles" contained in it.

[4] σὺ εἶπας ὅτι ἐγώ εἰμι, Θ f13 *pc* Or.

[5] Cf. B. H. Streeter, *The Four Gospels* (1936), 322; Taylor, *Mark* 568; Lohmeyer, op. cit. (above, p. 28, n. 1), 328, n. 2.

[6] On the earlier more inclusive conception of blasphemy see Lohmeyer, op. cit., 329; Blinzler, op. cit., 105f. According to E. Stauffer, *Jesus and His Story* (1960), 102f., 150, the blasphemy was the use of the theophanic formula '*anî hū*'. But "I am" does not have this meaning in Mark 14: 62, as it does in the Fourth Gospel (especially 8: 24, 58; 18: 6). It is simply an affirmation.

ance of Jesus: "*you* will see", "(the) Power" as a periphrasis for God, "*with* the clouds", following the Aramaic. Matt. 26: 64, "on the clouds", is secondary. As for the Lukan version (22: 69), its secondary nature seems clear. Its explanation of "the power" as "the power of God" does not encourage acceptance of the superiority of the absence of reference to the Son of man's coming to its presence in Mark and Matthew, any more than does the omission of "you will see". On all counts the Markan version is to be preferred.[1]

We have not hitherto found in Mark any saying about the coming or parousia of the Son of man which can be attributed to Jesus. Is Mark 14: 62 an exception? A widely favoured view is that it is no exception. Not that it is always rejected as unauthentic; but if it is accepted it does not, it is maintained, refer to a coming from God but a going to God. Thus Glasson, who does not allow any parousia utterances to Jesus, explains this one as referring to his assumption of glory and his exaltation to God's presence.[2] This view, in the form in which Glasson presents it, is acutely criticized by Tödt (who, however, refuses the saying to Jesus) on the ground that it is impossible to sustain a consistent parallelism between Mark 14: 62 and Dan. 7: 13.[3] J. A. T. Robinson, whose position resembles that of Glasson, writes on our passage that "Jesus affirms as the climax to his ministry of suffering and death an immediate translation into the glory of his Father. This is to be the *parousia* in its aspect of vindication, a coming to appear before the presence of God in exaltation and triumph—from then on".[4] Of this

---

[1] Stauffer, op. cit., 102, 142ff. (especially 150), 192, believes that the expression "I am" in Mark 14: 62 corresponds to "the most sacred formula of the divine self-revelation" [in the Old Testament]. Although this is unnecessary (see previous footnote), he accepts the genuineness *in toto* of the Markan version in preference to those in Matthew and Luke. On ἀπὸ τοῦ νῦν in Luke 22: 69 (so different from ἀπ' ἄρτι in Matt. 26: 64, which emphasizes the eschatological event), cf. Conzelmann, op. cit., 109, 116.

[2] Op. cit., 63ff.; cf. his article, "The Reply to Caiaphas (Mark XIV. 62)", NTS 7 (1960), 88–93; also Taylor, *Mark* 569.

[3] Tödt 35: "Zunächst ist die Parallelisierung zu Dan 7 nicht gut durchzuführen, weil dort das Gericht über den alten Äon bereits ergangen ist, ehe der Menschensohn auftritt und in die Regentschaft des Gottesreiches eingesetzt wird. Sodann ist aber auch die Reihenfolge der Zitate ein bedenkliches Hindernis: das Kommen mit den Wolken des Himmels schafft bei Dan 7 erst die Voraussetzung zur Inthronisation, in Mk 14, 62 hingegen folgt es der sessio ad dextram."

[4] *Jesus and His Coming* (1957), 130f.; cf. 43ff.

Mark 13: 26, he says, is a misunderstanding on the part of the early church, and is also at variance with the Markan theology as a whole. Schweizer does not accept the parousia passages as genuine, "but much is to be said in favour of the view that behind our texts a stage can be detected in which the coming of the Son of man with the clouds of heaven was related to the exaltation and vindication of Jesus". He thinks that since Mark interpreted the saying in 14: 62 in the sense of the parousia, he may "have inverted the original sequence of the two statements".[1] This last suggestion lacks force and is in any case sheer supposition. The difficulty of the order: session—coming with clouds, cannot be resolved so easily.

Much, however, still remains in favour of the more usual interpretation of Mark 14: 62. Thus Kümmel writes[2] of the "good tradition" according to which "Jesus, in the course of the hearing before the Sanhedrin after his arrest, gave his assent to the question about his Messiahship and illustrated it by pointing to the future coming of the Son of Man in divine glory. Without doubt it follows from this that Jesus expected that his future installation into the full messianic office would be the necessary preliminary to his participation in the coming judgment." He rejects attempts to avoid these facts by appeal to the parallel passages Matt. 26: 64 and Luke 22: 69, so that Jesus may be understood to have said nothing on this occasion about the parousia, and to have alluded only to exaltation.[3] It may be noted that it is not those who believe Mark 14: 62 to refer to exaltation or vindication, but some of those who see in it a definite allusion to the parousia as well, who entertain doubts of its genuineness. This is only to be expected, for it is more difficult to believe that Jesus spoke of the future advent of the Son of man than that he did not do more than refer to exaltation to God's presence as the Son of man.

Much has been made of the difficulty of the order of events in Mark 14: 62, in which the session of the Son of man precedes his coming, so that even if it is conceded that Dan. 7: 13 refers to a coming to God rather than a coming from God to

---

[1] Schweizer, *Lordship* 39 and n. 4; cf. *Menschensohn* 195.
[2] Kümmel 50.
[3] Ibid., 50, n. 102, on ἀπ' ἄρτι (Matthew) and ἀπὸ τοῦ νῦν (Luke).

earth, the order of the use of Ps. 110: 1 and Dan. 7: 13 rules this out here.[1]

It is by no means certain, however, that the Danielic passage does bear the meaning often attributed to it. Robinson[2] quotes with approval the statement of T. W. Manson: "It cannot be too strongly emphasised that what Daniel portrays is not a divine, semi-divine, or angelic figure coming down from heaven, to bring deliverance, but a human figure going up to heaven to receive it."[3] Robinson adds: "The important point is not whether in Daniel the scene is laid in heaven or earth: the locus of an apocalyptic vision, like that of a dream, is, literally, neither here nor there. What is indisputable is that it is a scene of vindication and that the Son of man comes *to* the Ancient of Days."[4] "[Such] spatial terms are in any case only an accommodation of language, and it is finally of no significance whether man is conceived as coming to God or God coming to man."[5] "Thus in Daniel 7 itself we have both representations: 'There came one like a son of man, and he came to the Ancient of Days' (v. 13) and, 'Until the Ancient of Days came, and judgement was given for the saints of the Most High' (v. 22)."[6] And his conclusion regarding the order session—coming in Mark 14: 62 is that "the two predictions of 'sitting at the right hand of God' and 'coming on the clouds of heaven' are to be understood as parallel expressions, static and dynamic, for the same conviction".[7]

This is a very convincing argument, with much in its favour. But there is another side to the question. Thus Dalman[8] thought that the assize "is held in the place where the animals have their being, i.e., upon the earth", so that verse 9 implies no change of scene, and the figure comes not from the earth, but from heaven. A possible objection to this interpretation, namely, that the description in Ezek. 1 of the divine chariot as the source of the wheeled throne in Dan. 7: 9 refers to God's

---

[1] Cf. C. E. B. Cranfield, *The Gospel according to Saint Mark* (1959), 444.
[2] Op. cit., 45.
[3] Manson, *Son of Man* 126.
[4] Ibid., 45, n. 2.
[5] Ibid., 51.
[6] Ibid., 51, n. 1.
[7] Ibid., 45.
[8] Op. cit. (above, p. 62 n. 1), 241.

throne in heaven, is countered by the fact that the divine chariot in Ezekiel was to serve God when he appeared on earth.[1] Beasley-Murray, combating what he terms "almost a new orthodoxy in Britain", points out that Dan. 7 does not imply that the saints were translated to heaven to rule the earth from there, and that verse 22 means that the Ancient of Days came *to earth* for judgement and deliverance, and concludes: "Neither in Daniel nor in the teaching of Jesus is there any ground for thinking that our passage [Mark 13: 26] and Mk. 14: 62 relate to anything other than a parousia to humanity on earth".[2]

Lohmeyer does not think that Dan. 7 has anything at all to do with exaltation;[3] but neither does he think that two separate events are meant in Mark 14: 62, which rather describes the Son of man's divine functions in two different ways.[4]

All these difficulties are removed if the whole saying is assumed to be unauthentic. Tödt[5] ascribes it to the post-resurrection church on the ground of the use of scripture which is lacking in authentic Son of man sayings [Luke 12: 8f., par.; Matt. 24: 27, 37, 39, par.]. W. Grundmann considers Mark's form of the utterance to be unauthentic and later than that of

[1] Glasson, op. cit., 14ff., has drawn attention to 1 En. 6–36. In this section of the book which according to Charles is pre-Maccabaean and therefore earlier than Daniel, there is a passage (14: 18–22) which closely resembles Dan. 7: 9f. in its description of the throne of God in *heaven*, and in Glasson's view is the source of the Son of man imagery in Daniel. 1 En. 14: 8 describes the ascent of Enoch to the divine presence in heaven in these words: "And the vision was shown to me thus: Behold, in the vision clouds invited me and a mist summoned me, and the course of the stars and the lightnings sped and hastened me, and the winds in the vision caused me to fly and lifted me upward, and bore me into heaven" (cf. later 2 En. 3: 1 (A): "It came to pass, when Enoch had told his sons, that the angels took him on to their wings and bore him up on to the first heaven and placed him on the clouds"). This suggestion is accepted by J. W. Bowman, *The Religion of Maturity* (1948), 225. But it is unconvincing. There is nothing about Enoch in the passage in Daniel. The imagery of Dan. 7 is certainly similar in some respects to that of 1 En. 14, but could be due to independent use of the same ideas by two different writers. Their subjects, however, are quite different—a corporate and symbolical figure in the one case, and the individual Enoch in the other. Glasson's explanation is examined and rejected by J. A. Emerton, JTS n.s. 9 (1958), 229f.

[2] *A Commentary on Mark Thirteen* (1957), 91.

[3] Op. cit. (above, p. 28 n. 1), 328: "Ein Gedanke, der der danielischen Vision und damit auch der von ihr getragenen jüdischen Apokalyptik unbekannt ist."

[4] Ibid., 329.   [5] Tödt 33–37.

Luke, and the product of Christian belief and application of scripture. The saying, however, has a historical basis in Jesus' confession of "seiner hochpriesterlichen [sic!] Sohnschaft vor seinen Richtern".[1]

I think that Mark 14: 62 can neither be dismissed as a community creation nor be divested of all reference to the parousia. Its superiority over Mark 13: 26 has already been remarked in the examination of that passage, especially in regard to the apparent distinction between Jesus and the Son of man and the Son of man's presence with God. In the former respect it is on a par with Mark 8: 38 as well as with the parallel in Luke 12: 8f., in the latter respect also especially with the Lukan saying. The tentative suggestion put forward earlier, that the second part of Mark 8: 38 may possibly refer not to the parousia but to the approach of the Son of man to the presence of God, is an idea which, as we have seen, is frequently favoured in regard to Mark 14: 62. But it is unsatisfactory.

If the saying is an utterance of Jesus, what did he mean by it? The difficulty involved in the order: session at the right hand of God—coming with the clouds, is not satisfactorily resolved by any of the expedients which have been proposed, i.e., the whole saying is a deposit of church doctrine, or the allusion to the passage in Daniel is a later addition, or the sequence was originally in the reverse order, or the two Old Testament passages are adopted as different expressions of the same fundamental conception, exaltation or vindication after the suffering and death of Jesus as at one and the same time both the Messiah-Son of God (Ps. 110: 1) and the Son of man (Dan. 7: 13).

The saying means, "Yes, I am, as you put it, the Messiah-Son of God; but this is only part of the truth of the matter. The total truth you do not comprehend. One of these days you will see the Son of man in the presence of God himself and coming with the clouds of heaven."[2] In 8: 38 it was sufficient

---

[1] *Das Evangelium nach Markus* (1959), 302. He distinguishes three stages in the growth of the saying: (1) ἐγώ εἰμι; (2) + Ps. 110: 1; (3) + Dan. 7: 13, for which addition Mark is responsible (n. 15).

[2] This does not create any fresh difficulty for the explanation of why the high priest declared this utterance to be blasphemy, for he and the other hearers assumed that Jesus was directly claiming for himself the right as Son of man to sit at God's right hand.

to refer to the Son of man as counsel for the prosecution. But now he is not addressing disciples,[1] some of whom might deny him or be ashamed of him, but his enemies who are, by that token, God's enemies. The Son of man, therefore, will be for them more than the counsel for the prosecution; he will be the eschatological judge.

The Son of man in Mark: conclusions

Of group A (the earthly activity of the Son of man) the sole instances (2: 10, 28) are probably not genuine words of Jesus, but Christological affirmations of the Palestinian church.

Jesus referred to his approaching passion, using the first person and metaphorical language in sayings which represent substantially authentic tradition (Mark 10: 38; 14: 22, 24; cf. also outside the Markan tradition, Luke 12: 50; 13: 33). But the predictions of the passion of the Son of man (8: 31; 9: 12, 31; 10: 33f.) are church formulations, and the same is true of the other members of this group. Nevertheless, it has been suggested, 14: 41 has been inspired by the expressed insight of Jesus that one of the disciples would betray him (14: 18); while 14: 21 and 10: 45 alone, although owing their present form to the community, are probably based directly on utterances of Jesus in the first person: "I go to him that sent me"; "I shall (or, "I came to") give my life as a ransom for many".

The sayings referring to the Son of man's resurrection (8: 31; 9: 31; 10: 34, and also 9: 9, included under category C) are valueless in themselves as a source of information on the thought of Jesus about resurrection. Mark provides no evidence that Jesus actually alluded either to the passion and death or to the resurrection of the Son of man. But their ultimate origin may be found not only in the faith of the post-resurrection church, but in the isolated logion in 14: 28, "After I am raised up, I will go before you into Galilee".

We arrive at the result that, according to the Markan tradition, Jesus did not refer to himself as the Son of man on earth at all, either as active in his ministry or as suffering and dying and being raised up. Yet he foresaw and referred to in the first person both his death and his resurrection. Nevertheless, there

---

[1] Mark 8: 34; Luke 12: 4; Matt. 10: 5.

must be an explanation for the choice of precisely the term Son of man in the sayings we have examined in groups A and B. The explanation is that Jesus did speak of the parousia of the Son of man according to the Markan tradition, and that this terminology has overlaid much of the reminiscences of Jesus' allusions to his ministry and his death and resurrection.

In the third group, C, two passages, 8: 38 and 14: 62, can be used with some confidence. 8: 38, it has been suggested, may not refer to the advent of the Son of man but to his approach *to* God, as so many exegetes demand for 14: 62. Be that as it may, 8: 38, while less good than the Q version in Luke 12: 8f., preserves, as does the genuine saying in 14: 62, the mystery of the relation between Jesus and the Son of man. By contrast, 13: 26 is sheer apocalyptic; this mysterious relationship is entirely absent, only the parousia of the Son of man is envisaged, and the verse is at best a distorted echo of Jesus' words. An important advance in the conception of the role of the Son of man was also noted, from that of counsel for (the defence [Luke 12: 8] and for) the prosecution (8: 38; Luke 12: 9) to that of the eschatological judge (14: 62).

In the tradition used by Mark, Christological development has already gone so far that for the most part what Jesus is believed to have said about his ministry and his death and resurrection has been radically affected by utterances about the Son of man's future activity as counsel or judge.

Chapter 3

THE SON OF MAN IN LUKE

The following sayings are peculiar to Luke.
A. 19: 10.
B. 17: 25; 22: 48; 24: 7.
C. 17: 22; 17: 30; 18: 8b; 21: 36.

A

Luke 19: 10. "For the Son of man came to seek and to save the lost."[1]

While the call of Zacchaeus is reminiscent of that of Levi (Mark 2: 14–17; Luke 5: 27–32), the only feature common to both narratives is, as B. S. Easton points out,[2] the presence of tax-gatherers in both, and Levi, unlike Zacchaeus, was called to follow Jesus. There is no reason to question that the story was derived by Luke from a special source quite independently of Mark. But the saying in 19: 10 presents difficulties.

It seems superfluous in its present position, which may be secondary. Not only is the narrative complete without it; the saying occurs, though in a slightly shorter version, at Matt. 18: (11): "For the Son of man came to save the lost."[3]

In verse 9a Jesus turns and addresses Zacchaeus himself:[4] "Today salvation has come to this house", and then adds, "since he also is a son of Abraham", as if referring to Zacchaeus in the third person. It may be suggested that the story ended with verse 9a, both 9b ("since he also is a son of Abraham") and verse 10 being later conclusions, inserted in that order, summing up the situation in different ways. Verse 9b is at first sight more narrowly Jewish ("to this son of Abraham,

---

[1] Luke 9: 56a is no part of the original text, but a secondary formation modelled on the analogy of 19: 10. 22: 48 is best assigned to group B.

[2] *The Gospel according to St. Luke* (1926), 279.

[3] DW 28 565 700 *pm* lat syc; cf. also the addition in Luke 9: 56 in some witnesses.

[4] J. Wellhausen, *Das Evangelium Lucae* (1904), 104, extrudes the words πρὸς αὐτόν as "ein falscher Zusatz".

too, salvation has come") than verse 10, but the latter is a clear allusion to Ezek. 34: 16, "I will seek the lost, and I will bring back the strayed".[1]

The partial resemblance of verse 10 to Mark 10: 45 gives ground for suspicion. It is inferior to that saying even in its present context,[2] where it is the Twelve who are addressed. Luke 19: 10 presents a "public and unambiguous use of 'Son of Man' ".[3] Only in these two passages does the expression "the Son of man came to" occur. It is a homiletical comment appended subsequently to the addition to Jesus' words to Zacchaeus in verse 9a, of verse 9b, "since he also is a son of Abraham", and is explanatory both of this addition, now assumed to be part of the utterance of Jesus himself, and of the whole story of the coming of salvation to Zacchaeus and his house.[4]

It was earlier pointed out that 1 Tim. 2: 5f. is a Hellenistic rewriting of the Semitic logion in Mark 10: 45.[5] Although the analogy is less clear, much the same can be said of the resemblance of 1 Tim. 1: 15, Χριστὸς Ἰησοῦς ἦλθεν εἰς τὸν κόσμον ἁμαρτωλοὺς σῶσαι[6] to Luke 19: 10. That the Son of man saying here, like Mark 10: 45, is the earlier, can hardly be doubted. But it does not represent the *ipsissima verba* of Jesus. It is another instance of the creation and attribution to Jesus by the early Palestinian church of a saying about himself as the Son of man. Although not a genuine word of Jesus, its ultimate basis may be some such utterance as Mark 2: 17 (parr. Matt. 9: 13; Luke 5: 32), "I came not to call the righteous, but sinners".

---

[1] E. Hirsch, *Frühgeschichte des Evangeliums*, ii: *Die Vorlagen des Lukas und das Sondergut des Matthäus* (1941), 231–33, thinks that the narrative itself originally concluded at verse 7, and that Jesus' answer to the criticism that he was associating with a sinner was, (and Jesus said), "He also is a son of Abraham", and that the remainder is later elaboration beginning with the intrusion of verse 8, which led to the expansion of Jesus' words to their present form in verses 9–10.

[2] The original setting may have been the Last Supper; see above, pp. 49f.

[3] Easton, op. cit., 279, who, while accepting the story itself as trustworthy, calls the utterance the evangelist's "generalization".

[4] Such homiletical comments are most familiar in the Fourth Gospel; cf. for example John 20: 29, where the words "blessed are those who have not seen and yet believe" are the homiletical comment on the word of Jesus, "Have you believed because you have seen me?"

[5] See above, p. 44.

[6] Cf. John 3: 17, εἰς τὸν κόσμον and ἵνα σωθῇ ὁ κόσμος.

B

Luke 17: 25. "But first he [the Son of man] must suffer many things and be rejected by this generation."

The Son of man is not actually named in this verse, but in the preceding one. There the Son of man may or may not be Jesus himself. This question can only be decided when we come to the Q sayings. But in the present sequence of the two verses Jesus is the Son of man as in the three Markan passion predictions reproduced by Luke.[1] Our saying intrudes into a Q context, and since Q does not report any sayings about the passion of the Son of man, it cannot come from that source; moreover, Matthew does not contain it. It may be assumed with some confidence that in Q Luke 17: 24 was followed immediately by verse 26. In Matt. 24: 27–37 these two Q sayings are separated by a long insertion (verses 29–36) of material derived from Mark 13: 24–32, which is preceded in verse 28 by a transposition of the ending of the Q material (Luke 17: 37).

According to Kümmel[2] "the πρῶτον shows that the saying must have stood originally in a pertinent connexion with a promise of the parousia". The word, however, is much more likely to be an editorial link.[3] The difficulty of maintaining that the saying is "a reliable old tradition"[4] is that in Luke 17: 24f. (or in the hypothetical "pertinent connexion") we find a close association of the passion and rejection of the Son of man with his future appearing in glory. An explicit association of this kind is unique, and must be secondary. The direct juxtaposition of the parousia glory of the Son of man and his (preceding) suffering must be the work of the evangelist, and the sole significance of the saying in Luke 17: 25 probably lies in its illustration of early Christian identification of the Son of man with the Jesus who suffered.[5]

[1] Luke 9: 22 = Mark 8: 31; Luke 9: 44 = Mark 9: 31; Luke 18: 32f. = Mark 10: 33f.

[2] Kümmel 70.

[3] So H. Conzelmann, *The Theology of Saint Luke* (1960), 124, n. 1: "πρῶτον is a typically Lucan term, especially in eschatological contexts".

[4] Kümmel 71.

[5] Cf. Tödt 98–100, who points in this connection to Mark 8: 31, 38 as an example of association in Christian thought of the suffering and the parousia of the Son of man.

importance for our purposes. But even if the second view is accepted, the utterance cannot come from Jesus. Jesus may well have addressed Judas at this critical moment; but everything goes to show that the word as recorded by Luke cannot be adduced as evidence that Jesus called himself, as a figure still active on earth, the Son of man. The saying is a dramatized form of the theme "the Son of man is betrayed".

Luke 24: 7. "(Remember how he told you, while he was still in Galilee), that the Son of man must be delivered into the hands of sinful men, and be crucified, and on the third day rise."

This saying has the distinction of being the only one peculiar to Luke which refers to both the death and the resurrection of the Son of man.

It has been regarded as a mere editorial combination of 9: 44 and 9: 22,[1] or as a remodelling of Mark 16: 7[2] necessitated by Luke's omission of Jesus' prediction in Mark 14: 28 that after being raised up he would precede his disciples to Galilee. The general resemblance of this saying to the Markan predictions of the Son of man's death and resurrection (Mark 8: 31; 9: 31; 10: 33f.) is admitted, but the differences are such as to make unlikely any theory of editorial composition alone. K. H. Rengstorf, for example, has pointed out[3] that since Lukan contact with Mark ceases at Mark 16: 8, that gospel as known to the third evangelist ended at that point, with the result that Luke 24: 1–11 (12) comes from another tradition. But a decision can only be reached by examination of the component parts of the saying.

1. δεῖ. On the use of this word to denote scriptural necessity, see above on Mark 8: 31.[4]

2. παραδοθῆναι. The theme "the Son of man is delivered up" is familiar from passages already discussed (Mark 9: 31; 10: 33; 14: 21, 41; Luke 22: 48). Of the Markan passages those which the present saying most closely resembles at this point are 9: 31, already used (in part) at Luke 9: 44 ("into the

---

[1] Easton, op. cit., 356; Kümmel 72, n. 175; cf. J. M. Creed, *The Gospel according to St. Luke* (1930), 293.

[2] Sjöberg 236n.; Schweizer, *Menschensohn* 197.

[3] *Das Evangelium nach Lukas*[8] (1958), 278f.

[4] Chapter 2, p. 32, n. 4.

hands of men"), and especially 14: 41 ("into the hands of sinners"), which Luke omits. It may be that Luke, having omitted the saying, reproduces some of its language here.[1] But this is uncertain; Luke could be quite independent here.

3. In only two other predictions of the Son of man's passion is the word "crucify" used, in Matt. 20: 19, where it replaces "kill" in Mark 10: 34, and in Matt. 26: 2, which introduces a saying of Jesus into a Markan context. In Luke 24: 7, as in both these places, the word "crucify" replaces the *terminus technicus* "kill", and is late.[2]

4. Is "on the third day" or "after three days" the older expression? Tödt thinks it is the latter, being pre-Markan (Mark 8: 31; 9: 31; 10: 34),[3] and compares its substitution by "on the third day" in Matthew and Luke (Matt. 16: 21* = Luke 9: 22;* Matt. 17: 23;* 20: 19* = Luke 18: 33) with the replacement of the verb "kill" by "crucify". More important is the association of the phrase "on the third day" (but not of "after three days") with ἐγείρεσθαι.[4] This association supports the view that ἐγείρεσθαι is more primitive than ἀναστῆναι.[5] "On the third day" is used with ἀναστῆναι only in Luke 18: 33 and 24: 7.

Luke 24: 7 is independent of the Markan sayings. Its terminology, however, is such that it cannot be a saying of Jesus; but it may preserve the knowledge that he referred to his death and resurrection while still in Galilee.

C

Luke 17: 22. "The days are coming when you will desire to see one of the days of the Son of man, and you will not see it."

Luke 17: 30. "So will it be on the day when the Son of man is revealed."

---

[1] Mark 14: 41, εἰς τὰς χεῖρας τῶν ἁμαρτωλῶν; Luke 24: 7, εἰς χεῖρας ἀνθρώπων ἁμαρτωλῶν.

[2] Cf. Tödt 141, 162f., 170f.; but also below, p. 164.

[3] Tödt 167–72.

[4] In the asterisked passages above.

[5] Cf. above, p. 57; Acts 10: 40, τοῦτον ὁ θεὸς ἤγειρεν ἐν τῇ τρίτῃ ἡμέρᾳ. Schweizer, *Lordship* 95: ". . . it was probably even longer before the raising of Jesus became the resurrection, an act of Jesus himself"; A. Oepke, TWNT ii. 334: "Der Gedanke der selbsttätigen Auferstehung Jesu wird erst in der johanneischen Theologie erreicht."

Although these two verses are peculiar to Luke, they cannot be treated in isolation from the whole section 17: 22–37, which has parallels in Matthew.

The teaching is addressed to the disciples, but this is stated in verse 22, which has no parallel in Matthew, and contains the unique expression "one of the days of the Son of man". Whether the words, "And he said to the disciples", are the work of the evangelist intended to indicate a change of audience, or come from a source, this unique expression is probably due to him. Verse 23 corresponds to Matt. 24: 26, but the two are so different that Luke has probably reshaped the original saying. This is supported by the close resemblance of its opening words to verse 21a. Verse 24 is from Q, but the differences from Matt. 24: 27 require explanation. Harnack[1] considered Matt. 24: 27ff. to be nearer Q, Luke's version being a revision. He also held that "the parousia of the Son of man" in Matt. 24: 27 stood in Q, for although confined to Matthew among the gospels, the expression occurs there only in Q sections (24: 37, 39; possibly also 24: 3). More usually and more convincingly it is thought that "parousia" in Matthew is secondary, and comes from the later language of the church.[2] If so, the question arises whether Luke's terms "the Son of man in his day" (verse 24) and "the days of the Son of man" (verse 26) are his own language or that of the common source; and if his own language, what has this replaced in the common source? Verse 25 we have seen to be an editorial insertion. Verses 26f. are from Q, but there is reason to believe that neither the Lukan nor the Matthaean form (24: 37–39) preserves exactly the wording of the common source. The strange expression "the days of the Son of man" recurs. Verses 28–30 have no counterpart in Matthew. Do they nevertheless come from Q?[3] It is unlikely that Matthew would have omitted them if he had known them. It has therefore been suggested that the saying about Lot stood in Q as known to Luke, but not in the form of

---

[1] A. Harnack, *The Sayings of Jesus* (1908), 106–108.

[2] Cf. Kümmel 38, n. 63; Tödt 8of., where the inferiority of the comparisons in Matt. 24: 37, 39 to Luke 17: 26 ("days" compared with "days") is pointed out.

[3] Cf. e.g. Klostermann, op. cit. (above, p. 79, n. 3), 175: omitted by Matthew; Manson, *Sayings* 141ff.: the whole section Luke 17: 22–37 is from Q.

it known to Matthew, and was added later as a parallel to the saying about Noah.[1] Is this really satisfactory? Apart from the more general consideration that new additions within Q would have been more likely by the time when Matthew's gospel, which is later than Luke's, was written, other factors render uncertain the derivation of these verses from Q. The rest of the section need not detain us.[2]

Concentrating on the expressions "the day" and "the days of the Son of man", we can use the following table for reference.

Luke 17		Matt. 24	
verse			verse
22, "one of the days of the Son of man".			
24, "the Son of man in his day".	Q	27, "the parousia of the Son of man".	
26, "the days of the Son of man".	Q	37, (39),[3] "the parousia of the Son of man".	
30, "the day when the Son of man is revealed".			

It is clear that Luke 17: 24, 26 are from Q, but whether the Lukan or the Matthaean form is the more original remains to be decided. A formidable difficulty is not only that Luke has the two expressions "the Son of man in his day" and "the days of the Son of man", but that the singular form corresponds to verse 30 and the plural to verse 22, neither of which verses has a parallel in Matthew, and neither of which may, despite the view of some scholars, have belonged to Q at all. If they did not, it would mean that both Q (verses 24, 26) and Luke's special source (verses 22, 30) independently represent Jesus as speaking both of "the day" and "the days" of the Son of man, or that one of these sources has influenced the wording of the other, or again that Luke himself is responsible for these expressions, or for one of them.

---

[1] Bultmann, *Tradition* 123; Vielhauer 66; Tödt 47.

[2] The theme of suddenness is resumed at verses 34f. after a reference to the fall of Jerusalem in verses 31f., with the name of Lot (verses 28f., 32) serving as a link between the two different themes (cf. Manson, *Sayings* 141f.). Verse 33, an independent saying out of its context, is adapted to the reference to flight in verses 31f. (cf. 9: 24 = Mark 8: 35 = Matt. 16: 25; Matt. 10: 39). Of this latter part of the pericope only verses 33(?), 34f., 37 are from Q.

[3] Strictly speaking 39b is an editorial repetition of 37b.

As we have seen, it is arguable that verses 28–30 are a secondary Q formation unknown to Matthew, a view at least preferable, despite its disadvantages, to the alternative that Matthew knew them but omitted them. It is not of vital importance whether they belong to a later recension of Q or were constructed by the evangelist himself. In any case their structure betrays their secondary origin, and therefore forbids the attribution of the words to the teaching of Jesus. The association of the references to Noah and Lot as outstanding examples of righteous men of the past saved by God in both 2 Pet. 2: 5–7 and Luke 17: 26–29 may be a case either of dependence of 2 Peter on Luke, or of independent allusions to these figures in the Jewish scriptures. Jesus is reported to have spoken about Sodom and Gomorrah,[1] and so could quite conceivably have spoken also of Lot, as he did of Noah. But this is sheer supposition, and is not borne out by the character of the section.

The structure of verses 28–30, although close superficially to that of verses 26f., is spoiled by the absence from verse 28 after the name of Lot of a conclusion corresponding to the words following Noah in verse 26. We have instead verse 30. This verse occupies the same position, at the end of the comparison, as does Matt. 24: 39b at the end of the comparison with the days of Noah, and means the same thing. In Luke the Son of man is "revealed", while Matthew refers to his parousia. The language of verse 30 shows it to be secondary. Nowhere else in the New Testament does the expression κατὰ τὰ αὐτά occur except in Luke 6: 23, 26; the parallel to verse 23 in Matt. 5: 12 has οὕτως, as has Matt. 24: 39. In verses 26f., life before the flood went on "until the day when Noah entered the ark"; in the days of Lot the even tenor of life ceased abruptly "on the day when Lot went out from Sodom". The same words (ᾗ ἡμέρᾳ) are used in verse 30 for the day on which the Son of man is revealed. The redactional nature of this verse is clear. It serves as a link between the reference to the story of Lot going out from Sodom on the very eve of disaster and the necessity for the inhabitants of Jerusalem, when calamity threatens, to leave the city forthwith without hesitation or turning back—

---

[1] Matt. 10: 15, par. Luke 10: 12; Matt. 11: 23f.; cf. Rom. 9: 29 (Isa. 1: 9); Jude 7; Rev. 11: 8; cf. SB i. 571–74.

"remember Lot's wife" (verse 32). "In that day" in verse 31 is interpreted as "the day when the Son of man is revealed" (cf. 21: 27), and verse 31 itself may come from Luke's special source.[1]

Do the expressions "the day of the Son of man" implied in verse 24, and "the days of the Son of man" in verse 26, mean the same thing? The former refers to the parousia, as is restated explicitly in Matt. 24: 27. The Son of man's appearing will be as sudden and unexpected as a flash of lightning, and not a final event prepared for by a series of premonitory signs. But in Matt. 24: 37, 39 the parousia of the Son of man is also equivalent to "the *days* of the Son of man" in Luke 17: 26. Is this double identification right, and is it to be assumed that Matthew read in Q what we read in Luke? Harnack's view that Matthew found "parousia" in Q is, as has been said above, not likely to be correct.

The actual expression "the day of the Son of man" is not found, but is clearly implied in Luke 17: 24. The usual explanation is that it is formed on the analogy of "the day of the Lord" in the Old Testament.[2] Transference of the idea of "the day" from God to a celestial messianic figure occurs in the Similitudes of Enoch. "On that day Mine Elect One shall sit on the throne of glory" (1 En. 45: 3). This figure is also called the Son of man in the Similitudes. The omission of "in his day" in Luke 17: 24 (BD it sa) would ease the problem, however, especially as verse 30 ("the day when the Son of man is revealed") is redactional. But the omission can hardly be accepted as sufficiently strongly attested.[3]

[1] Cf. the confusion of traditions about the coming of the Son of man and the fall of Jerusalem in Mark 13. Luke 21: 27 also illustrates, as does the present passage, the association in the mind of the third evangelist of the advent of the Son of man with physical disasters.

[2] See, however, the appended note to this section. On Jesus' eschatological use of "day" see Kümmel 36ff.

[3] A. R. C. Leaney, *The Gospel according to St. Luke* (1958), 69f., accepts the omission, urging "that Luke has stamped his own form of eschatology on material itself envisaging only one day of the Son of man" [thus Matthew's "parousia of the Son of man" is correct interpretation], in the interests of a conception of a number of "days of the Son of man": the transfiguration, resurrection, ascension, the appearances to Stephen and Paul, the restoration of Jerusalem and Israel, and the final consummation. The distinction between the singular and the plural is in principle correct, but the plural form is to be explained otherwise.

Is Matthew's "parousia of the Son of man" a conscious and deliberate interpretation and explication of what he read in Q, i.e., both of "the day" and "the days of the Son of man"? If so, the first evangelist must have read the same meaning into both expressions. Assuming for the moment that Luke reproduces Q in having the two expressions, do they in fact mean the same thing? Kümmel[1] thinks they do: Luke 17: 24 and 26 are "probably originally independent detached sayings" applied by the evangelist to the parousia, which may indeed have been their original meaning, and have come from the oldest tradition.

Identity of meaning, however, is unlikely (still on the present assumption that the phrases stood in Q). "The day of the Son of man" implied in Luke 17: 24 is an entirely eschatological expression. But "the days of the Son of man" in verse 26 must, on the analogy of "the days of Noah", denote a *period*, of which the term is the coming of the Son of man. Just as the days of Noah ended with the flood, so the days of the Son of man will culminate in his sudden advent. T. W. Manson wrote that " 'Days of the Son of Man' is not the plural of 'Day of the Son of Man', but a poetical way of describing the last days of the existing order".[2] This is an attractive suggestion; but such a meaning of the plural is only possible on the lips of Jesus if it is conceded that he spoke of himself as the Son of man in his earthly activity or if, with Manson, the Son of man is understood to be Jesus and his disciples. It is impossible for him if he referred to the Son of man only as a future, eschatological figure, because there is only one day of the Son of man, that of his parousia.

The difficulty of the expression in Luke 17: 22, "one of the days of the Son of man", is considerable. Manson accepted Torrey's explanation that the Aramaic adverb *laḥdhā'*, meaning "very much", has been misunderstood as the numeral "one" with the sign of the accusative, and that the original meaning was "you will greatly desire to see the day of the Son of man".[3]

---

[1] Kümmel 37f., approved by Vielhauer 66, n. 81.
[2] *Sayings* 143. This is the direct opposite of Leaney's suggestion.
[3] Manson, *Sayings* 142; C. C. Torrey, *The Four Gospels* 312; but in *Our Translated Gospels* 85, 89f., "of the days" (the messianic time) is suggested by Torrey, instead of "the day".

Certainly Luke's expression is not readily intelligible, and this may be the correct explanation (but see below).

"The days of the Son of man" in Luke 17: 26 is formed on the analogy of "the days of Noah". It is to be attributed not to Q, still less to Jesus himself, but to Luke. And that Matthew's equivalent, "the parousia of the Son of man", was also not in Q may be assumed because at Matt. 24: 27 it replaces the other phrase, "the day of the Son of man" implied in Luke 17: 24 (Q). In Matt. 24: 37, 39 also, therefore, it replaces an original "the day of the Son of man" in the common source. The word "parousia" occurs only in Matthew among the gospels (24: 3, besides the above references).

To sum up. "The day of the Son of man" stood originally both in the common source (verses 24, 26), and in Luke's special source (verse 22), where the plural is the result of Luke's substitution of it in verse 26. Verse 30 is editorial. All this leads to the conclusion that Jesus did not speak of "the days of the Son of man" but only of his "day".

Two questions remain. Why did Luke make these changes? What is the significance of the words of Jesus in the original form of the tradition?

The singular and the plural expressions, as we have seen, do not mean the same thing. "The day of the Son of man", correctly interpreted by Matthew's term "parousia", is the time of his appearance. The plural in Luke 17: 26, on the other hand, denotes the final period which will culminate in *the day* of the Son of man, in his sudden appearance. Just as the days of Noah were the closing period of the old era before the flood, so in due course will arrive the closing period of the present world order; and just as this period ended on the day of Noah's entry into the ark, so "the days of the Son of man", still to come, will end with his "day". Of verse 22, which says that the disciples will long to see "one of the days of the Son of man", it is suggested that, while the theory of misunderstanding of the Aramaic may be correct, it is equally possible that the plural is due to its occurrence in verse 26. In other words the evangelist has deliberately modified his source. Where the source reported Jesus as saying that the disciples would long to see "the day of the Son of man", Luke has altered this to their longing to see "one of the days of the Son of man", that is, in agreement with verse 26, some indication that that final era has at last arrived, which is bound to end with the coming of the Son of man.[1] Such an interpretation of Luke's procedure is fully in harmony with his general tendency to tone down the eschatological emphasis in the original material.[2]

If verse 22 is restored to what it is suggested may have been its original form, Jesus is warning the disciples that they will long to see the day of the Son of man, but in vain. This could be an authentic utterance, to be laid to heart in time of trial and persecution. No false trails are to be followed, for the day of his coming will be sudden like lightning. At the same time, it will be as in Noah's days. Completely unheralded to the unbelieving world as was the flood, the Son of man's day will be the end and climax of a period. But it is implied that, sudden though it will be, the faithful will not lack the opportunity of escape any more than did Noah and his people. This, it is urged, was the message of Jesus, a view supported by Matthew's version of the common source material which, though secondary in its wording, correctly interprets the original tradition which Luke has obscured in the interests of his own eschatological point of view.

Finally, the case for regarding the teaching in Luke 17: 22–27 in its proposed original form as substantially from the lips of Jesus himself, is very strong indeed. We have seen that the authenticity of the sayings in Luke 12: 8f. (par. Matt. 10: 32f.) and Mark 8: 38 (par. Luke 9: 26) is guaranteed by the relationship, not defined as identity, between Jesus and the Son of man. What is determinative at the judgement, where the Son of man acts as counsel for the defence or for the prosecution, is a man's attitude to Jesus on earth. The case here is, if

---

[1] This would mean that Luke's plural form may correspond formally to the Rabbinical "days of the Messiah"; cf. SB iv. 826ff., 857ff.

[2] Tödt 98 places the emphasis somewhat differently. "The days of the Son of man" are the coming kingdom. The Son of man already sits at God's right hand (cf. 22: 69, which omits the coming with the clouds in Mark 14: 62), but this rule is not yet visible to the church. "Dementsprechend kommt die Kraft für die Jünger nicht nur daraus, dass sie in jene Ferne vorwärtsblicken dürfen, sondern vielmehr daraus, dass sie auf das Reich, welches in Jesus mitten unter ihnen war [cf. Luke 17: 21], zurückblicken können." But the main concern is with the *coming period* of the Son of man, his "days", of which the "day" is the culmination. That this is Luke's intention is shown by the comparison with the days of Noah.

anything, even more firmly grounded, for there is no overt hint at all of any relationship between them: the eschatological figure, the Son of man, will come. But a similar kind of relationship is nevertheless implied, but in a different way and without any use of the first person singular. This is achieved by the comparison with the days of Noah. Just as deliverance depended then on trust in God displayed by Noah and his people, so, without being expressed in so many words, the thought can hardly be absent that the Son of man in his day will act in support of or against a man according to his attitude to Jesus. Indeed, in one respect Luke 17: 24, 26 are even more definite than the other sayings (Luke 12: 8f.; etc.), and go a step further. For the very fact that the *day* of the Son of man is envisaged—in place of the day of the Lord (Yahweh)—means that the Son of man's function is greater than that of counsel for the defence or prosecution; he is himself the judge. It is true that, if this is accepted, there is inconsistency in the utterances of Jesus about the role of the Son of man: at one time he is a counsel or advocate, at another the judge himself. I fail to see any fundamental objection to this. It is well known to what straits critics have been driven by Jesus' far from consistent teaching about the presence and the coming of the kingdom of God, and what distortions of that teaching have been produced by the desire to achieve at all costs a rigid consistency ("realized eschatology", "futurist eschatology").

Appended Note on "the day(s) of the Son of man"

Direct influence of the Rabbinical expression "the days of the Messiah" on Luke in his choice of the term "the days of the Son of man" is most improbable (see above, p. 89 n. 1). The Rabbinical conception belongs to a different circle of ideas, and is besides post-Christian, perhaps based on 2 Esdras 13: 52, ". . . no one on earth can see my Son or those who are with him, except in the time of his day" (RSV, following the Syriac; cf. SB ii. 237). This, however, is the singular. "The day of the Son of man" in Luke resembles "the day of the Messiah", which was formed on the analogy of the day of Yahweh. But we look in vain for an exact parallel to the Lukan phrase. It is true that "it is in keeping with the eschatological character of the Son of Man that a day of this kind should await him", and so Mowinckel (392) does not think it necessary to derive the idea from the day of Yahweh, as in the case of the day of the

Messiah, because it belongs to the Son of man concept. "The day of the Elect One" (1 En. 61: 5; cf. 45: 3), who is the Son of man, corresponds closely to "the day of the Son of man" (which we have maintained was the conception entertained by Jesus), and may have been known to him, as well as the concomitant idea of the revealing of the Son of man (cf. Mowinckel 388, and especially 1 En. 69: 29, "that Son of Man has appeared") which occurs in Luke 17: 30, although this saying seems to be of secondary origin. On the other hand, the absence in Jewish writings of any real parallel to "the *days* of the Son of man" (Luke 17: 22, 26) supports the case for its unauthenticity, in sharp contrast to the singular form.

Luke 18: 8b. "Nevertheless, when the Son of man comes, will he find faith on the earth?"

Easton thought these words "can be understood perfectly as a saying of Christ's".[1] This confidence is not widely shared, and the weight of critical opinion seems to be decisively against acceptance of the saying.[2]

If, however, the saying is regarded as a genuine utterance of Jesus, the question arises as to whether it refers to the future coming of the Son of man at the parousia, or to the earthly ministry of Jesus. These alternatives are discussed by Manson,[3] who prefers the latter, and takes Son of man as equivalent to the first personal pronoun, comparing Luke 7: 34 = Matt. 11: 19 (Q), "the Son of man *came*"; and we may note also the I-saying in Q at Luke 7: 9 = Matt. 8: 10, "Not even in Israel have I found such *faith*". Deferring for the moment the meaning of "faith" in this saying, the "Lucan stylistic peculiarities (πλήν, ἄρα)" mentioned by J. Jeremias[4] do not in themselves entirely rule out its derivation from good tradition, because they could have been introduced by Luke after translation from Aramaic.

Some writers regard the saying as secondary because, whereas in the parable itself God is the judge (verses 7, 8a), here the

---

[1] Op. cit. (above, p. 76, n. 2), 268; cf. W. L. Knox, *The Sources of the Synoptic Gospels* ii (1957), 114: an isolated saying of Jesus no longer understood, but which originally may have reflected "a half-ironic expression of regret that the hope that the Pharisees would accept the kingdom of heaven had proved illusory".

[2] Cf. Bultmann, *Tradition* 189; Kümmel 59, n. 126; Vielhauer 57. Sjöberg, 237n., is doubtful as to its authenticity.

[3] *Sayings* 308.

[4] *The Parables of Jesus* (1954), 84.

Son of man is the judge.[1] In itself, however, this is not a decisive objection if, as has been suggested above, Luke 17: 24, 26 may be taken as evidence that Jesus referred to the judicial functions of the Son of man.

To return to the meaning of "faith", it is widely held that it is faith in the Pauline sense.[2] Against this is the conviction, firmly rooted in the tradition, that Jesus spoke of faith in the sense of trust in God.[3]

Nevertheless, the saying must be regarded as an interpretative addition intended to explain the parable of the unjust judge.[4] The mention of the Son of man is, however, totally alien to the preceding parable and, as Tödt points out,[5] this is the sole example in the synoptics of the direct association of the coming of the Son of man and faith. The conclusion must be that the faith which the Son of man should expect to find on the earth when he comes is faith or belief in Jesus. The Son of man is Jesus. This equation makes it impossible for the saying to belong to the earliest stratum, much less to be a word of Jesus himself. Despite its Lukan phraseology, it is uncertain whether it should be attributed to the evangelist himself. It sounds very much like a preacher's homiletical comment, but it is impossible to say whether it was already appended to the parable in Luke's source.

Luke 21: 36. " ... and to stand before the Son of man."

This saying concludes verses 34–36: ". . . But watch at all times, praying that you may have strength to escape all these things that will take place, and to stand before the Son of man." The section is a late Hellenistic formation with no

---

[1] J. Wellhausen, *Das Evangelium Lucae* (1904), 99; Jeremias, op. cit., 84.

[2] Cf. Jeremias, op. cit., 84; Klostermann, op. cit. (above, p. 79, n. 3) 179: πίστις is "das rechte Christentum, nicht die gläubige Aufnahme des Menschensohnes".

[3] E.g. Luke 7: 9 = Matt. 8: 10. Cf. Knox, op. cit., 114, n.1, for the view of the equivalence of "faith" in Luke 18: 8 to the Rabbinical '₍e₎mûnāh.

[4] Hirsch, op. cit. (above, p. 77, n. 1), 159, thinks that it really belongs to 17: 37, but has been separated from it by the parable, 18: 1–8a; that it fits 17: 20–37 better than 18: 1–8a, because the former section also deals with the coming of the Son of man; and that its present function is that of a transition to the parable of the Pharisee and the publican, 18: 9–14. Certainly the question (only here at the end of a parable) is intended by Luke as also a conclusion to this whole section beginning at 17: 20.

[5] Tödt 93.

claim to be the words of Jesus.[1] Nevertheless, and although the primary purpose of our investigations is to attempt to determine the extent of genuine use by Jesus of the concept and term Son of man, the saying cannot be summarily dismissed. Although a later composition, it shows the living force of the Son of man concept in non-Palestinian circles and, if our approach is correct, preserves an element of the teaching of Jesus about the Son of man.

The eschatological outlook of the passage is, however, that of the third evangelist. It is conditioned by the problem of the delay of the parousia.[2] "That day" (verse 34) will still come suddenly, but it is not near. Meanwhile life continues on its usual course; and although the suddenness of the irruption of "that day" is stressed, in view of this expectation the life of the Christian must be regulated by unceasing watchfulness in prayer in order that he may be able to escape "all these things that will take place", that is, the trials and tribulations immediately preceding the end, and "to stand before the Son of man".[3]

Thus the thought of Luke 21: 36 is precisely that of 18: 1, 8b, only in the latter case the thought is expressed, as it were, in two stages. The need for continuous prayer (18: 1) corresponds to the admonition to "watch at all times, praying . . .", and the question whether the Son of man will find faith on the earth when he comes (18: 8b) corresponds to standing before the Son of man. The time when the Son of man comes seeking faith on the earth and the time when the faithful will be able to

---

[1] Cf. Bultmann, *Tradition* 126; Vielhauer 57; Schweizer, *Menschensohn* 192 (details of Lukan language). Jeremias, op. cit., 62, n. 76, however, while agreeing that the pericope is a late composition, considers it to be "made up of early material worked over".

[2] H. Conzelmann, *The Theology of Saint Luke* (1960); on Luke 21 see pp. 131f.

[3] Cf. Conzelmann, op. cit., 132: "As the End is still far away, the adjustment to a short time of waiting is replaced by a 'Christian life' of long duration, which requires ethical regulation and is no longer dependent upon a definite termination. The virtue of ὑπομονή comes to the fore. The appeal is no longer based on the time, but on the fact of a future Judgement." Tödt 91: "Nicht das Verhalten angesichts des *nahen* Endes wird bedacht, sondern die *allezeit* anhaltende Wachsamkeit im Gebet, die es dem Gläubigen ermöglichen wird, in jener Epoche der Drangsalszeichen zu entrinnen, die nach Auffassung des Lukas noch nicht das Ende selbst bedeuten, sondern erst seine Nähe ankündigen."

stand before him are "the day of the Son of man", the culmination of what Luke understands by "the days of the Son of man", on the analogy of "the days of Noah" (17: 22ff.). It is clear, therefore, that in 21: 34–36 the same eschatological theme is presented as in 17: 22ff. and 18: 1–8.

Is the Son of man in 21: 36 the judge or the advocate before God as the judge? Tödt[1] does not think that 21: 36 is any exception to the rule that none of the Lukan Son of man passages depicts the figure as the eschatological judge; he is rather the advocate on behalf of Christians. His reasons for this conclusion, however, are not decisive.[2] On the contrary, in Luke 18: 8b the evangelist views the Son of man as judge. That he does so here also is very probable, not only because of the expression "to stand before"[3] the Son of man, but also because of "that day", which is equivalent to the day of the Son of man. We have suggested that "the day of the Son of man" implied in Luke 17: 24 originally stood in Luke's special source (17: 22) and in the common source (17: 26), and that Jesus himself spoke of the Son of man's role as judge.

If this is accepted, Luke 21: 36, although not an utterance of Jesus himself, agrees with the older Palestinian traditions and is evidence of the tenacity of Jesus' teaching about the eschatological role of the Son of man. Moreover, as in a strand of older tradition (Luke 17: 22–27), Jesus is reported as speaking of the Son of man without any direct hint of identification, or even of any relationship at all, of himself with that figure.

The Son of man in Luke: conclusions

Luke's peculiar material contains only one example of sayings of group A, 19: 10, and this is a community creation. Although Jesus may well have spoken in the first person of his having come to seek the lost (cf. Mark 2: 17), Luke like Mark provides no evidence that he spoke of his earthly ministry as the Son of man.

[1] Tödt 91; cf. W. Grundmann, *Das Evangelium nach Lukas* (1961), 387. Schweizer, *Menschensohn* 192, sees the Son of man as judge in this passage.

[2] The absence of the idea of the angels as the entourage of the Son of man; Luke 9: 26; 12: 8f.; 21: 27f. (as against Mark 13: 27).

[3] The regular expression for the intercession of priests (Deut. 10: 8; 2 Chron. 29: 11; Jer. 15: 1; Ezek. 44: 15) and of prophets (1 Kings 17: 1; 18: 15; 2 Kings 3: 14; 5: 16; Jer. 18: 20) before God. The Christian is his own advocate. Cf. K. H. Rengstorf, TWNT vii. 235, n. 252.

Luke's special material also has no authentic sayings about the suffering of the Son of man. 17: 25 is editorial; 22: 48 is a narrative form of the theme of the Son of man's betrayal; and 24: 7 is on a par with the Markan predictions of the death and resurrection of the Son of man, though independent of them. Like Mark, therefore, Luke's special material has no saying which can be claimed as evidence that Jesus referred to his passion and resurrection as the Son of man.

We have seen reason to suppose that in Luke's special source and in Q Jesus spoke not of the "days" of the Son of man, which is Lukan eschatology, but of his "day" (Luke 17: 22, 24, 26), when the Son of man would be the judge. If this is correct, then the idea of the coming (Mark 14: 62) or of the day of the Son of man are two different expressions of the teaching of Jesus on the same theme. That his teaching should have been preserved in two rather different forms in different strands of tradition is to be expected, and it is urged that these two divergent forms of the thought of Jesus are correctly recorded in them.

The result would then be that Jesus spoke only of the *eschatological* role of the Son of man, according to Mark, Luke's own source, and Q. In none of them, be it noted, is there any explicit identification of Jesus and the Son of man, although there exists some relationship between them.

The two Lukan parallels to Mark which alone call for any comment here confirm the impression that the Lukan eschatology is the evangelist's own, that it is reduced and toned down when compared with that of Mark, and that preference for Luke, when he differs from Mark, is unwarranted.

Although Luke 21: 27 reproduces Mark 13: 26 almost if not quite exactly,[1] the eschatological outlook of verses 25–28 is virtually the same as in 17: 22ff. The cosmic signs which inspire distress and fear in the hearts of men are not themselves the end, but are indications for the faithful that that period has dawned which will end with the coming or the day of the Son of man, the period called "the days of the Son of man" in 17: 22, 26. What is distress for the world will be for believers what they have longed for, "the days of the Son

---

[1] The only significant change, ἐν νεφέλῃ instead of the plural, is due according to Conzelmann (op. cit., 183, n. 1) to the analogy between the parousia and the ascension (Acts 1: 9, 11).

of man", and so they can now take courage, for their redemption draws near.

Luke 22: 69 is an abbreviation of Mark 14: 62. The reason for the abbreviation is partly the evangelist's tendency to tone down the parousia idea which he describes in other terms (17: 22ff.; 18: 8b), and partly and perhaps especially the desire not to depict Jesus as telling the unbelieving members of the sanhedrin that *they* will *see* the day of the Son of man. The Lukan emphasis is here specially prominent. The stress is on the session of the Son of man at the right hand of God, and since this session is "from now on", the exaltation of Jesus is the central thought for Luke.[1]

---

[1] Cf. Tödt 95: "ihm ist an dem gelegen, was der Gemeinde durch Jesu Wort vor dem Synedrium gesagt wird: von jetzt an sitzt der Menschensohn zur Rechten Gottes." Cf. Luke 24: 26.

Chapter 4

THE SON OF MAN IN MATTHEW

The following sayings are peculiar to Matthew.
A. 13: 37; 16: 13.
B. 26: 2.
C. 10: 23; 13: 41; 16: 27; 16: 28; 19: 28; 24: 30; 24: 39b;[1]
25: 31.

A

Matt. 13: 37. "He who sows the good seed is the Son of man."

The explanation of the parable of the tares (Matt. 13: 37–43) (and perhaps also the parable itself)[2] is not from Jesus, but is the work of the evangelist. Jeremias's linguistic analysis alone proves this, for the passage is composed in distinctively Matthaean terms.[3] Moreover, two of its conceptions (verse 41) are peculiar to Matthew in the New Testament: the angels of the Son of man (16: 27; 24: 31), and the kingdom of the Son of man (16: 28). This kingdom is clearly distinguished from the kingdom of God (verse 43), a distinction used by Vielhauer[4] in support of his thesis that the synoptic tradition knows no connection between the Son of man and the kingdom of God. Certainly Matthew saw no such connection in the current traditions; and it may be that the differentiation between the kingdom of God and the kingdom of the Son of man was sug-

[1] See above, p. 84, n. 3.
[2] So Manson, *Sayings* 192–96: the parable or rather allegory was composed to fit the explanation. J. Jeremias, *The Parables of Jesus* (1954), 20, 64, 155–57, accepts the authenticity of the parable.
[3] Jeremias, op. cit., 64–67, with which cf. his paper, "Die Deutung des Gleichnisses vom Unkraut unter dem Weizen (Mt. xiii 36–43)", *Neotestamentica et Patristica* [O. Cullmann Festschrift] (1962), 59–63: verses 40–43a are the evangelist's adaptation of Jewish Christian tradition. Cf. G. Bornkamm, "Enderwartung und Kirche im Matthäusevangelium", *The Background of the New Testament and its Eschatology: Studies in honour of C. H. Dodd*, ed. W. D. Davies and D. Daube (1956), 253f.
[4] Vielhauer 55.

gested by the belief in the temporary kingdom of Christ or the Son which would give way to the kingdom of God (1 Cor. 15: 24–28). The sphere of the kingdom of the Son of man, however, is confined to the church, out of which will be removed all save the sons of the kingdom of God (verses 38, 43). The relationship between the Son of man as the one who sows the seed and as the one who purges his kingdom through the agency of his angels is to be understood in the sense that the historical activity, the sowing, of the Son of man who is Jesus, is part of the eschatological event.[1] Matt. 13: 37 is aptly described as "primitive Church dogma",[2] and not a saying of Jesus.

Yet the saying has some importance for our purpose in that it admirably illustrates the process whereby Jesus came to be identified with that Son of man whose coming he proclaimed. Once the identification was made it was inevitable that his earthly activities should be described as those of the Son of man. The *basic idea* of the future activity of the Son of man in verse 41 is more primitive than the notion of the Son of man as the one who sows the good seed.

In this particular instance the Markan parable of the sower has suggested to the evangelist the metaphor of Jesus, the Son of man, as the sower. Matthew, however, does not repeat the beginning of the explanation of that parable in Mark 4: 14, "The sower sows the word", but is more interested in the rest of the explanation from Mark 4: 15 on (which he in fact modifies to read, "This is he who was sown by the road", Matt. 13: 19b), which confusedly compares the seed not with the word which is preached, but with the various kinds of hearers who are sown in different kinds of soil.[3] In precisely the same way the good seed sown by the Son of man is not the word, but "the sons of the kingdom". The Son of man is the sower and also, through his angels, the reaper; he is the founder of the church and at the end its judge when all intruders, the tares sown by the devil, will be rooted out.

[1] Cf. E. Lohmeyer-W. Schmauch, *Das Evangelium des Matthäus* (1956), 223, n. 2.

[2] Manson, *Sayings* 194.

[3] Jeremias, op. cit., 62f., explains this as the result of fusion of the two concepts of the Word as God's seed and of men as God's planting (2 Esdras 9: 31; 8: 41).

Matt. 16: 13. "Who do men say that the Son of man is?"

This is an editorial modification of Mark 8: 27. The evangelist, adopting, as in 13: 37, the point of view reached by the church of his day, represents the disciples as already knowing Jesus as the Son of man. Consequently he also rewrites the first Markan prediction of the passion and resurrection of the Son of man (Mark 8: 31): he (Jesus) must suffer, be killed, and be raised up (Matt. 16: 21).

B

Matthew has only one saying concerning the suffering of the Son of man which is not taken from Mark.

Matt. 26: 2. "You know that after two days the Passover is coming, and the Son of man will be delivered up to be crucified."

The first verse of the chapter concludes, with the characteristic formula, the last of the five main blocks of teaching material. Verse 2a is a modification of Mark 14: 1 which follows the apocalyptic chapter Mark 13, expanded in Matthew to the dimensions of chapters 24 and 25. The statement in Mark about the proximity of the passover becomes in Matthew a reminder on the lips of Jesus himself about this, "when[1] the Son of man will be delivered up to be crucified".

The theme of the delivering up of the Son of man is, of course, familiar (Mark 9: 31; 10: 33; 14: 21, 41; Luke 22: 48; 24: 7). The passage which this one most closely resembles is Luke 24: 7, "the Son of man must *be delivered* into the hands of sinful men, and *be crucified*, and on the third day rise".[2] The word "crucify" is a late substitution for "kill",[3] and occurs elsewhere in predictions of the passion of the Son of man only in Matt. 20: 19, where it replaces "kill" in Mark 10: 34. Moreover, the absolute use of the verb "to deliver up", with no mention of those to whom the Son of man is delivered up, is almost unique.[4]

The saying is a Matthaean insertion into a Markan context,

---

[1] Semitic use of the conjunction καί?

[2] Matt. 26: 2, παραδίδοται εἰς τὸ σταυρωθῆναι; Luke 24: 7, δεῖ παραδοθῆναι . . . καὶ σταυρωθῆναι.

[3] See above, p. 82, n. 2.

[4] But cf. Mark 14: 21, parr.

and a formulation of the evangelist himself. He has constructed it and placed it here by way of introduction, on the lips of Jesus himself, to the passion narrative proper. The second part of the verse may possibly be the heading for the passion lection.

C

Matt. 10: 23. "For truly I tell you, you will not have gone through the cities of Israel before the Son of man comes."

This saying has given rise to the most diverse interpretations, and opinion is sharply divided as to its authenticity.

A. Schweitzer accepts it as a genuine utterance of Jesus. This is due to his regarding the discourse in Matt. 10 as "historical as a whole and down to the smallest detail", so that he summarily dismisses all theories of composite structure.[1] "The Parousia of the Son of Man, which is logically and temporally identical with the dawn of the Kingdom, will take place before they [the Twelve] shall have completed a hasty journey through the cities of Israel to announce it."[2] On their return with this not having happened, Jesus came to the conclusion that he would have to suffer death in order to force the coming of the kingdom, by enduring in his own person the sufferings preliminary to its coming. So he went to Jerusalem to meet his death. The fatal weakness of this approach is the refusal to accept the composite nature of this Matthaean discourse. H. G. Wood pertinently asks: "How could Schweitzer assert that a discourse containing 'Go not into the way of the Gentiles' and 'Ye shall be brought before rulers and kings for my sake for a witness to them and to the Gentiles' is historical as a whole and in every detail?"[3] As others have remarked, literary criticism has made vast strides forward even since the year 1906, when Schweitzer wrote, and it has now become even more impossible than before to do anything but accept the composite structure of the discourses in Matthew.[4]

Attempts have been made on other grounds, however, to

[1] *The Quest of the Historical Jesus*[3] (1954), 361.
[2] Ibid., 357.
[3] *Jesus in the Twentieth Century* (1960), 79, n. 2.
[4] Schweitzer's "thorough-going" eschatology is supported by M. Werner, *The Formation of Christian Dogma* (1957), a shortened English version of *Die Entstehung des christlichen Dogmas* (1941, 1954[2]).

include Matt. 10: 23 among the genuine utterances of Jesus.[1]

J. Schniewind[2] regards it, like Matt. 10: 5f. and 15: 24, as an authentic word fitting the situation of Jesus and not that of the early church. It means that when the Son of man appears from heaven the mission to the Jews will still be incomplete because they have rejected the message. The saying expresses a last hope, in the sense that Israel will recognize the one she has rejected when the Son of man comes, and will turn to him (cf. Rom. 11: 25). This exegesis can only be described as forced and as reading into the text a meaning it does not bear.

J. Jeremias[3] also connects this saying with Matt. 10: 5f. and 15: 24, which he views as authentic restrictive utterances of Jesus derived from Matthew's special material. Its antiquity and Palestinian origin are guaranteed by the Semitic structure, and "by its incompatibility with Matthew's universalistic outlook, and by the dismay which it must have caused as an unfulfilled prediction". This approach is integral to Jeremias's thesis that Jesus, confining his own preaching to Israel, both criticized the contemporary Jewish mission to the Gentiles and forbade his disciples to exercise any similar mission in their work. Vielhauer,[4] however, points out that Jeremias's second and third criteria, while signs of great age, are no proof of authenticity, and rejects the syllogism: a saying displays Aramaisms; the Aramaic-speaking church did not create *Herrenworte*; therefore a saying with Aramaisms is genuine, on the ground that the primitive community made no hard and fast distinction between *ipsissima verba* of the historical Jesus and the words of the exalted Lord delivered through the preaching of Christian prophets.

Another expedient is to separate the two parts of the saying, as is done by Kümmel,[5] on the ground that the second part is not smoothly attached to the first. According to Kümmel the second part of the verse, "for truly, I tell you . . .", is an isolated and authentic logion, of which the meaning is that the parousia of the Son of man will take place before the com-

---

[1] Sjöberg 236, n. 2, includes Matt. 10: 23 among Son of man logia with some claim to be genuine.

[2] *Das Evangelium nach Matthäus*[8] (1956), 7, 131.

[3] *Jesus' Promise to the Nations* (1958), 20ff.

[4] Vielhauer 59f.

[5] Kümmel 61ff.

pletion of the disciples' preaching of the kingdom of God in Israel. The first section of the verse is a secondary intrusion designed to introduce this detached logion. But there seems no good reason for bisecting the verse.[1]

In sum, the various attempts to claim Matt. 10: 23, in whole or in part, as an utterance of Jesus, are not very satisfactory or convincing. The key to the solution of the problem is the recognition that the saying is isolated in its present context in the mission charge.

Matt. 10: 17–22 is a reproduction of Mark 13: 9–13 (cf. Luke 21: 12–19), which is not reproduced in Matt. 24, the chapter corresponding to Mark 13, except that Mark 13: 13 ("and you will be hated by all for my name's sake; but he who endures to the end will be saved") is repeated not only in Matt. 24, the first part in verse 9 (with the addition of "the nations" to "all"), the second part in verse 13, but also in Matt. 10:22, precisely as in Mark. It is clear that the setting of Matt. 10: 17–22 is the work of the evangelist. Moreover, Mark 13: 13 is followed immediately by the reference to the abomination of desolation, implying persecution, and by the advice to flee. In the same way Matt. 10: 22 (the same saying as Mark 13: 13) is followed by advice to flee from persecution in verse 23a. Since Mark 13: 13b in its position in Matt. 24: 13 is followed by a saying which implies the direct opposite of its sequel in Matt. 10: 23 (24: 14, "And this gospel of the kingdom will be preached throughout the whole world, as a testimony to all nations; and then the end will come"), this might be thought to support the originality of 10: 23, or at least of the second part of it, because 24: 14 is based on Mark 13: 10. But the restriction of the mission to Israel both here and in Matt. 10: 5f. and 15: 24 is incompatible with being brought before rulers and kings in 10: 18.

The saying is widely regarded as having arisen out of the

---

[1] Cf. Vielhauer 59, n. 43; Tödt 56. F. V. Filson, *The Gospel according to St. Matthew* (1960), 131f., adopts the position that what is important is the meaning attached to the saying by the evangelist and the early church. While Matthew applies it to the church's missionary task which will still be unfinished when the Son of man is fully and finally revealed, it may mean "that as the Apostles do the works of Christ and win men to accept his Kingdom message, the Kingdom comes and the Son of Man is manifested". But this modernistic approach can hardly be correct.

problem either of persecution or of the Gentile mission in the early church.[1]

Vielhauer,[2] viewing the saying as probably not authentic, believes that the problems vanish if it is regarded as a community formulation, a word of encouragement of some prophetically inspired Christian to his brethren in time of persecution. The main point of the saying lies in its first part, in the reference to persecution and flight.[3]

Those, on the other hand, who decide that the chief source of the saying is early Christian missionary experience, naturally emphasize the second part. Here again, however, there is a difference of view as to whether the background is the mission to Gentiles or to Jews. Schweizer,[4] connecting the saying with that in 10: 5f., attributes both of them to the period when, in the absence of unambiguous guidance in the teaching of Jesus, the church was divided on the question of the propriety of a mission to Gentiles, and they both illustrate the narrower, exclusive view.

On the other hand, Kilpatrick[5] thinks that the saying need not be restricted to Palestinian cities, but includes cities in which Jewish communities were to be found, and should be read in the light of Paul's custom of first preaching in the local synagogues. Thus "the restrictive implication of the verse disappears", and so far from being a relic of the conservatism of the Palestinian church (much less a word of Jesus), reflects contemporary practice and *acceptance* of the Gentile mission.

Tödt[6] represents the viewpoint that the saying comes from a

---

[1] It is quite correct but insufficiently precise to say that "it reflects the experience and the expectations of the primitive Palestinian Church", Manson, *Sayings* 182, cf. *Teaching* 221f.

[2] Vielhauer 59–61; cf. T. F. Glasson, *The Second Advent* (1945), 104.

[3] Vielhauer 59, n. 43: "Diese Weissagung der baldigen Parusie des Menschensohnes hat ihr Akumen nicht in der Zusicherung, Israel könne aus Zeitmangel nicht vollständig missioniert werden, sondern in dem Trost an die verfolgten und fliehenden Jünger." E. Bammel, "Matthäus 10, 23", *Studia Theologica* 15 (1961), 79–92, argues that a saying concerning eschatological distress (cf. the shortening of the days, Matt. 24: 22 (= Mark 13: 20)) has been transformed into a word of consolation in time of persecution.

[4] *Menschensohn* 191.

[5] G. D. Kilpatrick, *The Origins of the Gospel according to St. Matthew* (1946), 119.

[6] Tödt 56f.

situation of persecution in the midst of a mission to the *Jews* and is, as others have suggested, a creation of some Christian leader rather than an utterance of the historical Jesus. This is the most probable explanation. Nowhere else is Jesus reported to have expected the coming of the Son of man so soon as this saying seems to suggest.[1] This conclusion is in harmony with the place of the Son of man both in Matthew's special source and in the evangelist's editorial work.

Matt. 13: 41. "The Son of man will send his angels, and they will gather out of his kingdom all causes of offence and evil-doers."

As we have seen in the discussion of 13: 37 above, the explanation of the parable of the tares is the work of the evangelist. All that is necessary here is to note that the conceptions of the angels of the Son of man and of the kingdom of the Son of man are peculiar to Matthew in the New Testament. As regards the former, Matthew in the two other places (16: 27 and 24: 31) describes the angels mentioned by Mark (8: 38 and 13: 27) as belonging to the Son of man. Matthew's idea of the kingdom of the Son of man is not consistent. In the present passage it is obviously the church, comprising good and evil among its members. But in 16: 28 ("until they see the Son of man coming in his kingdom") it is the eschatological kingdom, and the expression is an editorial modification of "the kingdom of God" in Mark 9: 1.[2] Matt. 13: 41, therefore, is a perfect example of a saying constructed by the evangelist out of ideas which are shown to be his from their use in his modifications of Markan passages.

---

[1] This difficulty would be removed if the saying referred not to the parousia but to the preliminary triumph of the Son of man as the prelude to the final coming. So A. Feuillet, "Les origines et la signification de Mt 10, 23b", *The Catholic Biblical Quarterly* 23 (1961), 182–98. Pointing to resemblances with Luke 12: 11f., he accepts Matt. 10: 23 in both its parts as a genuine logion, a word of consolation closely connected with the other saying, and an announcement of divine judgement on Israel which for the church will be deliverance. But this pre-parousia interpretation is not convincing.

[2] Tödt 64, n. 83, also notes Matt. 20: 21, "your kingdom", and remarks that although the expression Son of man is not used, the thought is of the kingdom of Jesus as the future Son of man. Here again we have an editorial change, for Mark 10: 37 has "your glory".

Matt. 16: 27. "For the Son of man will come in the glory of his Father with his angels, and then he will recompense each man for what he has done."

Although an editorial remodelling of Mark 8: 38, this saying has its own importance. Comparison of Mark 8: 38 with the Q form in Luke 12: 8f. (of which, in its removal of the distinction between the Son of man and Jesus, Matt. 10: 32f. is an inferior version) establishes the superiority of Luke.[1] Matt. 16: 27 is still further removed from the original saying. It was tentatively suggested earlier that in Mark 8: 38 the parousia doctrine may not be intended, largely on the ground that the saying is reproduced in essentials by Luke (9: 26), who apparently did not see in it the parousia doctrine which he omits in his version of Mark 14: 62 at 22: 69. However this may be, Matthew, as we might expect, not only sees the parousia doctrine in Mark 8: 38, but makes it quite explicit and unambiguous by transferring it from a subordinate clause to form the main sentence. Moreover, the role of the Son of man as witness (still more apparent in Luke 12: 8f.) becomes in Matthew that of the eschatological judge.

This change seems to have followed the pattern of such passages as the following.

Ps. 61 (62): 13, σὺ ἀποδώσεις ἑκάστῳ κατὰ τὰ ἔργα αὐτοῦ.
Prov. 24: 12, ἀποδίδωσιν ἑκάστῳ κατὰ τὰ ἔργα αὐτοῦ.
Ecclus. 32: 24, ἕως ἀνταποδῷ ἀνθρώπῳ κατὰ τὰς πράξεις αὐτοῦ.

But it is much more than a matter of verbal similarities. There is the influence of Jewish thought of the Son of man as judge.[2] Belief in the Son of man as judge, however, seems to be firmly embedded in the gospel traditions.[3] The historical basis of this belief is to be found in the teaching of Jesus himself, who sometimes regarded the role of the Son of man as that of a witness, and sometimes as that of the eschatological judge.[4] But Matt. 16: 27 is not part of the evidence for the teaching of

[1] See above, pp. 57ff.
[2] 1 En. 62: 5; 69: 27, 29 (the Elect One is judge in 45: 3; 51: 3; 55: 4; 61: 8; 62: 2f.).
[3] See the discussions of the following texts: Matt. 16: 27; 24: 30; 25: 31; Mark 14: 62*; Luke 11: 30*; 17: 22*, 30 (including 24* and 26*); 18: 8b; 21: 36; John 5: 27. The asterisked passages may be genuine words of Jesus.
[4] Cf. Cullmann, *Christology* 158.

Jesus. Its importance lies in its reflection of the growing emphasis on the thought of Christ as the judge.[1]

Matt. 16: 28. "Truly, I tell you that there are some of those standing here who will not taste death until they see the Son of man coming in his kingdom."

The saying in Mark 9: 1 about the kingdom of God is transformed into a prophecy of the very near advent of the Son of man in his kingdom. This is an editorial change in accordance with the evangelist's predilection for the Son of man Christology. Jesus did not proclaim himself as Son of man, but the coming of the kingdom of God. The idea of the kingdom of the Son of man is deducible from Dan. 7: 13f., and also from 1 Enoch.

> ". . . When they see that Son of Man
> Sitting on the throne of his glory.
> And the kings and the mighty and all who possess the
>   earth shall bless and glorify and extol him who rules
>   over all, who was hidden.
> For from the beginning the Son of Man was hidden,
> And the Most High preserved him in the presence of
>   His might,
> And revealed him to the elect" (62: 5–7).

In our passage the kingdom of the Son of man is an eschatological conception, and corresponds to the kingdom of Christ elsewhere in the New Testament,[2] and in this sense is equivalent to the kingdom of God.[3] But the idea is not consistent with 13: 41, where the kingdom of the Son of man is the church. Further, while the saying in Mark 9: 1 does not belong to what precedes but is out of its context, Matthew's revision (16: 27f.)

---

[1] Acts 10: 42; 17: 31; 1 Cor. 4: 5; 2 Cor. 5: 10; 2 Tim. 4: 1, 8; 1 Pet. 4: 5. Connected with the change of outlook in Matthew is the fact that the totally un-Jewish idea of the Son of man accompanied by angels (SB i. 973; A. H. McNeile, *The Gospel according to St. Matthew* (1938), 247, says "the Parousia with the angels is based on Zech. xiv. 5") is carried still further in that the accompanying angels of Mark 8: 38 become the angels of the Son of man, for which see also Matt. 13: 41, and 24: 31 compared with Mark 13: 27.

[2] Luke 22: 30; 23: 42; John 18: 36; 2 Tim. 4: 18; 2 Pet. 1: 11.

[3] Cf. Eph. 5: 5; Rev. 11: 15. K. L. Schmidt in TWNT i. 581f.

creates a new and consistent picture of the Son of man as judge in his kingdom.

Matt. 19: 28. "Truly, I tell you that in the regeneration when the Son of man shall sit on the throne of his glory, you also who have followed me shall sit on twelve thrones judging the twelve tribes of Israel."

There is a parallel passage in Luke 22: 28–30. To what sources do these passages belong? If they both come from Q, either the presence of the Son of man in Matthew and his differentiation from Jesus are more original features, or the introduction of the Son of man is a secondary Matthaean feature, as in 16: 13, 28; 26: 2.[1] The differences between them, however, and the presence of only two tolerably close resemblances—the mention of following Jesus in Matthew, and continuing with him in his trials in Luke, and in both the promise to the disciples that they will sit on thrones judging the twelve tribes of Israel—tell strongly against their derivation from a common source.[2]

The case for the superiority of Matthew[3] is not strong. Neither is that for Luke.[4] A decision is not important, because the Lukan version is not a Son of man saying.[5] It remains to evaluate Matt. 19: 28.

This can hardly be an utterance of Jesus. The word παλινγεν-εσία is Greek, and untranslatable into Hebrew or Aramaic.[6] The expression "the Son of man shall sit on the throne of his glory" is only in Matthew (25: 31). "The throne of (his) glory" is an apocalyptic phrase (1 En. 45: 3; 55: 4; 61: 8; 62: 2, 3, 5; 69: 27). Likewise the idea of the throne of the Son of man is apocalyptic (1 En. 62: 5; 69: 27, 29). Thrones in the plural are mentioned in the gospels only in our passage and in

---

[1] So Schweizer, *Menschensohn* 189; cf. the succinct summary of both possibilities in Fuller 97, n. 5.

[2] Cf. Vielhauer 61–64; earlier B. H. Streeter, *The Four Gospels* (1936), 288, and Manson, *Sayings* 216f., assigned the sayings to M and L respectively.

[3] Urged by Kümmel 47 and Vielhauer 61.

[4] Supported by Schweizer, *Menschensohn* 189, attributing the word to Jesus.

[5] Nevertheless the Lukan saying, independently of any comparison with that in Matthew, betrays later features, e.g. the idea of the kingdom of Christ.

[6] Vielhauer 62; G. Bornkamm, *Jesus of Nazareth* (1960), 209f.

Luke 22: 30. This also is an apocalyptic feature. "And I will bring forth in shining light those who have loved my holy name, and I will seat each on the throne of his honour", 1 En. 108: 12; cf. Rev. 3: 21.

But the objection has also been raised that the mention of *twelve* thrones in Matt. 19: 28 cannot go back to Jesus, because the Twelve were probably "ein Phänomen der nachösterlichen Gemeinde".[1] This is unwarranted, for old evidence like the report of a resurrection appearance to the Twelve in 1 Cor. 15: 5 shows that they were certainly instituted by Jesus himself. On the other hand, the reflection that the primitive church could hardly "have invented a saying which promises a throne, amongst others, to Judas Iscariot",[2] is not decisive. No doubt Judas, as the references to him in the gospels show, was a source of embarrassment to the early church. Yet it would have been impossible for the post-resurrection church to avoid speaking of twelve thrones,[3] and to speak instead of eleven, because there were not eleven tribes of Israel, but twelve.[4]

These considerations suggest that Matt. 19: 28 is a creation of the church in support of the supremacy of the Twelve as the leaders of the new Israel. It is put into the form of a prophecy by Jesus, and is given the authority of an utterance of his not so much by the distinction between the speaker and the Son of man, but rather by the equation of the two so characteristic of Matthew and his special material. The Jesus of history and the eschatological Son of man have become identified in Christian belief. If not the work of the evangelist himself, the saying comes from that climate of thought about Jesus as the Son of man which was so congenial to him.

Matt. 24: 30. "And then will appear the sign of the Son of man in heaven, and then all the tribes of the earth will mourn, and they will see the Son of man coming on the clouds of heaven with power and great glory."

This verse is commonly regarded as an editorial expansion of

---

[1] Vielhauer 62.

[2] Manson, *Sayings* 217.

[3] The omission of the number of thrones in Luke 22: 30 may therefore be another sign of inferior tradition.

[4] We do not need to pursue here the connection of the election of Matthias in order to restore the number of twelve apostles (Acts 1: 21–26).

Mark 13: 26. Thus E. Hirsch[1] thinks that the evangelist's objection to Mark's limitation of the coming of the Son of man to the gathering of the elect has led him to introduce the reference to the mourning of the tribes of the earth.[2] There is much to be said, however, in favour of the view that the verse contains elements from tradition other than that of Mark.[3] Although our primary interest is in "the sign of the Son of man", this enigmatic feature cannot be isolated from the rest of the verse.

The editorial structure of the verse itself is clear. The first καὶ τότε is taken from Mark 13: 26, and the second (καὶ τότε κόψονται) repeats it. Then follows, with minor changes, the saying in Mark.[4] It is further to be observed that Matthew appears to intend three sentences in this chapter to be taken in conjunction with one another. In verse 3 he modifies Mark 13: 4, "When will these things be, and what will be the sign when these things are all to be accomplished?" to read, "When will these things be, and what will be the sign of your coming (τὸ σημεῖον τῆς σῆς παρουσίας) and of the end of the age?" Secondly, this importation of the term παρουσία into a Markan passage bears a certain deliberate resemblance to the substitution of "the *parousia* of the Son of man" for "the *day* of the Son of man" in the original common source.[5] Thirdly, "the sign of the Son of man" which will be revealed in heaven is the answer to the question asked in verse 3, "what will be the sign of *your* parousia?"[6] To Matthew and his readers "Son of man" is another name for Jesus.

[1] *Frühgeschichte des Evangeliums*, ii: *Die Vorlagen des Lukas und das Sondergut des Matthäus* (1941), 313f.

[2] Hirsch, ibid., notes that this agrees with the outlook of Matthew, "der Jesus so oft vom Wehklagen und Zähneknirschen in der Hölle sprechen lässt".

[3] Thus Manson, *Teaching* 223, was inclined to assign Matt. 24: 30 to the M tradition.

[4] This is introduced by καί which might have the force of "when": "and then all the tribes of the earth will mourn when they see the Son of man coming". But against this is the meaning of "the sign of the Son of man"; see below.

[5] Matt. 24: 27 compared with Luke 17: 24; see above, pp. 82ff.

[6] This was already seen by W. C. Allen, *The Gospel according to S. Matthew*[3] (1922), 258f., who admitted the possibility that the sign of the Son of man could be a portent, perhaps an appearance of the crucified Christ, preceding the actual parousia of the Son of man, but decided in favour of identifying the Son of man as himself the sign predicted in Dan. 7: 13.

The problem is the identity of this sign, which is also the sign of the end of the age. The appearance of the sign of the Son of man in heaven *is* the sign of Jesus' coming (or parousia) and of the end of the age. To the question "when?" (verse 3) the answer is "and then", after the tribulations and cosmic upheavals previously described. But, as against Mark, the actual parousia of the Son of man is preceded by his sign and then by the lamentation of the tribes of the earth. Both παρουσία and συντελεία (Matt. 24: 3) are confined to Matthew among the gospels.[1] The probability is strong that Matt. 24: 3, couched in church language,[2] was written by the evangelist in the light of and in anticipation of 24: 30. If, therefore, the sign of the parousia of Jesus and of the end of the age *is* the sign of the Son of man himself, what precisely is this sign?

Q has a saying (Luke 11: 29f.; Matt. 12: 39f.) of which Luke preserves the more original form. "This generation is an evil generation; it seeks a sign, but no sign will be given to it except the sign of Jonah. For as Jonah became a sign to the Ninevites, so will the Son of man be to this generation."[3] It is tempting to see a direct connection between this and Matt. 24: 30.[4] This sign of Jonah has as its counterpart the Son of man (Luke 11: 30). Certainly the two expressions "the sign of Jonah" (τὸ σημεῖον Ἰωνᾶ) and "the sign of the Son of man" (τὸ σημεῖον τοῦ υἱοῦ τοῦ ἀνθρώπου) are identical in form. It is not so certain whether there is also a correspondence in meaning.

Tödt[5] rightly stresses the future tense in Luke 11: 30, "For as Jonah became a sign to the Ninevites, so will the Son of man be to this generation." But by that time it will be too late. A generation which rejected the preaching of Jesus and failed to see in it something greater than Jonah, namely, the *final* sign, will be ready to repent when the Son of man appears as judge.

---

[1] παρουσία, Matt. 24: 3, 27, 37, 39; συντελεία (τοῦ) αἰῶνος, Matt. 13: 39, 40, 49; 24: 3; 28: 20; cf. Heb. 9: 26.

[2] On παρουσία in this connection as a Hellenistic technical term in primitive Christianity since Paul, see Kümmel 38, n. 63; Tödt 80f.

[3] See below, pp. 133ff.

[4] Cf. J. Schniewind, *Das Evangelium nach Matthäus*[8] (1956), 244. According to A. Vögtle, "Der Spruch vom Jonaszeichen", *Synoptische Studien* [A. Wikenhauser Festschrift] (1953), 276f., the sign of Jonah refers to the resurrection of the Son of man, of which the sign of the Son of man, the appearing of the risen Christ, is the fulfilment.

[5] Tödt 49.

This appearance, the sign of the Son of man in heaven, is the real answer to the request of this generation for a sign from heaven. But this exegesis is only partially correct in my opinion.

It is to be observed that it is not Matthew but Luke which is followed here, for Matthew replaces the comparison of Jonah and the Son of man as signs with an analogy between Jonah's being in the whale's belly three days and three nights and the lying of the Son of man in the heart of the earth for the same period. Nor can the suggestion that the sign of the Son of man in heaven is the real answer to the request for a sign from heaven be sustained as a Matthaean idea. In Matthew the request for a sign *from heaven* is in a passage (16: 1, par. Mark 8: 11) which says nothing about the Son of man as a sign, and the sign of Jonah is not defined (16: 4). Luke links the request for a sign from heaven with the sign of Jonah (11: 16, 29), but of course makes no reference to the sign of the Son of man in heaven. The connection is thus missing also in Luke. It is therefore necessary to approach Matt. 24: 30 from another angle, and separately both from the request for a sign from heaven and from the idea of the Son of man as, up to a point, a sign in the same sense as the sign of Jonah.

While the elect will be gathered together by the angels of the Son of man, the tribes of the earth will mourn when the sign of the Son of man appears in heaven. Why will they mourn? Precisely because of the appearing of this sign. It is not correct to say that the actual manifestation of the Son of man himself, interpreting "the sign of the Son of man" as equivalent to the Son of man, causes the mourning,[1] for this manifestation comes after the lamentations have begun. The sequence is: appearing in heaven of the sign of the Son of man, mourning of the tribes, their vision of the coming of the Son of man on the clouds.

The omission in Matt. 24: 30 of the words ἐπ' αὐτόν from a sentence which otherwise is verbally identical with that in Rev. 1: 7, is due to the fact that the Son of man as such is not mentioned until the third clause, when "they will see him". In Rev. 1: 7 the Son of man coming with the clouds is seen by every eye and by those who pierced him, and consequently all

---

[1] Cf. Tödt 74, who thinks the wailing is caused by the realization that the appearing of the Son of man is the sign of judgement; it is now too late for repentance.

the tribes of the earth will mourn (for themselves) because of him (NEB, "shall lament in remorse"). Both passages use the *testimonia* Zech. 12: 10ff. and Dan. 7: 13, although not in the same order, and both in an eschatological context. Since John 19: 37, "And again another scripture says, They shall look on him whom they pierced", quotes a part of the passage in Zechariah as a scriptural testimony within the passion framework, and in view of the general tenor of Zech. 12: 10ff., Matt. 24: 30 and Rev. 1: 7 may represent independent adaptations of the *testimonium* to an apocalyptic framework, or at least are evidence of a parallel use of it in association with Dan. 7: 13 in an apocalyptic sense. The reversal of the order of the quotations from Daniel and Zechariah in Matt. 24: 30 is due to the desire to introduce another element of tradition, the appearing of the sign of the Son of man in heaven.

B. Lindars, in an interesting discussion of Zech. 12: 10 in Christian apologetic, remarks that if the sign of the Son of man "was intended by Matthew to mean the sight of 'him whom they pierced', then perhaps the old patristic idea that it is the cross may be right after all".[1] One part of Zech. 12: 10 is reflected both in John 19: 37 and Rev. 1: 7.

John 19: 37, ὄψονται εἰς ὃν ἐξεκέντησαν.

Rev. 1: 7, καὶ οἵτινες αὐτὸν ἐξεκέντησαν.[2]

Since Matthew, like the author of Revelation, is familiar with the association of the Zechariah passage with Dan. 7: 13, the absence in Matthew of any allusion to piercing is somewhat surprising. But it is replaced by "the sign of the Son of man".[3]

In the Epistle of the Apostles 16 the risen Christ says that the sign of the cross[4] will go before him when he returns to the

---

[1] *New Testament Apologetic* (1961), 126; the earliest patristic example occurs in Cyril of Jerusalem, *Catecheses* 15.22, σημεῖον δὲ ἀληθὲς ἰδικὸν τοῦ Χριστοῦ ἐστιν ὁ σταυρός.

[2] On the textual complexities see K. Stendahl, *The School of St. Matthew* (1954), 212–14; Lindars, op. cit., 122ff.; F. F. Bruce, "The Book of Zechariah and the Passion Narrative", *Bulletin of the John Rylands Library* 43 (1961), 341f.

[3] The expression is unique, as is also its meaning unless it means the Son of man himself. A somewhat distant analogy is the light which, in a late Rabbinic exegesis of Isa. 60: 1, was thought to accompany the Messiah, *Pesikta Rabbati* 36 (see SB i. 954–56).

[4] So the Coptic; the Ethiopic version has "my cross"; cf. E. Hennecke-W. Schneemelcher, *New Testament Apocrypha*, Eng. trans. ed. R. McL. Wilson, i (1963), 200.

earth to execute judgement. In the Didache 16: 6, in a clear allusion to Matt. 24: 30, we read, καὶ τότε φανήσεται τὰ σημεῖα τῆς ἀληθείας· πρῶτον σημεῖον ἐκπετάσεως ἐν οὐρανῷ . . . The phenomenon will be the Son of man with hands outstretched on the cross.[1] To these early interpretations of the passage is to be added the elaboration in the Gospel of Peter of the account of the rolling away of the stone from the sepulchre in Matt. 28: 2–4, in itself an enhancement of the simple statement in Mark 16: 4, that the women found it already removed.

". . . they [the soldiers] saw again three men come out of the sepulchre, and two of them sustaining the other, and a cross following after them. And of the two they saw that their heads reached unto heaven, but of him that was led by them that it overpassed the heavens. And they heard a voice out of the heavens saying: Hast Thou preached unto them that sleep? And an answer was heard from the cross, saying: Yea."[2]

Here we have the strange conception that the cross was entombed with Jesus, and that after the resurrection and ascension it was seen in the sky. Although a legendary accretion in its details, it is possible that its ultimate basis, like that of the other examples cited (and all occur in second-century writings), is already present in Matt. 24: 30. It is unlikely that the sign of the Son of man is simply the Son of man himself.[3] The expression is some kind of allusion to the passion. It replaces the reference to the piercing in Rev. 1: 7. The substitution is due to the desire of the evangelist to utilize a Christian apocalyptic idea which does not come to expression elsewhere except in subsequent exposition of our passage.[4] That it is the sign of the *Son of man* is probably due to the evangelist, and is certainly what we should expect in view of evidence elsewhere in his gospel of

[1] Cf. K. H. Rengstorf, TWNT vii. 26of. But J. P. Audet, *La Didachè* (*Études Bibliques*, 1958), renders "le signe de l'ouverture dans le ciel" (243), and thinks that if the cross had been intended something more than ἐν οὐρανῷ would have been added (473); cf. Rev. 6: 14.

[2] Gospel of Peter 10: 39–42 (M. R. James, *The Apocryphal New Testament* (1945), 92f.; Hennecke-Schneemelcher, op. cit., 186). Cf. the Apocalypse of Peter (Ethiopic text as translated by James, 511), "with my cross going before my face will I come in my majesty", with which also compare especially the Epistle of the Apostles 16 (Ethiopic).

[3] Cf. K. H. Rengstorf, TWNT vii. 236 (lines 19–21), against Schniewind, op. cit., 244f.

[4] On which see W. Bousset, *Der Antichrist in der Überlieferung des Judentums, des Neuen Testaments und der alten Kirche* (1895), 154–59.

his interest in this title and Christology. He has taken the title from Dan. 7: 13 which he is going to use. The sign of the Son of man is thus an enigmatic description of the cross. Its appearance in the sky will cause the tribes of the earth to mourn (for themselves), because it is the premonitory sign of the approach of the Son of man as judge.[1]

There are some who, while sharing my disinclination to identify the sign of the Son of man with the Son of man himself, would not go as far as to equate the sign with the cross, but would be content to regard it as a premonitory sign whose precise form cannot be determined. This is a reasonable point of view; and it is true that the explanation of the sign here supported is incapable of proof. Some further support for it may, however, be found in the three apocalyptic signs appearing in heaven in the book of Revelation.

12: 1, καὶ σημεῖον μέγα ὤφθη ἐν τῷ οὐρανῷ—a woman clothed with the sun, etc.;

12: 3, καὶ ὤφθη ἄλλο σημεῖον ἐν τῷ οὐρανῷ—a great red dragon, etc.;

15: 1, καὶ εἶδον ἄλλο σημεῖον ἐν τῷ οὐρανῷ μέγα καὶ θαυμαστόν—seven angels with the plagues, etc.

The writer describes what these signs in heaven are, because he is bound to do so. Matthew's failure to say precisely what the sign of the Son of man is may simply be due to the fact that it was well known from the apocalyptic tradition adopted by him. The sign of the Son of man was the greatest of all signs, the cross.[2]

Matt. 25: 31. "When the Son of man comes in his glory, and

[1] NEB renders, "the sign that heralds the Son of man". Glasson, op. cit. (above, p. 103, n. 2), 189–91, points out that the great trumpet mentioned in Matt. 24: 31 is associated, as in the Old Testament (Isa. 27:13), with the gathering of the dispersed, as is also the raising of a standard (Isa. 11: 12), and that in the Old Testament the trumpet and the ensign or standard (LXX σημεῖον) are found together (Isa. 18: 3; Jer. 51: 27). But σημεῖον in Matt. 24: 30 seems not to bear this meaning, and is connected with the mourning of the tribes of the earth rather than with the trumpet.

[2] Is there already some connection with the devotional use of the cross and the orientation of prayer towards the east as the quarter of heaven from which Christ would return? The latter practice has been held to be possibly earlier than the end of the first century; see E. Peterson, "Das Kreuz und das Gebet nach Osten", *Frühkirche, Judentum und Gnosis* (1959), 15–35; also C. E. Pocknee, *Cross and Crucifix* (1962), 36.

all the angels with him, then he will sit on the throne of his glory."

This saying enjoys the distinction of being the only Son of man saying in a gospel parable. This fact in itself may arouse suspicion, for we should certainly expect more than a single instance of association of this favourite expression on the lips of Jesus with his characteristic parabolic style of teaching. It is, of course, widely agreed that 25: 31–46 is not, in its entirety, a parable at all. C. H. Dodd finds the only truly parabolic element in "the simile of the shepherd separating the sheep and the goats" in verses 32f.[1] Again, as Jeremias and others have shown, the parables of Jesus did not originally refer to the parousia while, according to our findings so far, the evidence is not at all weighty that he spoke about the Son of man in other than future terms. This last consideration would at first sight appear to be a point in favour of the present saying; an impression, however, totally invalidated by closer examination. The nearest analogy to the presence of the Son of man figure in this parable or rather (in its present form) allegory, occurs in the explanation of the parable of the tares (13: 37, 41). But this explanation (and perhaps the parable also) does not go back to Jesus. The beginning of it is clearly modelled on the opening words of the Markan explanation of the parable of the sower.

Mark 4: 14, ὁ σπείρων τὸν λόγον σπείρει.

Matt. 13: 37, ὁ σπείρων τὸ καλὸν σπέρμα ἐστὶν ὁ υἱὸς τοῦ ἀνθρώπου.

Curiously enough, Matthew does not reproduce Mark 4: 14 in his version of the explanation of the parable of the sower. In his own parable, as explained by him, the sower *must* be the Son of man because the Son of man does the sifting between all who are causes of offence and evildoers, and the righteous who will shine in the kingdom of their Father, just as the king, identical with the Son of man, separates the goats from the sheep who alone inherit the kingdom of his Father. The sudden transition from the Son of man in the opening sentence to the king in verses 34 and 40 arouses suspicions both as to the connection of verse 31 with the rest of the pericope, and as to the authenticity of these references to the king.

[1] *The Parables of the Kingdom* (1936), 85, n. 1.

Elsewhere in Matthew it is God who is called the king (5: 35; 18: 23; 22: 2, 7). Nowhere else is Jesus reported to have referred to the Son of man as a king. The alternative is to take the Son of man as a corporate figure comprising the king and his brethren.[1] But this is not a possible solution of the difficulty because no passage in any of the gospels requires a corporate interpretation of the Son of man.

It is undeniable, however, that parts of the pericope have the ring of authentic teaching of Jesus. The centre and core of the whole structure is to be found in the two amen-pronouncements in verses 40 and 45. "Truly, I say to you, inasmuch as you did it . . ."; "Truly, I say to you, inasmuch as you did it not . . ."[2] They make quite a similar point to that in other sayings which rest on good tradition: Mark 9: 37 (parr. Matt. 18: 5; Luke 9: 48); Matt. 10: 40; Luke 10: 16; Matt. 10: 42; Mark 9: 41. All these I-sayings have or originally had as their common theme, despite much divergence of detail ("children", "you", "little ones"), the thought that treatment good or bad meted out to others[3] is actually tantamount to treatment of Jesus himself.

There is, however, another group consisting not of I-sayings but of Son of man words: Luke 12: 8f.; (Matt. 10: 32f.); Mark 8: 38; Luke 9: 26. Of these, the bracketed passage is a secondary version of Luke 12: 8f., because it has lost the distinction between Jesus and the Son of man. This distinction still remains in Mark 8: 38, but there has been added the parousia doctrine. Luke 9: 26 basically reproduces Mark. What is important in the present connection is that only Luke 12: 8f. (since Mark 8: 38 is admittedly doubtful) can be relied upon as evidence of the nature of Jesus' reference to angels in connection with the Son of man. They are not the retinue of the Son of man, but stand as a periphrasis for God himself. In Matt. 25: 31, however, the angels are introduced in much the same way as in three other passages already discussed. Matt. 13: 41 is a later

---

[1] Manson, *Teaching* 265; *Sayings* 249f.

[2] This is not to limit possibly authentic words of Jesus to these two verses. For an analysis see J. A. T. Robinson, "The 'Parable' of the Sheep and the Goats", NTS 2 (1956), 225–37, who suggests verses 32f., 35–40, 42–45 as the original core.

[3] On the Christianization of ἀδελφός characteristic of Matthew, see J. Jeremias, *The Parables of Jesus* (1954), 84, n. 96.

construction, 16: 27 is an editorial remoulding of Mark 8: 38, and 24: 31 is derived from Mark 13: 27 (the angels become the angels of the Son of man; cf. 13: 41; 16: 27). Moreover, exactly the same phrase, ἐπὶ θρόνου δόξης αὐτοῦ, occurs in 19: 28, which we have seen good reason to classify as a *Gemeindebildung*. It is a Jewish apocalyptic expression borrowed from the Similitudes of Enoch, where the closest analogy is found in 62: 5, "When they see that Son of Man sitting on the throne of his glory."[1]

If traces of authentic teaching of Jesus remain embedded in the rest of the passage, its opening verse contains none. The non-recurrence of the title Son of man after the opening verse requires explanation. Jeremias suggests "stylization of the introduction by Matthew".[2] In this connection it is thought that the evangelist has transformed a parable about God as the judge in order to represent Jesus as judge.[3] Although a probable view, some uncertainty remains in view of evidence elsewhere that in the teaching of Jesus the Son of man, while depicted as a witness or advocate at the last judgement, is sometimes regarded as the judge.[4]

The parable is an echo of the teaching of Jesus that men's attitude to him will determine the attitude to them of the Son of man at the judgement. It is Matthew's intention to portray Jesus as the Son of man who is the judge which has led him to introduce the pericope with the picture of the Son of man taking his place on his throne. Although the Son of man is not again named in the parable, he is the centre of it. At the same time he is addressed as the Lord (verses 37, 44), and the purpose of the parable is to show what is meant by men's attitude to Jesus on earth. Their attitude to him is revealed by their willingness or their failure to help others in distress. The parable, therefore, is the deposit of early Christian ethical instruction, and serves as a climax after the two preceding parables of the virgins and of the talents. Verse 31 is not only the opening of the third in the series, but serves also as the link which joins it to the two other parables, which are also parables

[1] Cf. also the association of the Son of man and the throne of his glory in 1 En. 69: 27, 29.
[2] Jeremias, op. cit., 142.
[3] Cf. Schweizer, *Menschensohn* 191; Vielhauer 58.
[4] See the discussions of the asterisked passages listed in n. 3, p. 105 above.

of judgement exercised by the Lord (χύριε in verses 11, 20, 22, 24, as in verses 37 and 44) who, it is made plain, is the Son of man.

The Son of man in Matthew: conclusions

In group A, 13: 37 is part of the later explanation of the parable of the tares, and 16: 13 is editorial. This confirms results already reached, for we now see that not only in Mark and in Luke's special material, but also in Matthew's, there is not a single undisputed saying of Jesus about the earthly activity of the Son of man.

The sole instance in group B, namely 26: 2, has been shown to be an insertion into a Markan context. Matthew, therefore, has nothing to contribute which can modify our conclusions in regard to Mark and Luke. Neither in Mark nor in the special material of the other two synoptists is there a single saying to be produced as evidence that Jesus spoke of his passion and resurrection *as the Son of man*.

The position is not quite the same as regards group C. While both Mark (14: 62) and Luke (17: 22) seem to preserve correct tradition that Jesus spoke of the eschatological activity of the Son of man as judge, Matthew provides no genuine sayings. Of course, even the secondary Matthaean formations testify indirectly to the knowledge that the teaching of Jesus included allusions to the eschatological role of the Son of man. But Matthew, so far from preserving the mark of authenticity, that is, the distinction between Jesus and the Son of man (Mark 14: 62; 8: 38; Luke 12: 8f.), equates the two. The reason for this is predilection for the Son of man Christology. To the evangelist and the circle to which he belonged the Jesus of history and the eschatological Son of man are one and the same as the object of faith.

We have seen that, although to a lesser extent than has often been thought, both Mark and the Lukan material provide valuable data for the understanding of the problem of Jesus and the Son of man. But Matthew, while shedding light on the development of the Son of man Christology in the church, has nothing to contribute towards the solution of this problem.

Chapter 5

THE SON OF MAN IN Q

A. Luke 6: 22 (par. Matt. 5: 11); 7: 34 = Matt. 11: 19;
9: 58 = Matt. 8: 20; 12: 10 = Matt. 12: 32.
B. None.
C. Luke 11: 30 (par. Matt. 12: 40); 12: 8 (par. Matt. 10:
32); 12: 40 = Matt. 24: 44; 17: 24 (par. Matt. 24: 27);
17: 26 (par. Matt. 24: 37).

A

Luke 6: 22. "Blessed are you when men hate you, and when
they expel you and insult you, and cast out your name as evil
because of the Son of man."

Matt. 5: 11. "Blessed are you when men insult you and
persecute you and speak every kind of evil against you falsely
because of me."

Despite considerable verbal differences, it is clear that these
two passages are variant forms of the same underlying Aramaic
beatitude.[1] For our immediate purpose the important variation
is that of "because of the Son of man" in Luke and "because
of me" in Matthew. It is not very easy to decide which is the
more original. Matthew has a tendency to make a clear
identification of Jesus and the Son of man, either by intro-
ducing the title (Matt. 16: 13; Mark 8: 27), or by replacing it
by the personal pronoun (Matt. 16: 21; Mark 8: 31). It would
therefore be quite in accordance with his outlook that, finding
"Son of man" in his source, he should have changed it to the
first person pronoun, which certainly appears at first as more
natural in the context. It is possible, although not likely, that

---

[1] On the translation variants in the second part of the beatitude in its two
forms see J. Jeremias, *The Sermon on the Mount* (1961), 18; for more detailed
discussion of the relationship between Luke 6: 22f. and Matt. 5: 11f. see
Black, *Aramaic Approach.*

the common source did read "because of me". In this case Luke would be responsible for the title Son of man.

Harnack[1] called attention to the omission of ἕνεκεν ἐμοῦ in Matt. 5: 11 by "a succession of ancient Western authorities"[2] (and also to the variant reading ἕνεκεν δικαιοσύνης),[3] and concluded that the omission, representing the true Matthaean text, proves that the words "because of the Son of man" in Luke could not have stood in Q. The textual evidence for the omission in Matthew, however, is much too weak to support this contention.

The conclusion must be that the common source had "because of the Son of man". But it is the character and origin of this last beatitude which is determinative for the evaluation of this feature of it. In Matthew there were originally seven beatitudes (verses 3–9), in the third person plural. The eighth (verse 10) seems to have been modelled on that in verse 11, of which it is an abbreviation, in order to round off the series, for it has the same conclusion, "for theirs is the kingdom of heaven", as the first beatitude. Luke's three beatitudes (6: 20f.) are supplemented by the much longer Q-beatitude, and this in turn seems to have led to the addition to the corresponding three woes (verses 24f.) of a fourth, the conclusion of which is structurally identical with that of the fourth beatitude.[4]

The greater detail of the last beatitude in both the Lukan and Matthaean forms has to be explained. It is not sufficient to postulate another source, and to leave the matter there. The persecutions referred to are inflicted for discipleship of Jesus *as the Son of man*[5]—not the Son of man who will come in glory, but the Son of man active here on earth. Clearly, therefore, it is the church which is speaking, the church which believes that the Jesus for faith in whom persecution has broken out is the Son of man in heaven. It can therefore speak of persecution

---

[1] *The Sayings of Jesus* (1908), 52f.

[2] According to S. C. E. Legg's edition of Matthew (1940), ad loc., these comprise one Vulgate manuscript, Epiphanius, and Lucifer.

[3] D a b c g¹ k; Legg cites D, Hilary, and Augustine. This later Western variant is due to the occurrence of the same phrase in the preceding verse.

[4] κατὰ τὰ αὐτὰ γὰρ ἐποίουν τοῖς (ψευδο)προφήταις οἱ πατέρες αὐτῶν.

[5] Cf. Tödt 115: "Die Hoheit und die Radikalität seines Anspruches wird durch den Menschensohnnamen unterstrichen; insofern ist der Name hier ein *Titel*, der die besondere, einmalige Vollmacht seines Trägers bezeichnet."

"because of the Son of man". Matthew's substitution of "because of me" is his clarification of what he found in the common source. To him Jesus and the Son of man are equivalent names. Tödt[1] rightly describes the beatitude as an *eschatological* promise ("reward in heaven"). It is a *Gemeinde-bildung* formed on the analogy especially of the authentic utterance of Jesus in Luke 12: 8f., in which loyalty to himself on earth will be rewarded by the Son of man in heaven.

The next three sayings (Luke 7: 34; 9: 58; 12: 10, and parr.) are, along with Mark 2: 10, 28, attributed by Bultmann "to a mere misunderstanding of the translation into Greek".[2] This series of sayings is, therefore, quite different from the other two groups (those which speak of the future coming of the Son of man and go back to old tradition, and those concerning his sufferings, death, and resurrection, which are all *vaticinia ex eventu*), because "Son of man" is a mere mistake for "man" or "I". This is surely an inadequate explanation. Why were just *these* utterances mistranslated, and not many more where Jesus speaks in the first person concerning his work on earth? It is equally unsatisfactory to suppose that these sayings are I-words deliberately assimilated to the Son of man type.[3] It might be asked, Why precisely *these* sayings?

Each of these three sayings has its own difficulties and characteristics, as is the case with others of the same category examined earlier. But what is in general true of the latter must be taken into account when approaching this group of three Q sayings. Those other sayings are all solemn pronouncements about the status or mission of the Son of man. "The Son of man has authority on earth to forgive sins" (Mark 2: 10); "the Son of man is lord even of the sabbath" (Mark 2: 28); "the Son of man came to seek and to save the lost" (Luke 19: 10).

Luke 7: 34. "The Son of man has come eating and drinking, and you say, Behold, a glutton and a drunkard, a friend of tax collectors and sinners."

Matt. 11: 19. "The Son of man came eating and drinking,

---

[1] Tödt 115.
[2] *Theology* i. 30.
[3] Cf. W. Manson, *Jesus the Messiah* (1943), 117, who seems to recognize the deficiencies of this explanation.

and they say, Behold, a glutton and a drunkard, a friend of tax collectors and sinners."[1]

That the actual theme of contrast between the asceticism of John the Baptist and the freer relationships of Jesus is old and authentic is proved by other elements in the synoptic tradition. Mark 2: 18 (parr. Matt. 9: 14; Luke 5: 33) records the criticism that the disciples of Jesus did not fast like those of John and the Pharisees.[2] The charge of friendliness towards tax collectors and sinners was brought against Jesus (Mark 2: 16). Moreover, the rejection by "the men of this generation" of John and Jesus alike, and for opposite reasons, and the absence of any allusion to John as either opponent of or as witness to Jesus as the Messiah, are evidence of the antiquity of the saying.[3] Also, as Jeremias points out,[4] "Jesus places himself on an equality with John, whereas the primitive Church always emphasized the subordination of John". That Jesus spoke in the first person of his coming to the world of men is an element of the tradition which can hardly be dismissed as completely unhistorical.[5] It follows that this saying about his own coming and the earlier coming of John stems from authentic tradition and not from the creative impulse of the early church. On the other hand, the term Son of man may not belong to the oldest form of the logion. The contrary view can only be upheld if "Son of man" is not the apocalyptic term but represents the Aramaic *bar nāš*, "a certain man", and has the same meaning as ἄνθρωπος immediately afterwards.[6] Manson points out[7] that the *general* meaning of "man" is quite impossible in this context. He envisages two possibilities. Either the expression "Son of man" is here redactional, or Jesus used *bar nāšā'* "in the special sense". Setting aside both these possibilities, the second for the excellent

[1] Matthew's form is probably to be preferred. Luke has introduced stylistic improvements: ἐλήλυθεν for ἦλθεν, λέγετε for the indefinite λέγουσιν; cf. Harnack, op. cit., 18f.

[2] Note especially Luke 5: 33, οἱ δὲ σοὶ ἐσθίουσιν καὶ πίνουσιν.

[3] Cf. Schweizer, *Menschensohn* 200.

[4] J. Jeremias, *The Parables of Jesus* (1954), 121, n. 75.

[5] Cf. Schweizer, *Menschensohn* 199 on the unwarranted rejection of all such sayings.

[6] Jeremias, op. cit., 121, n. 75. The suggestion of Théo Preiss, *Le fils de l'homme* (1951), 30, is most unlikely to be correct, namely, that "la traduction grecque essaye de rendre le sens ambivalent du 'barnash'", "Son of man" and "man".

[7] *Teaching* 217f.

reason that it is difficult to comprehend why Jesus should have used "the apocalyptic counter *bar nāshā*" in a contrast between his own personal character and that of John, Manson decides (like Jeremias later) in favour of a misunderstanding of the Aramaic *bar nāš*, "a certain man", equivalent to "I". This widely adopted solution would permit acceptance of the whole saying in its present form as genuine.[1] But this explanation should be rejected.

This does not mean, however, that the saying as a whole must be set aside as a *Gemeindebildung*.[2] Rather, the presence of the title Son of man in this undoubtedly genuine utterance[3] is the result of early Christian interpretation of an original I-word. The Son of man is Jesus as the object of the church's post-resurrection faith. Jesus is the glorified and exalted Son of man. The term here is, therefore, a *Hoheitsbezeichnung*[4] of the Jesus of Christian faith, the Jesus who in his life upon earth was rejected as a glutton and a drunkard and as a friend of tax collectors and sinners, but who was raised up by God to the dignity of the status of the Son of man.

Luke 9: 58 = Matt. 8. 20. "Foxes have holes and the birds of the air have nests; but the Son of man has nowhere to lay his head" (Greek identical).[5]

The contrast between the lot of the Son of man and the happier state of the foxes and birds has exercised the ingenuity of scholars. Bultmann sees in this saying an adaptation into a word of Jesus, made in the Greek-speaking church, of a sup-

[1] I do not think that such sayings can be satisfactorily explained by the theory that Jesus deliberately employed the ambiguous expression *bar nāš*, meaning either Son of man (Messiah) or simply "one" ("I myself"); cf. M. Black in ET 60 (1948), 34f.

[2] Cf. W. Grundmann, *Das Evangelium nach Lukas* (1961), 168.

[3] The accusation "a glutton and a drunkard" is doubtless authentic, and a familiar description of a ne'er-do-well; cf. Deut. 21: 20.

[4] So rightly Tödt 106–9.

[5] The Gospel of Thomas preserves the saying (No. 86) in a slightly different form. "[The foxes have their holes] and the birds have their nest; but the Son of man has no place to lay his head and to rest." The reference to rest may be a gnostic addition, expressing the thought of rest as the state of blessedness (see R. M. Grant with D. N. Freedman, *The Secret Sayings of Jesus according to the Gospel of Thomas* (1960), 172; R. McL. Wilson, *Studies in the Gospel of Thomas* (1960), 59; B. Gärtner, *The Theology of the Gospel of Thomas* (1961), 60f.). But the saying in the Gospel of Thomas is more important for us as its sole example of a Son of man saying.

posed Jewish proverbial saying about men in general and the animal world.[1] Such a suggestion has been rightly rejected by a number of critics,[2] and most trenchantly by T. W. Manson, who wrote:

"The view that *v.* 58 is a popular proverb put into the mouth of Jesus may be dismissed. Proverbs, in order to survive, must contain some element of truth: and this proverb is required to say that man, in contrast to foxes and birds, has no home; which is plain nonsense. For man, of all the living creatures, has provided himself with the most elaborate and permanent lodgings."[3]

Manson's own suggestion is based on the felt necessity of taking into account not only "the Son of man" but "the strange conjunction of foxes and birds". The foxes are "the Edomite interlopers" (Jesus calls Herod Antipas "that fox", Luke 13: 32), and the birds are the Romans, so that the effect of the saying is: "everybody is at home in Israel's land except the true Israel". This interpretation bears all the marks of Manson's acute and original mind, and can find support from the use of "birds" as a symbol for Gentiles, and of "foxes" as a symbol for Ammonites (1 En. 89).[4] But it fails in the most important particular, for the term Son of man in the gospels never has the corporate sense.[5] Moreover, it is a mistake to attach so much significance to the foxes and birds. Yet some explanation is required. It seems most likely that these were associated in popular Palestinian speech—"foxes and birds".[6] If so, but only in this particular detail, there may be an element of truth in the view that some proverbial saying underlies the logion.

[1] *Tradition* 27, 102, cf. *Jesus and the Word*, 42f. [Fontana edn., 1958]; also Grundmann, op. cit., 204, who further suggests (referring to Luke 7: 35, immediately following the preceding Son of man saying) that Son of man here replaces Wisdom; cf. 1. En. 42: 1f., "Wisdom found no place where she might dwell; then a dwelling-place was assigned her in the heavens."

[2] E.g. J. M. Creed, *The Gospel according to St. Luke* (1930), 142; W. Manson, *Jesus the Messiah* (1943), 59f.; Schweizer, *Menschensohn* 199; G. Bornkamm, *Jesus of Nazareth* (1960), 229.

[3] *Sayings* 72.

[4] Cf. R. H. Charles, *The Book of Enoch translated*, etc. (1912), 195.

[5] *Pace* my late revered teacher's well-known theory. Tödt 113 calls Manson's interpretation of this passage "zu weit hergeholt".

[6] Cf. our "cats and dogs", though admittedly this phrase has a *domestic* flavour!

Cullmann, who is curiously uncritical in his general approach to the Son of man sayings, accepts this one as an authentic utterance of Jesus, and sees its importance in the fact that it calls attention to his humiliation as the Heavenly Man incarnate and living upon earth.[1] Cullmann's reference to the Christological hymn in Phil. 2: 6ff. is out of place. Important though the hymn is, it cannot be connected with the thought of Jesus concerning himself.

There are two other possible ways of attributing the saying to Jesus. The first would take quite literally the reference to the Son of man having nowhere to lay his head. In favour of this may be the consideration that the saying is not likely to have been formulated by the church, because there are no other examples of the church speaking of Jesus exercising his ministry without material resources or lodging-place.[2] The plausibility of this approach, however, vanishes when it is recalled that in fact Jesus did often receive lodging.[3] The saying, therefore, has alternatively been understood as a figurative allusion by Jesus to his final rejection,[4] rather than a reference to the conditions of his itinerant ministry. It has been regarded as an indirect prediction of the sufferings of the Son of man, and therefore as a Q parallel to the Markan passion predictions.[5] Fuller argues on the analogy of other sayings in which Jesus utters warnings on the cost of discipleship and on the necessity of taking up one's cross and following him.[6]

But it is hard to maintain that this saying is a particularly close parallel to such sayings, still less to the Markan predictions of the passion of the Son of man. The former are in the first person, whereas in the present saying the subject is the Son of man. Every Son of man saying requires explanation. This one, although suitable to the context, may owe its position to secondary causes. It differs from Luke 7: 34 = Matt. 11: 19, where the contrast between John the Baptist and Jesus corresponds to the *Sitz im Leben* of Jesus. Moreover, the understand-

---

[1] *Christology* 162.
[2] Cf. Schweizer, *Menschensohn* 199.
[3] Cf. Mark 1: 29–35; 11: 11; and in Luke 8: 3 the mention of the women who provided maintenance for Jesus and the Twelve.
[4] Cf. Mark 9: 12 which, however, is not a saying of Jesus.
[5] Cf. Fuller 104f.; Preiss, op. cit., 30.
[6] Mark 8: 34–37, parr.; Matt. 10: 38f.; Luke 14: 27.

ing of the saying as an indirect passion prediction is greatly weakened by the absence from Q of any other sayings which could be so described. Whatever the true explanation of Q's lack of Son of man passion predictions,[1] it would be very surprising if the sole exception were so indirect, or even ambiguous, that some scholars do not recognize it as a prediction of the passion at all.[2]

The teaching of Jesus includes warnings that to follow him involves the severing of certain human relationships.[3] It is significant that immediately after the saying under discussion Q reports Jesus' answer to another aspirant to discipleship, "Leave the dead to bury their own dead", to which Luke alone appends a third example (Luke 9: 61f.). I see no reason to question the substantial authenticity of both these sayings. But they are not in the category of Son of man sayings. Luke 9: 58 = Matt. 8: 20 stands as the opening of the pericope concerning candidates for discipleship. The subject is not Jesus in the first person, but the Son of man.[4] What is the reason for this arrangement? Although the saying, if taken quite literally to refer to the conditions of Jesus' earthly ministry, would not be altogether in accordance with the facts, the resurrection faith in Jesus as the glorified and exalted Son of man, recalling that earthly ministry and its at first seemingly tragic and hopeless end, realized that the outcome was rejection. The same thought was expressed a little later by the fourth evangelist. "He came to his own home, and his own people received him not" (John 1: 11).

Our saying reads like a preacher's exhortation concerning discipleship of Jesus the Son of man. As Jesus on earth was rejected by his people and wandered homeless, so must the disciple expect to be. The detail of the foxes and birds may well have been derived from some popular Palestinian proverbial

---

[1] See below, pp. 132f.

[2] For what it is worth there is the fact that in the Gospel of Thomas, a collection of sayings of Jesus probably derived from an earlier collection and partially expanded in a gnosticizing direction (see my article, "Non-gnostic Sayings in the Gospel of Thomas", *Novum Testamentum* 4 (1960), 292–306), the version of our saying has nothing to do with the death of Jesus.

[3] Matt. 10: 37; Luke 14: 26; Mark 10: 28 parr.

[4] Tödt 114 asks, "Warum heisst es nicht einfach: 'aber ich habe nicht, wohin ich mein Haupt lege'? " His answer appears to be on the right lines.

Morning came
and Jesus was standing on the shore.....

THOMAS KILDUFF, O.C.D.

BORN: AUGUST 29, 1907

PROFESSED: SEPTEMBER 29, 1928

DIED: OCTOBER 23, 1986

" Tell them that I love them"

saying which was thought to be appropriate and calculated to impress the exhortation on the minds of the hearers.

Luke 12: 10. "And every one who speaks a word against the Son of man will be forgiven; but he who blasphemes against the Holy Spirit will not be forgiven."

Matt. 12: 32. "And whoever speaks a word against the Son of man will be forgiven; but whoever speaks against the Holy Spirit will not be forgiven either in this age or in that to come."

Despite verbal differences due partly to Luke's style and partly to Matthew's expansions, the sayings are identical in meaning. The problem of the Son of man is complicated by a parallel saying in Mark 3: 28f. which does not mention the Son of man. In Mark the distinction is drawn between blasphemies or insults against *the sons of men*, which are forgivable, and blasphemy against the Holy Spirit, which is unforgivable. In Q the distinction is between blasphemy against the Son of man, which is forgivable, and blasphemy against the Holy Spirit, which is not. Many scholars[1] have followed Wellhausen in giving the preference to the Markan form of the saying.[2] At first sight this does seem to be the easiest solution. A clear distinction is made between mere slanders which men aim at one another and the infinitely more serious sin of blasphemy against the Holy Spirit. In Q, on the other hand, a natural difficulty is at once felt in the differentiation between the Son of man and the Holy Spirit. Why should Jesus have made this distinction between himself and the Spirit, in view of his august claims to a unique filial relationship to God and a unique mission? The difficulty is, if possible, still further increased if he is held to refer to the Son of man as a heavenly figure in some way related to but, so far as concerns his ministry on earth, distinct from himself.

The advantages of the Markan form of the saying, however, become less convincing on closer examination. What are the sins and blasphemies against men? Perhaps deliberate hyperbole is expressed—human slanders contrasted with blasphemy against the Holy Spirit himself—to drive home the heinousness of such blasphemy against the Spirit manifested in the

---

[1] E.g. Bultmann, *Tradition* 138; Manson, *Sayings* 110; Taylor, *Mark* 242.
[2] J. Wellhausen, *Das Evangelium Matthaei* (1904), 62f.

charge of the scribes that Jesus was performing exorcisms through the power of Beelzebul. No doubt that is the meaning intended by the evangelist and, as is probable, by an earlier compiler who had appended verses 28f. to this section. But this does not mean that the verses belonged here originally; they may have formed a separate saying[1] in some unknown context. But on the assumption that an actual word of Jesus is reported, it must be conceded that the Markan form appears to be nearer to the original. It has been suggested that in the original saying Jesus used the term "a son of man" in the generic sense, meaning man or men in general, and that the change to the plural in Mark was intended to clarify this, while in Q the expression was misunderstood as a messianic title, the Son of man. Alternatively, by "Son of man" Jesus, it is thought, meant himself, but not in a messianic sense. In Mark this is generalized by transformation into the plural, in Q it is particularized into the title Son of man. The disadvantage of this second view is the supposition that Jesus was in the habit of speaking of himself as "the Son of man" in a personal way, while at other times he used the first person singular. This is logically not very likely. The attempt to justify the Markan version as retaining essentially the original meaning of Jesus is also unsatisfactory, for where is the evidence that Jesus employed the expression "a son of man" in a generic sense? We cannot get very far by postulating a saying *of Jesus* with this expression behind the Markan version. Moreover, the unconscious tendency of the attempts to defend Mark is to gravitate in the direction of Q, which at least actually has the term "the Son of man" in the singular.

The suggestion that the saying in its different forms originated in the very early church is not new.[2] And there is a much more probable explanation of the differences than the hypothesis of misunderstanding of Aramaic. Two preliminary points may be made. If one form developed out of the other,

---

[1] Cf. Taylor, *Mark* 241, who, however, adds that "Mark has rightly divined, or was guided by good tradition, in connecting it with the charge of possession by Beelzebul".

[2] B. H. Branscomb, *The Gospel of Mark* (1937), 74; C. K. Barrett, *The Holy Spirit and the Gospel Tradition* (1947), 105–7; E. Schweizer, *Spirit of God* (1960), 25, n. 6: "the saying can hardly go back to Jesus" (= TWNT vi. 395, n. 407).

the case for Q as prior is much stronger than for Mark,[1] whose version of the saying E. Lohmeyer[2] called "ein ungeheures Wort" because it removes differentiation among sins other than that of blasphemy against the Holy Spirit, and by making them all certain of forgiveness abolishes the need for a final judgement. Secondly, it is not too much to say that the two versions formally contradict one another, for in Mark blasphemy against the Holy Spirit, which in Q is clearly distinguished from blasphemy against the Son of man, is actually the same thing as blasphemy against Jesus in his earthly ministry, who now in the post-resurrection era is known as the exalted Son of man, although he is not given that name here. This would be clear even without the evangelist's comment in verse 30, "for they had said, He has an unclean spirit".

Barrett[3] calls attention to the normal patristic exegesis, according to which blasphemy against the Son of man is a sin of the heathen, but is forgivable in baptism for those who are converted to Christianity, whereas post-baptismal sins are unforgivable because they are committed against the Holy Spirit who had been received in baptism, and the most heinous of such sins is blasphemy against the Spirit. Up to a point this approach undoubtedly does justice to the New Testament church's vivid consciousness of possession of the Spirit as "the absolutely constitutive factor" of its life,[4] so that blasphemy against him was the unforgivable sin of apostasy.[5]

The saying about blasphemy, however, is in its origin more closely bound to the soil of Palestine than is allowed for by

[1] Cf. Percy 253–56. The saying occurs in the Gospel of Thomas (No. 44) in the following form. "He who blasphemes the Father will be forgiven, and he who blasphemes the Son will be forgiven, but he who blasphemes the Holy Spirit will not be forgiven, either on earth or in heaven." Wilson, op. cit. (above, p. 123, n. 5), 147, explains this as the final stage in the development, of which the first and second stages are the Markan and Q forms. Be that as it may, the version in Thomas, while reflecting Christian thought in the sequence Father/Son/Holy Spirit (cf. Grant-Freedman, op. cit., 148), is a modification not of Mark but of Q. Since Thomas like Q is a collection of sayings, this may support the superiority of the Q version as the generally current and accepted one.

[2] *Das Evangelium des Markus* (1954), 80.

[3] Op. cit., 106f.

[4] Barrett, op. cit., 106; cf. Branscomb, op. cit., 74.

[5] Cf. especially Heb. 6: 4–6; in 1 John 5: 16f. the "sin unto death" is probably apostasy; cf. Acts 7: 51; Eph. 4: 30; 1 Thess. 4: 8, for allusions to resistance or opposition to the Spirit.

the traditional exegesis. In Q the section begins with an exorcism (Matt. 12: 22; Luke 11: 14), and apparently at an earlier stage in its history closed with the pronouncement, "He who is not with me is against me, and he who does not gather with me scatters" (Matt. 12: 30; Luke 11: 23). Luke 12: 10 has the saying about blasphemy in a different context from that in Matthew. The Lukan position is due to the evangelist, who thus brings together two Son of man sayings, despite the unsuitability of a saying about blasphemy against the Son of man being forgivable coming immediately after the declaration that he who denies Jesus will be disowned in the presence of God (by the Son of man, as is implied from verse 8). The Q position of the declaration about blasphemy is preserved in Matthew. That is, at a later stage in the development of Q, or perhaps in another recension than that known to Luke this saying, originally independent, was introduced immediately after the conclusion of the pericope (Matt. 12: 30, 32) as a new conclusion. As an independent saying it referred to the difference between those who spoke against the Son of man from outside the church and apostates within who sinned against the Holy Spirit. Justification for the suggestion that the saying was originally independent of its context in Q (as given in Matthew) may be found in the fact that while it forms a tolerable link with the accusation that Jesus performed his exorcisms by demoniac power (Matt. 12: 24; Luke 11: 15), this accusation is *interpreted* as not only constituting a charge against Jesus, but as involving blasphemy not only against the Holy Spirit whose operation made the exorcisms possible, but also against Jesus *understood as the Son of man*. Yet there remains the inconsistency of the two kinds of blasphemy, one forgivable and the other not. Be that as it may, the fact that the *Son of man* is an object of blasphemy establishes the Palestinian provenance of the saying, and so it is not hostile outsiders in general who are intended, but the Jews. In other words, a pronouncement which arose in the early church in order to meet a current problem —Jewish opposition to and rejection of the church's offer of the gospel—has been given a concrete situation in the life of Jesus himself. We can see that the choice of context was most apt—an incident typical of Jewish opposition which Jesus himself had had to face. The attitude of the church would have been that blasphemy against its Lord, serious though it was, could be forgiven those Jews who were converted and came in baptism to confess Jesus as the exalted Lord and Son of man.[1]

The Markan version of the saying is secondary. It is not the result of misunderstanding, but is a deliberate alteration of the singular "Son of man" into the plural "sons of men" in order, so it was thought, to make it fit the context better. This does not, however, imply dependence of Mark upon Q, but knowledge of the saying in a form similar to that in Q. We may also assume that the pre-Markan parallel (Mark 3: 22–30) to the whole Q section which (unlike Q) begins not with an exorcism but with the accusation of scribes from Jerusalem that Jesus had Beelzebul, already included the saying in verses 28f. as its conclusion when Mark took it up. This saying had originally, like the parallel one in Q, been independent, and was in a form resembling Q. To it the evangelist has appended the explanatory remark in verse 30, "for they had said, He has an unclean spirit", referring back to verse 22.[2] Matthew reproduces the Markan form of the saying on blasphemy in an abbreviated form immediately before the Q version, and presumably regarded them as of different content. The most important modification of Mark's saying, the substitution of "men" for "sons of men", is intended not only to clarify the meaning, but also to mark off as clearly as possible the saying derived from Mark from that in Q. The Markan version, though secondary, still fits the context tolerably well, but not well enough, for the pericope deals with attacks on Jesus and requires something resembling the Q version. In Mark the emphasis has shifted. The contrast between blasphemy against the Son of man and blasphemy against the Holy Spirit has disappeared. The central thought has now become the enormity, the unforgivableness of blasphemy against the Spirit, in contrast to which all other sins pale into relative insignificance and will be forgiven. In other words, the change is in the direction of other expressions of similar thought about op-

[1] Cf. Acts 15: 5 for converted Pharisees. In Matt. 12: 24 the charge of exorcism through Beelzebul is made by Pharisees (cf. Mark 3: 32, scribes). Even if "some of them" in Luke 11: 15 more accurately represents Q, Jews are still intended.

[2] The unclean spirit is Beelzebul, which may not be a name for Satan; cf. C. E. B. Cranfield, *The Gospel according to Saint Mark* (1959), 136.

position to the Spirit and sins that cannot be remitted,[1] and is evidence of a later stage of development. The prefixing of "amen" in Mark supports this view. The saying has become a solemn pronouncement, regarded as coming from the Lord, of a principle of permanent validity for the church: blasphemy against the Holy Spirit is the one unforgivable sin. The saying acquired the form it has in Mark when its earlier independent form, akin to that in Q, was no longer fully understood. It acquired this secondary form when it was added to the preceding sayings at the pre-Markan stage.

In short, in both traditions, in that represented in Q (Matthew) and in that represented in Mark, the same saying gravitated to the corresponding context, but in the latter case this involved alteration and reinterpretation as a word of Jesus, of a saying whose origin is in fact to be sought in a somewhat earlier stage of the life of the church itself. The risen, glorified, and exalted Jesus had become the object of faith as the Son of man. How then, it was felt, could blasphemy against him ever be forgiven?[2]

B

Q has no saying of this type at all. No doubt the reason for this is very largely the nature of Q as a collection of sayings of an ethical and religious character.[3] The fact that Q contained no passion narrative would naturally account for the absence of sayings resembling Mark 14: 21 and 14: 41, which occur within the passion narrative itself. But neither does Q contain any predictions of or allusions to the coming passion of the Son of man.[4] In itself this is not adequately accounted for by the absence of a passion narrative. There is, however, one passage, the lament for Jerusalem (Luke 13: 34f. = Matt. 23: 37–39), which may be regarded as an exception to the absence from

---

[1] See above, p. 129, n. 5.

[2] Cf. Tödt 111. Schweizer also (see above, p. 128, n. 2) attributes the Q logion to the early church. But I do not accept the inference he draws from his conclusion (that there is no longer any possibility of forgiveness for a wrong decision about the earthly Jesus): "Dann bestätigt dies aber, dass 'Menschensohn' in erster Linie Titel des Irdischen war", Menschensohn 200.

[3] Cf. V. Taylor, Jesus and His Sacrifice (1943), 79. The same thing is true of the special Matthaean sayings tradition.

[4] Luke 9: 58 = Matt. 8: 20 is no exception; see above, pp. 125f.

Q of sayings of any kind relating to the passion. Its position in
Q cannot be determined. In its Matthaean context, however,
the reference to the passion is unmistakable, for Jesus is speaking on the eve of the passion.[1] In Luke the context is even
more striking, for the words follow Jesus' reference to the
necessity of his going away by death,[2] and to Jerusalem as the
scene of the martyrdom of a prophet. Both evangelists, therefore, understood the saying to refer to the passion. Even in
isolation the words can hardly be understood otherwise. By
contrast, Q has no suffering *Son of man* sayings; but the passage
just discussed shows that the passion did not lie completely
outside the interests of Q. The upshot is that the absence of
sayings of this category from a source which is almost entirely
a collection of sayings may be adduced as further corroborative
evidence for the unauthenticity of sayings about the passion
of the Son of man elsewhere such as we have encountered in
Mark and Luke.

C

Luke 11: 30. "For as Jonah became a sign to the Ninevites,
so will the Son of man be to this generation."

Matt. 12: 40. "For as Jonah was three days and three nights
in the belly of the whale, so will the Son of man be three days
and three nights in the heart of the earth."[3]

---

[1] Cf. Creed, op. cit., 187; A. H. McNeile, *The Gospel according to St.
Matthew* (1938), 342, paraphrases: "God is deserting you, because I am
about to depart by death; and you will not see Me till I return as the
heavenly Messiah."

[2] Cf. Black, *Aramaic Approach* 152f.

[3] See P. Seidelin, "Das Jonaszeichen", *Studia Theologica* 5 (1951), 119–31:
Matt. 12: 40 (like Luke 11: 30) owes its present form to the evangelist,
but should be preferred as probably containing the substance of Jesus'
meaning, if not his actual words. The saying is the result of application of
the psalm in Jonah 2 to the death of Jesus; A. Vögtle, "Der Spruch vom
Jonaszeichen", *Synoptische Studien* [A. Wikenhauser Festschrift] (1953),
230–77: Luke 11: 30 corresponds to Q, Matt. 12: 40 being an alteration of
this. Both forms are later explanations of Jesus' reference to the sign of
Jonah, the former interpreting it in terms of the parousia of the Son of
man, the latter in terms of the resurrection; O. Glombitza, "Das Zeichen
des Jona (zum Verständnis von Matth. xii. 38–42)", NTS 8 (1962), 359–
66 (see below, p. 138, n. 3). The suggestion that "Jonah" should be "John"
(the Baptist) (J. H. Michael, " 'The Sign of John' ", JTS 21 (1920), 146–
59) is most improbable; cf. Vögtle 234, 246f. J. Howton, "The Sign of
Jonah", *Scottish Journal of Theology* 15 (1962), 288–304, argues that, since

A number of scholars have supported the Matthaean version of the saying as superior to that in Luke.[1] The idea that the sign is Jonah's deliverance from the whale certainly corresponds to Jewish thought,[2] although this in itself, in view of the Jewish nature of Matthew's gospel, could be taken as militating against its priority over Luke. Similarly, it is thought, the Son of man is the object of the miracle of deliverance from death.[3] J. Schniewind[4] describes the saying as a *Rätzelspruch* in which the sign is the world judge who will have died and been raised from the dead. So far from being a later interpretation of Luke 11: 30, the Matthaean version, according to Schniewind, is the more original one, even to the extent that the Lukan form is to be regarded as an abbreviation of it motivated by the inaccuracy of the prophecy that the Son of man would be in the heart of the earth for three days and three nights, whereas Jesus was raised up on the third day after *two* nights in the tomb.

But there are formidable difficulties in the way of taking Matt. 12: 40 as the older form. It would be the only allusion in Q to the death and resurrection of the Son of man. The explicit identification of Jesus with the Son of man is characteristic of Matthew, and is not a feature of the oldest sayings. In Luke 11: 30, on the other hand, this identification remains indeterminate.[5] In Matthew the connection of verses 41f. with the saying is not perspicuous, whereas in Luke verses 31f. constitute a tolerable link with verse 30. In fact Matt. 12: 40

---

in Aramaic Jonah means a dove, the word was misunderstood for the proper name and left untranslated. Jesus offered "the sign of the dove". But the application of the Jewish symbolism of Israel as the dove (cf. Ps. 74: 19) to Jesus the Son of man as the redemptive remnant is too subtle to be convincing, and is rendered superfluous by the writer's acceptance of Luke 11: 30 as a word of Jesus.

[1] Cullmann, *Christology* 62f., inclines to this view, but leaves the matter open.

[2] Grundmann, op. cit. (above, p. 123, n. 2), 242. A. Schlatter, *Der Evangelist Matthäus* (1948), 416, stated that the sign must be "ein Eingriff der göttlichen Allmacht in den Verlauf der Ereignisse". Cf. the material in SB i. 644ff.; also Seidelin, op. cit., 122ff.

[3] Barrett, op. cit. (above, p. 128, n. 2), 90, accepts Matt. 12: 40 as an utterance of Jesus, who meant that the only sign this generation would receive would be his death and resurrection.

[4] *Das Evangelium nach Matthäus*[8] (1956), 162.

[5] Cf. Sjöberg 180, n. 1.

bears all the marks of a secondary formation,[1] and has a completely different meaning from Luke 11: 30. Jeremias,[2] however, although agreeing as to the secondary nature of Matt. 12: 40, suggests that its meaning is basically identical with that of Luke 11: 30, but with a change of emphasis. He holds that in Luke the meaning is that as Jonah was a sign to the Ninevites as one who appeared to them after having been saved from the belly of the whale, so Jesus will appear to this generation after being raised from the dead. The claims of Jesus, as of Jonah, will be established by deliverance from death. Matt. 12: 40 is a secondary explanation in that the emphasis has shifted from this central theme to the length of time involved —three days and three nights. This approach is not convincing. Q has no other saying foretelling the passion and resurrection of the Son of man. Such predictions are primarily Markan, and they are not constructed out of Q material, and they derive some details from the passion kerygma and the scriptures utilized in association with it.[3] Luke 11: 30 cannot be explained in this manner by comparing it with Matt. 12: 40. The two sayings are entirely different. Whatever may be the meaning of the former, the second clearly depicts Jonah's "submarine adventures"(!)[4] as a prefiguration of the death and resurrection of Jesus. We conclude that Luke 11: 30 is the older form of the saying, and stood in Q.

It is at least possible, of course, that Luke 11: 30 also may be secondary,[5] and that both it and Matt. 12: 40 are independent attempts to explain "the sign of Jonah".[6] This involves the central problem of the authenticity of Luke 11: 30, even though, as we have urged, it is superior to Matt. 12: 40. The authenticity of Jesus' refusal of a sign "except the sign of Jonah" is also involved, because in Mark 8: 11f. the refusal of a sign is absolute. Matt. 16: 4 adds the words "except the sign of Jonah" from Q, without any explanation of their meaning. But the readers would be expected to recall the explanation already given in 12: 40. Evidently Mark and Q followed variant traditions about the refusal of a sign. Possibly, however,

[1] Cf. Sjöberg 179, n. 1, 238, n. 1; Bultmann, *Tradition* 124; Tödt 196f.
[2] TWNT iii. 412f.   [3] Tödt 196f.   [4] Manson, *Sayings* 89.
[5] Cf. J. Jeremias, *The Parables of Jesus* (1954), 83.
[6] Cf. Creed, op. cit., 163.

there is no essential difference between them (see further below).

Closer examination of Matt. 12: 39–42 may shed further light on this question of Luke 11: 29f. The addition in Matt. 12: 39 supplies the clue to Matthew's interpretation of the Q passage as a whole. "No sign will be given to it except the sign of Jonah *the prophet*." The Ninevites repented at the preaching of Jonah the prophet. From this point of view the sign of Jonah was his preaching. But this generation has failed to respond to the presentation of a still greater kerygma, namely, the proclamation of the imminent kingdom of God by Jesus— "something greater than Jonah is here". Yet the preaching of Jesus, vastly superior though it was to that of Jonah, because it not only called for repentance but announced the imminence of the judgement and the kingdom of God, can justifiably be called "the sign of Jonah". But then the comparison between Jonah as a sign in the past and the Son of man as a sign in the future (ἔσται) required explanation. Matt. 12: 40 is the earliest attempt to explain Q (Luke 11: 30). The evangelist was not conscious of any inconsistency in thus producing a second explanation of "the sign of Jonah" by changing the Q saying into a prediction of the death and resurrection of the Son of man. Further, Matthew makes the saying about the repentance of the Ninevites, in which Jonah is mentioned twice, follow immediately the two occurrences of the name in verses 39f. By contrast the similarly constructed saying about the queen of the south seems to be tacked on as an afterthought. This is because Matthew's treatment of the Q section (Luke 11: 29–32) involved not only the substitution of the saying in verse 30 by an explanatory comment, but also the transposition of the sayings about the queen of the south and the Ninevites from their chronological order in Q for the sake of effect, and in order to achieve a still closer connection.[1]

Although it may be assumed that Luke 11: 29–32 represents the passage substantially as it stood in Q, it contains elements which did not originally belong together. The mention of Jonah both in verses 29f. and in verse 32 led to their subsequent association, especially as the Ninevites feature along with

---

[1] Manson, *Sayings* 91; Bultmann, *Tradition* 118; per contra Schniewind, op. cit., 162. The omission of verse 32 in Luke by D d r² is due to the similar ending of the preceding verse.

Jonah both in verse 30 and in verse 32. This latter fact would not altogether rule out the possibility that verse 30 is secondary and is an attempt to explain "the sign of Jonah" (but see below). The original non-association of verses 29f. and 31f. is betrayed by the fact that in verse 30 Jonah and the Son of man are compared as signs to their respective generations, whereas in verse 32 Jonah is inferior to what is being manifested now. The latter saying comes from some other unknown context, but is probably genuine.[1] The relevance of verse 31 to its present context is much less satisfactory, and it may have been retained here simply because of its established association with the next saying in the source.[2]

This composite nature of the passage invalidates some of the attempts to discover the meaning of Luke 11: 30 as a saying of Jesus. Thus the conclusion that "the sign of Jonah" must denote the preaching of Jesus and of Jonah (κήρυγμα, verse 32) as the point of comparison depends on taking Luke 11: 29–32 as a unity. The only sign vouchsafed to this generation is then Jesus' proclamation of the coming kingdom of God, and this proclamation is the πλεῖον, the something greater than Jonah.[3] Admittedly it would be just possible, although forced, to arrive at a similar conclusion even apart from verse 32. But apart from the fact that a description of Jesus' preaching as a "sign" would be unusual,[4] there is the difficulty of the future tenses in verses 29f.: "no sign will be given (δοθήσεται) ..."; "so will the Son of man be (ἔσται) ...". The former future tense might, it is true, be understood in the sense that no further sign will be given[5] than that already given, the sign of Jonah—that is, the preaching of Jesus or alternatively Jesus as a preacher of

---

[1] Cf. Matt. 12: 6, τοῦ ἱεροῦ μεῖζόν ἐστιν ὧδε, and Manson's comment (*Sayings* 187): "The fact that [these verses] appear in the matter peculiar to Matthew is a strong argument in favour of the genuineness of the saying. The conservative Jewish Christians who gathered this material together were not the people to invent sayings of this kind." The saying also closely resembles Luke 10: 13–15 = Matt. 11: 21–24, where again unrepentant Israel is contrasted with the heathen; cf. Bultmann, *Tradition* 118; Seidelin, op. cit., 121.

[2] Even its authenticity is perhaps less certain than that of verse 32; but cf. Grundmann, op. cit. (above, p. 123, n. 2), 242.

[3] So Fuller 34, 40 who, however, includes Jesus' miracles as "part and parcel of his kerygmatic activity".

[4] J. Jeremias, TWNT iii. 412: "ganz ungewöhnlich".

[5] I.e., by God, K. H. Rengstorf, TWNT vii. 231.

judgement.[1] But unless Luke 11: 30 is not a word of Jesus but an attempt to explain "the sign of Jonah", the second future tense is not susceptible of a parallel explanation, i.e., that as Jonah as a preacher of judgement was a sign to the Ninevites, so this generation will receive no sign other than that it has already, the Son of man as a preacher of judgement. In fact, however, full weight must be given to both future tenses. The Son of man *will be* to this generation what Jonah was to the Ninevites, namely, a sign, and he will be the *only* sign to be given to it. There is therefore no essential difference in meaning between the prediction of the sign of Jonah in Q and the outright refusal of any sign at all in Mark 8: 12.[2]

The saying in Luke 11: 30 refers to the coming of the Son of man as judge (cf. Mark 14: 62). The sign will be the Son of man himself in this capacity. Naturally there is not an *exact* correspondence between Jonah as a sign and the Son of man as a sign. How could there be between a mere prophet like Jonah and the eschatological figure of the Son of man himself? A critical difference is intended between the time of Jonah and the Ninevites and the time of this generation, and so between the "signs". This generation has not responded to the preaching of Jesus, since it is an evil generation (Luke 11: 29; Matt. 12: 39). It *will* get a sign, but not of the kind it expects, not what it means by a "sign"—a proof from Jesus of the correctness of his claims—but the sign of Jonah. By then, however, the last chance of repentance will have passed.[3]

The authenticity of Jesus' refusal of any sign except the sign of Jonah and of the perhaps deliberately somewhat enigmatic explanation of what this sign would be, is supported by another Q passage, Luke 17: 23f., 26f. which, it has been urged, contains valuable information on Jesus' eschatological outlook.[4] More-

---

[1] Kümmel 68f.

[2] Par. Matt. 16: 4 adds "except the sign of Jonah".

[3] References to "the sign of the Son of man in heaven" (Matt. 24: 30) by some exegetes (Jeremias, TWNT iii. 413, n. 31; Bultmann, *Tradition* 124, n. 2; Tödt 49) seem to me to be irrelevant, because, although the expression is identical in form with "the sign of Jonah", it does not mean the Son of man as himself a sign, but the sign which precedes the advent of the Son of man; see above, pp. 108ff. Glombitza, op. cit., 363f., also brings in Matt. 24: 30, which he explains as denoting the manifestation to all of the sign *given to* the Son of man, that is, his deliverance from death.

[4] See above, pp. 82ff.

over, there is good ground for the authenticity also of the saying peculiar to Luke in verse 21, the burden of which is equivalent to saying that the kingdom of God is not preceded by any premonitory signs, but that on the contrary all of a sudden it will be present "in your midst".[1] The resemblance to the denial of any sign in our present passage is obvious, although this does not mention the coming of the kingdom. The other passage at verse 22 leaves the subject of the kingdom for the Son of man. Although the kingdom of God and the Son of man do not seem to be directly associated in Jesus' sayings, his whole outlook nevertheless suggests that the coming of the kingdom in its full consummation is connected with the appearing of the Son of man as the eschatological judge. In the discussion of the passage in Luke 17 it was suggested that in verse 24 the concept "the day of the Son of man" is clearly implied, and that both verse 22 (L) and verse 26 (Q) originally contained this expression. The advent of the Son of man would overtake the unbelieving world suddenly and unheralded, as the flood overwhelmed the world of Noah's day. But just as faithful Noah and his people found timely refuge in the ark, so believers will be spared the dire consequences of the coming of the Son of man *in his day* —as judge, for "the day of the Son of man" refers to his judicial functions. The similarities to Luke 11: 29f., 32 are striking. The Ninevites were spared because they repented at the preaching of Jonah. Noah and his people escaped the universal calamity.[2] But even apart from verse 32, a saying originally independent of its present context, there is a similar comparison.

Luke 11: 30, "For as Jonah became a sign to the Ninevites, so will the Son of man be to this generation."

Luke 17: 26, "And as it was in the days of Noah, so it will be in the days (originally "day") of the Son of man."

The day of the Son of man, when he comes as judge, is precisely what is meant by the sign of Jonah which the Son of man will be to this generation. In both passages there is that lack of specific identification of Jesus with the Son of man which is a strong mark of an authentic saying.[3] In Luke 11: 29f. the

[1] Manson, *Sayings* 304.
[2] The saying about Lot (Luke 17: 28–30) is probably secondary, just as is that about the queen of the south (11: 31).
[3] Cf. Mark 8: 38; Luke 12: 8f.

sign of Jonah, the Son of man as judge, will be the authentication of the preaching of Jesus.

Luke 17: 24 (par. Matt. 24: 27), 17: 26 (par. Matt. 24: 37)

For discussion of these texts see (besides the preceding section) the examination of Luke 17: 22, 30,[1] where it was shown that in the Q source Jesus spoke of "the day of the Son of man", and by this expression alluded to the Son of man as judge. There is no equation of Jesus with this figure.

Luke 12: 8 (par. Matt. 10: 32)

See on Mark 8: 38,[2] and the result reached there that it is inferior to this Lukan form of the Q saying. (Matthew's version is secondary, and identification of Jesus and the Son of man has caused the disappearance of the title.) The Son of man acts as witness or counsel before God as judge, and as in Luke 17: 24, 26 there is no equation of this figure with the Jesus who speaks.

Luke 12: 40.[3] "Do you also be ready, for the Son of man comes at an hour you do not expect."

Matt. 24: 44. "Therefore do you also be ready, for the Son of man comes at an hour you do not expect."

Jesus' parable of the burglar appears to be the basis of other New Testament passages because, as Jeremias says, this metaphor "is foreign to the eschatological imagery of late Jewish literature".[4] According to Jeremias[5] the parable was addressed by Jesus to his contemporaries as a warning of the approaching "eschatological catastrophe", the day of the Lord (Amos 5: 18), and is echoed in the thought of the day of the Lord coming as a thief (1 Thess. 5: 2, 4; 2 Pet. 3: 10; cf. Luke 21: 34f., "that day"). The "Son of man" was substituted for "the day of the Lord" by the church when it applied the parable to the delay of the parousia, and changed it into an admonition to its members

---

[1] Above, pp. 82ff.
[2] Above, pp. 57ff.
[3] The verse is omitted by 1 118 209, but there is little reason to suppose, with Blass, that it is spurious (F. Blass–A. Debrunner–R. W. Funk, *A Greek Grammar of the New Testament*, etc. (1961), sect. 294(5), p. 154).
[4] *The Parables of Jesus* (1954), 40.
[5] Ibid., 39–41.

to be ever watchful. If this is correct, we find a still later stage in Rev. 3: 3; 16: 15, where Christ says, "I will come as a thief".[1] A different view is that the parable is a *Gemeindebildung* directed to the problem of the delayed parousia, and always was Christological.[2] In either case the conclusion that Luke 12: 40 = Matt. 24: 44 cannot be included among Jesus' own references to the Son of man is supported by the lack of any other statements by him that "the Son of man comes", with no descriptive details of any kind.[3]

The conclusion, therefore, is that this saying (appended to the parable of Jesus) is neither an utterance of Jesus, nor an alteration of a reference by him to the coming day of the Lord, nor the conclusion of a short parable itself created by the church. It is probably best understood as a preacher's hortatory comment on the genuine parable of the burglar. The sayings mentioned above about the day of the Lord coming like a thief and about Christ coming as a thief are variant applications of the central idea in the parable of Jesus, only in the second instance, "I will come as a thief" (Rev. 3: 3; 16: 15), use has also been made of the explanatory comment about the Son of man understood as part of the parable of Jesus.

The Son of man in Q: conclusions

Since Q has no sayings of category B (sufferings of the Son of man), the problem is that of the coexistence in one and the same source of sayings of the other two groups, A and C. It has been established that in Q Jesus speaks of the Son of man as of another figure connected with the future order, and that authentic sayings of this kind are to be found in Luke 11: 30; 12: 8; 17: 24, 26. The natural presumption would be that Jesus could not also have referred to himself as the Son of man in his ministry upon earth. In Q, as elsewhere, this presumption is fully justified by the conclusion reached regarding the sayings in group A, that none of them is an actual saying of Jesus.[4]

---

[1] Cf. also Schweizer, *Menschensohn* 191.
[2] Cf. Vielhauer 66, and his criticism in n. 79 of Jeremias' view of the parable as an adapted "crisis-parable".
[3] Neither Matt. 10: 23 (see above, pp. 100ff.), nor Luke 18: 8b (see above, pp. 91f.) is a genuine saying.
[4] Luke 7: 34 = Matt. 11: 19 is probably based on a saying in the first person.

The full significance of the two types of sayings in Q, however, can only be assessed in relation to the other synoptic evidence. This will be undertaken in chapter 8, where the results of the preceding studies will be coordinated, and suggestions will be offered towards a solution of the problem of "Jesus and the Son of man". But first, in the next two chapters, we must consider the Son of man concept elsewhere in the New Testament and in the Fourth Gospel.

Chapter 6

THE SON OF MAN ELSEWHERE THAN IN THE GOSPELS

1. *In the form "Son of man"*

Acts 7: 56. "Behold, I see the heavens opened, and the Son of man standing at the right hand of God."

This is the sole New Testament example outside the gospels of the title in its full form, ὁ υἱὸς τοῦ ἀνθρώπου, and on the lips of another than Jesus.

E. Lohmeyer[1] postulated a Galilean origin for the Son of man Christology. This view has been criticized on the grounds that the title Son of man (or Kyrios) does not imply a different Christology from that of Messiah, assigned by Lohmeyer to the Jerusalem church,[2] and that Christologies cannot thus be differentiated geographically.[3] Cullmann supposes that this passage is important not only because Stephen is correctly reported to have used the term Son of man, but because he was a Hellenist,[4] and the Hellenists belong to the same circle of thought as Jesus, who is himself the source of this Christology in the sense that he used the term as a self-designation. What is involved is a series of associations: esoteric Judaism (1 Enoch, the Qumran community),[5] Jesus, the Hellenists, the Fourth Gospel, the Epistle to the Hebrews.[6] But there are missing links. While criticism of or opposition to the temple and its cultus may

---

[1] *Galiläa und Jerusalem* (1936), followed by F. C. Grant, *The Gospel of the Kingdom* (1940), 54, and in *The Interpreter's Bible* vii (1951), 641, 849.

[2] Bultmann, *Theology* i (1952), 52f.; Percy 244n.

[3] Cullmann, *Christology* 164f.

[4] Ibid., 155, n. 3.

[5] Cf. Cullmann, "The Significance of the Qumran Texts for Research into the Beginnings of Christianity" in *The Scrolls and the New Testament*, ed. K. Stendahl (1958), 18ff.

[6] Cullmann, *Christology* 181ff.; see also in ET 71 (1959), 8–12, 39–43. F. F. Bruce, " 'To the Hebrews' or 'To the Essenes'?" in NTS 9 (1963), 217–32, provides a valuable corrective to recent attempts to relate too closely the addressees of the epistle to the Hebrews and the men of Qumran.

fairly be said to unite all these members, 1 Enoch is an exception, and the Qumran texts do not mention the Son of man.[1]

Elsewhere I have written that if the Son of man seen by Stephen stood at the right hand of God as his advocate, "the passage assumes quite extraordinary importance as supplying an explicit formulation of the intercessory (but not necessarily priestly) role of the Son of man".[2] This conclusion is independent of the quite secondary question of whether Stephen actually shared this belief. If Luke is not himself responsible for the words attributed to Stephen, the passage proves the existence of a Son of man Christology at a very early date.[3] I do not think, however, as Cullmann does,[4] that Stephen's vision reflects Jesus' thought of himself directly as the Son of man, but rather depends on Jesus' interpretation of the conception of the exalted Son of man (as the heavenly advocate), which is one of the few aspects of his thought on the subject on which the synoptics may be supposed to preserve reliable information. Of course, Stephen's vision adds something new— the precise identification of Jesus with the Son of man. Although, if the protomartyr was to be portrayed as seeing a vision of the Son of man, it was bound to be a vision of the Son of man in heavenly glory, it is significant that the sole New Testament example of ὁ υἱὸς τοῦ ἀνθρώπου outside the gospels should be of this kind.

What is the connection between Stephen's vision and Luke 22: 69? "But from now on the Son of man shall be seated at the right hand of the power of God." Assuming that Luke 22: 69 is based on Mark 14: 62, has it influenced Acts 7: 56, which would then be Lukan in origin? The crux of the matter is that in Acts the Son of man is seen standing, and not sitting.[5]

---

[1] At the most the *idea* of the Son of man may be indirectly present in its corporate aspect. Cf. F. F. Bruce, *Biblical Exegesis in the Qumran Texts* (1960), 63ff., who holds that the figure in Dan. 7 "was from the first intended to be identical with the Isaianic Servant", and that the sect identified itself with both figures.

[2] CJT 209; on the origin of the high priest Christology in Jesus' thought of the Son of man as the heavenly intercessor, see CJT 206ff.

[3] Cf. Schweizer, *Menschensohn* 202, n. 60.

[4] *Christology* 183.

[5] In verse 55 the singular "the heaven", along with the plural "the heavens" in verse 56, suggests the possibility of Luke's use of a Semitic source for the word of Stephen; cf. E. Haenchen, *Die Apostelgeschichte*[12] (1959), 243, n. 3.

The common explanation that the Son of man rises to greet his witness is inadequate,[1] unless it be supposed that this was in order to vindicate him.[2] It has been suggested that the Son of man was originally thought of as standing *before* God, like the intercessory angels.[3] But this is sheer supposition. Nor is it very profitable to reduce ἑστῶτα ("standing") so as to denote mere situation.[4] Another way is to invest the word of Stephen with fuller eschatological meaning by inferring a reference to the parousia, so that what he sees is a proleptic vision of the parousia.[5] The passage, however, will not bear the weight of this construction, and we must fall back upon the fact that here (as in Luke 22: 69) the glorified Son of man is not associated with the parousia, nor with *explicit* intercessory functions.

Despite the resemblances between the two passages, neither has influenced the other. The absence of any mention of the coming of the Son of man in Luke's version of Mark 14: 62 is due to his tendency to tone down the eschatology of his sources. This is not the case with Stephen's vision, and we ought not to attempt to give it a parousia reference it does not possess. Such a reference is absent because it is irrelevant. But the idea of the Son of man as an intercessor or advocate is clear, even if implicit. He does not sit as a judge, but stands. Like other intercessors, the angels, he stands in the presence of God to present his case; unlike them, however, whom he has superseded, not directly before him,[6] but at his right hand, in accordance with the *testimonium* Ps. 110:1, and precisely because he is uniquely the Son of man.

The vision of Stephen, therefore, consists of an identification of Jesus with that Son of man of whom Jesus said, "Everyone who acknowledges me before men, the Son of man also will

---

[1] Nor can we accept the suggestion of E. M. Sidebottom, *The Christ of the Fourth Gospel* (1961), 76, that the standing is to be explained by the bidding of the son of man in Ezek. 2 to stand on his feet.

[2] C. S. C. Williams, *The Acts of the Apostles* (1957), 112; see also for the advocate theory C. F. D. Moule in *Studiorum Novi Testamenti Societas Bulletin* 3 (1952), 46f.

[3] Dan. 7: 13 (LXX), καὶ οἱ παρεστηκότες παρῆσαν αὐτῷ; cf. Tödt 274.

[4] Dodd, *Scriptures* 35, n. 1.

[5] H. P. Owen, "Stephen's Vision in Acts VII. 55–6", NTS 1 (1955), 224–26, thinks that the Son of man here is the Christ about to return; that is why he rises.

[6] Cf. 1 En. 89: 76; 99: 3; 104: 1.

acknowledge before the angels of God."[1] This tells against the view that Acts 7: 56 has no contact with the synoptic Son of man,[2] even though the thought of the parousia does not appear because, as has been said above, it is irrelevant to the situation. The importance of the vision of Stephen is that the Son of man is represented as not only exalted to God's right hand, but as playing the role of advocate for those who confess him. It is proof of a living Christology. There is also a close similarity with the future vision of the opening of the heaven and the Son of man in John 1: 51.

Hebrews 2: 6. "What is man that thou art mindful of him, or the son of man, that thou carest for him?"

The Son of man Christology cannot claim to be prominent in Hebrews like that of the Son of God (1: 8; 4: 14; 6: 6; 7: 3; 10: 29), for it occurs but once, and then only in this quotation from Ps. 8. But the context shows that the writer was quite familiar with it,[3] and assumed knowledge of it in his readers. The promise of sovereignty held out to man has been fulfilled in Jesus as the Son of man (υἱὸς ἀνθρώπου), whom we see "crowned with glory and honour because of the suffering of death". It is the same conception as in Stephen's vision—the exaltation of Jesus as Son of man. The author of Hebrews is not alone in using Ps. 8 to express this belief, for Paul also uses verse 6 of the Psalm ("thou hast put all things under his feet") in 1 Cor. 15: 25–27, linking it to the familiar *testimonium* Ps. 110: 1. The author of Hebrews interprets the psalm Christologically as best suiting his purpose of contrasting Christ as Son of man with the angels, as in the first chapter he has contrasted him with them as Son of God.[4]

The writer brings together the Christologies of the Son of God and the High Priest by his interpretation of Ps. 2: 7 and Ps. 110: 4 (Heb. 5: 5f.). The dominance of the Son of God Christology is shown also by its strategic introduction at the

---

[1] ἔμπροσθεν and ἐνώπιον, used as synonyms here in Luke 12: 8f., may have the more general meaning "in the presence of" rather than "in front of". But in any case in this authentic logion the church's use of Ps. 110: 1, "at the right hand", is not present as it is in Acts 7: 56.

[2] Tödt 276.

[3] Cf. O. Michel, *Der Brief an die Hebräer*[10] (1957), 71.

[4] On Jewish messianic use of Ps. 8 see Mowinckel 357.

beginning of the argument, "he has spoken to us by a Son" (1: 2), and by the first quotation from scripture, "Thou art my Son, today I have begotten thee" (1: 5, from Ps. 2: 7). It may be surmised that the link between the two Christologies is provided by the idea of the Son of man. God spoke "by a Son", and the Son of man made for a short time lower than the angels is therefore the *pre-existent* Son of man. The Son of man's role as advocate is carried a step further, to that of the priestly intercession of the exalted Jesus (7: 25). The High Priest Christology[1] is the fruit of reflection on the belief in the exaltation to the heavenly world of Jesus as the Son of man. But its ultimate origin may be sought in the teaching of Jesus about the Son of man as the advocate.[2]

All this is a considerable advance on Stephen's vision in Acts. Yet the line of development in thought is logical and clear, with basically the same emphasis—the Son of man exalted to heavenly glory, and vindicating his own. Although the author of Hebrews stresses the real humanity of Jesus, he never uses the term Son of man in this connection, except in citing Ps. 8 in order to illustrate his theme of exaltation after humiliation. To these he has, however, prefixed that of pre-existence, with the result that the idea of the Son of man can no longer be confined within the limits set by the synoptics and Stephen's vision, and resembles the Johannine pre-existent Son of man and the ἄνθρωπος in Paul.[3]

Revelation 1: 13; 14: 14, "one like a son of man".

Both passages contain allusions to Dan. 7: 13. The curious expression ὅμοιον υἱὸν ἀνθρώπου[4] is virtually equivalent to ὁ υἱὸς τοῦ ἀνθρώπου in the gospels and Acts 7: 56, but Revelation retains the distinctive apocalyptic form "like a son of man", which the gospels have discarded.[5] As in Acts 7: 56, the Son of

[1] Cf. also John 17: 19; Rom. 5: 2; Eph. 2: 18; 5: 2; 1 Pet. 2: 24; 3: 18; 1 John 2: 1.

[2] Cf. further CJT.

[3] Cf. J. Héring, *L'épître aux Hébreux* (1954), 31.

[4] Explained as an exact reproduction of the Aramaic by C. C. Torrey, *The Apocalypse of John* (1958), 96. The variant υἱῷ in some MSS., including C in both passages, is an obvious correction; see T. Holtz, *Die Christologie der Apokalypse des Johannes* (*Texte und Untersuchungen* lxxxv, 1962), 118 n. 1.

[5] R. H. Charles, *The Revelation of St. John* ii (1920), 20; cf. i (1920), 27. For agreement in essentials with the Son of man in Jewish apocalyptic, cf. Mowinckel 358.

man is seen in a vision, and therefore as reigning in glory (1: 13); but also as reaping the earth in judgement.[1] The exaltation of Christ as the Son of man is presupposed, as in Stephen's vision, but the humiliation and suffering which preceded it are attached not to the figure of the Son of man, except indirectly in 1: 7 ("Behold, he is coming with the clouds, and every eye will see him, every one who pierced him; and all tribes of the earth will wail on account of him"),[2] but to the slain and conquering lamb. It would have been surprising had the seer made no use of the apocalyptic Danielic Son of man. Nevertheless, in view of other contacts of thought and expression between the two books, the presence of the figure of the Son of man in both Johannine writings, the Gospel and the Apocalypse, however great the difference of content, can hardly be accidental. It suggests a living interest in the Son of man Christology as such.

Appended Note. The Son of man after the New Testament

Survival of the term Son of man as a true apocalyptic title is naturally to be expected in Jewish Christianity.[3] Elsewhere it almost entirely loses its original sense, and is employed to describe not the divinity of Jesus, but his humanity.[4]

In the Gospel according to the Hebrews the risen Lord appears to James, and says to him, "My brother, eat your bread, for the Son of man is risen from among them that sleep."[5] Since it is the *risen* Christ who speaks, we have a curious development of the usage in the canonical gospels, where it is the historical Jesus who uses the title. But here his words take on the form of a fulfilment of the synoptic predictions of the resurrection of the Son of man. In the Fourth Gospel, although the earthly Jesus formally speaks of himself as the Son of man, as in the synoptics, he is at the same time the

---

[1] Rev. 14: 14ff.

[2] On the association of Dan. 7: 13 and Zech. 12: 10ff., see on Matt. 24: 30.

[3] Cf. H. J. Schoeps, *Theologie und Geschichte des Judenchristentums* (1949), 78–82.

[4] Cf. H. Lietzmann, *Der Menschensohn* (1896), 69–80; G. Dalman, *The Words of Jesus* (1902), 252f.; E. A. Abbott, *Notes on New Testament Criticism* (= *Diatessarica* part VII, 1907), 214–29; E. Stauffer, *New Testament Theology* (1955), nn. 800, 838; J. M. Robinson, *A New Quest of the Historical Jesus* (1959), 102, n. 2.

[5] Jerome, *De viris illustribus* 2: "Frater mi, comede panem tuum, quia resurrexit Filius hominis a dormientibus."

eternal Christ, the Son of man who has not only descended, but has also ascended to where he was before (John 3: 13). Moreover, this not so very distant resemblance to the Fourth Gospel is also a development away from the canonical gospels in the same direction, if by another route, as the otherwise normal tendency, illustrated by the passages in Acts, Hebrews, and Revelation which we have examined, to restrict the title of Son of man more and more to the risen, vindicated, and exalted Christ.

The other passage occurs in the account of the martyrdom of James given by the Jewish Christian Hegesippus (c. 180).[1] In answer to the scribes and Pharisees James says, "Why do you ask me about the Son of man? He sits in heaven on the right hand of the great power, and he will come on the clouds of heaven." This seems to be modelled on Jesus' reply to the high priest,[2] and also forms a Jewish Christian counterpart to the declaration of Stephen. Whether a genuine tradition is preserved is doubtful. At any rate, the present form of the story has also been constructed with an eye on the Lukan passion narrative, for James offers the same prayer as Jesus for forgiveness of his enemies (Luke 23: 34). But these are secondary matters, as is also the question whether James or Stephen actually entertained a Son of man Christology.

The importance of the two passages is that they place James in the centre and that, whatever their literary connection may be, they both witness to the survival of the Son of man Christology well into the second century.[3]

2. *In the form "Man"*

Paul is the only New Testament writer, apart from the evangelists, with a consistent and thorough-going Son of man Christology.[4]

---

[1] Eusebius, *H.E.* ii. 23. On the relationship to this of the similar account in codex V of the Nag Hammadi texts, see A. Böhlig, "Zum Martyrium des Jakobus", *Novum Testamentum* 5 (1962), 207–13. Böhlig does not say whether the title Son of man occurs also in this narrative.

[2] In its Matthaean form (Matt. 26: 64) rather than the Markan one (Mark 14: 62): ἐκ δεξιῶν τῆς μεγάλης δυνάμεως, ἐπὶ τῶν νεφελῶν.

[3] Cf. M. Simon, *St. Stephen and the Hellenists* (1958), 71–74: the title Son of man was a kind of *terminus technicus* in the early church, descriptive of "the exalted and eschatological Christ" (74).

[4] See especially Cullmann, *Christology* 166–81, whose order in treating the passages is here followed. J. Weiss, *Earliest Christianity* [= *The History of Primitive Christianity*] ii (1959), 485ff., strongly emphasizes the identity of "the Man" in Paul with the Son of man, of which it is a Hellenization. Cf. A. M. Hunter, *Paul and his Predecessors*[2] (1961), 86f., who remarks that in his reference to Ps. 8: 6 at 1 Cor. 15: 27, "the title Son of Man trembles on Paul's lips".

It is widely held that in 1 Cor. 15: 45–9 Paul is contradicting a Jewish doctrine of the two Adams in some form similar to that known to us from Philo. According to Philo there are two Adams. The Adam in Gen. 1: 27 is the heavenly man made in God's image, the Adam in Gen. 2: 7 is the historical first member of the human race, of earthly as distinct from the heavenly origin of the other man.[1] But the incarnation of Christ understood by Paul as the Son of man, "the second man from heaven", made this doctrine totally untenable. Paul sees in both the passages from Genesis a reference to the first human being. There is, indeed, a second man, but he is the last Adam (ὁ ἔσχατος Ἀδαμ), the eschatological Son of man, and he is from heaven.

Rom. 5: 12ff. is to be interpreted on similar lines. Although Paul here does not directly apply the name Adam to Christ, Adam is the type of "the one who was to come" (verse 14), and Jesus Christ as "the one man" who brought life is contrasted with the one man whose sin involved death for all (verses 15, 17).

The question that arises is this. If it is conceded that Paul was well aware of the Son of man Christology, but employed the terms Adam and Man instead, was the choice of the substitute entirely his own? The choice of terminology in 1 Cor. 15: 45ff., it might be said, was determined by the Jewish doctrine he was attempting to refute, and is also reflected in the passage in Romans. But this does not necessarily mean that Paul was the first to use the term "Man" in this sense, and chose to do so because it was more suitable than Son of man in pointing the contrast between Adam and Christ (1 Cor. 15: 21f.).[2]

Into the variety of views concerning the Christological hymn in Phil. 2: 6–11 it is unnecessary to enter here.[3] But among them are two which are irreconcilable. F. W. Beare[4] agrees that the hymn is not Paul's own composition. But neither is it "pre-Pauline". Rather, it is "a hymn composed in Pauline circles, under Pauline influence", in terms of the Man from heaven (1 Cor. 15: 47), who "though he was rich, yet for your sake

---

[1] Philo, *Legum allegoria* I. 31f.; *De opificio mundi* 134ff.
[2] Perhaps this contrast was itself earlier than Paul; cf. Hunter, op. cit., 123.
[3] See R. P. Martin, *An Early Christian Confession* (1960).
[4] *The Epistle to the Philippians* (1959), 74ff.

became poor" (2 Cor. 8: 9). The hymn is a Christianized form of the Heavenly Man-Redeemer myth, and the background of thought is therefore predominantly Hellenistic and syncretistic. In this case the hymn can make no contribution to knowledge of Christological thought before Paul wrote.

On the other hand, E. Lohmeyer held the hymn to be a translation from an Aramaic original, and in particular regarded the words "as a man" in verse 7 as rendering the Aramaic *kᵉbhar nāš*, "as Son of man".[1]

What has to be decided is the connection between Phil. 2: 6–11 and the other two passages. That the dependence is on the part of the Christological hymn is hard to believe. At the same time, it is to be interpreted in the light of 1 Cor. 15: 45ff. and Rom. 5: 12ff.[2] It seems probable that in Phil. 2: 6–11 Paul is adapting, and not necessarily repeating verbatim, a Greek form of an Aramaic hymn. If the thought appears to be Pauline—the second Adam as the true image of God, his obedience contrasted with the disobedience of the first man, the association of Servant and Son of man—this could be due partly to the process of adaptation, which is most obvious in the addition of the words "even death on a cross" in verse 8, which stand outside the rhythmical structure, but mostly to the influence of the hymn on Paul's thought.[3] It may be suggested

---

[1] The results of his earlier study, "Kyrios Jesus. Eine Untersuchung zu Phil. 2, 5–11" (*Sitzungsberichte der Heidelberger Akademie der Wissenschaften, Phil.-Hist. Klasse*, 1928) [on Son of man see 39f., 68], are summarized in *Der Brief an die Philipper* (1956), 90ff. (95 for this particular point). Cf. the opinion of J. Jeremias in *The Servant of God* (W. Zimmerli and J. Jeremias, 1957), 88f. (= TWNT v. 703f.), that the hymn belongs to the category "pre-Pauline stock of tradition"; cf. 97 (= TWNT v. 708f.). C. F. D. Moule, *Studiorum Novi Testamenti Societas Bulletin* 3 (1952), 49, writes: "... when one comes to think of it, the very terms of Phil. 2 are themselves not far from Danielic: *en homoiomati anthropou* and *schemati heuretheis hos anthropos* – what are these phrases if not equivalent to 'like unto a son of man?'" Lohmeyer's suggestion, however, is not accepted by most critics; cf. Holtz, op. cit., 16, n. 3.

[2] Cf. Cullmann, *Christology* 175, who emphasizes, against E. Käsemann, the uncertainty of direct influence from the gnostic redeemer myth, and finds the primary reference to be to the story of the creation of man in Genesis.

[3] Cf. P. Bonnard, *L'épître de saint Paul aux Philippiens* (1950), 48, to the effect that the Pauline and Johannine Christologies are developments of ideas in the hymn. V. Taylor, *The Person of Christ in New Testament Teaching* (1958), 63, quotes Bonnard with approval, but leaves open the question of the hymn's pre-Pauline authorship.

that this Greek form of an Aramaic hymn provided Paul with the suitable word for use in contrasting Christ as the "Man" with Adam. It is scarcely credible that Paul was the originator of the substitution of Son of man by Man, important though the conception is in his thought. It must have taken place quite early, and the new term replaced Son of man, which was reserved for use on the lips of Jesus in the gospels.

A somewhat later illustration of this very point is to be found in 1 Tim. 2: 5f. "There is one Mediator of God and men, the man Christ Jesus, who gave himself as a ransom for all." This is a Hellenistic rewriting, for a non-gospel context, of the original Semitic form in the saying, "The Son of man came (not to be served but to serve, and) to give his life as a ransom for many" (Mark 10: 45). Our earlier discussion of this text concluded that its original Aramaic form did not have the bracketed words.

All this would seem to show that the Son of man Christology persisted for some time as an influential concept, both within the New Testament period and beyond. It is not the case that the church had no theology of the Son of man, for it is present both in its original form and in the adaptation "Man".[1] If this Christology is the basic one because it goes back to Jesus, this is not surprising. Yet we have to define what we mean by this. It is arguable that the Son (of God) Christology also has its ultimate roots in Jesus' own thought of God as Abba, that is, in his unique filial consciousness, and that the High Priest Christology characteristic of but not altogether confined to Hebrews is derived from Jesus' idea of the Son of man as an advocate or intercessor. In both these cases radical interpretative elaboration erected by the church on the original data forbids the easy conclusion that Jesus actually spoke of himself either as the Son (of God) or as the High Priest. The same seems to be true of the Son of man. Jesus said much about the Son of man in his teaching, but this concerned the Son of man as exalted in glory to the right hand of God as mediator and intercessor, and as coming at some future time as the agent of judgement.

[1] J. A. T. Robinson, *Jesus and His Coming* (1957), 57, n. 2, dismisses the matter rather too summarily.

Chapter 7

THE SON OF MAN IN THE FOURTH GOSPEL

The survey in the preceding chapter of the Son of man as a living Christological concept outside the canonical gospels is an indispensable preliminary to the study of the Johannine Son of man, because this cannot be isolated from the Son of man in other writings.

In the Fourth Gospel we find two circles of thought. What may be called the "synoptic Son of man" is overlapped in varying degrees by a "non-synoptic Son of man".

The Fourth Gospel is a real and genuine *gospel*. It belongs to that literary-religious *genre* created by the church. This is not merely to state the obvious, but is intended as a reminder against any tendency to view it as a theological treatise more or less successfully disguised as a gospel. Whatever else it may be, it is first and foremost a gospel. It is therefore to be expected that it should resemble the other gospels in many features, including the attribution to Jesus of the title Son of man. But the Son of man in John is both like and unlike the synoptic figure. This is due not only to the greater interpretative element in John, but also to the use of different sources. Nowhere does there appear any clear trace of the fourth evangelist's having used any of the synoptic Son of man sayings.

I have already mentioned resemblances between the Son of man in the Fourth Gospel and in Acts, Hebrews, Revelation, and the Gospel according to the Hebrews. But there are also affinities with the Hellenistic idea of the heavenly Man (ἄνθρω-πος), a radical difference from the synoptics. C. H. Dodd, referring especially to 1 Cor. 15, points out that Paul uses the term "man" "in connection with *testimonia* which elsewhere are associated with the expression 'Son of Man' ".[1]

The Fourth Gospel frequently calls Jesus "the man",[2] but only two of the instances appear to have any Christological

[1] *Interpretation* 243.
[2] Cf. E. M. Sidebottom, *The Christ of the Fourth Gospel* (1961), 96.

153

significance. In 10: 33, "We stone you for no good work but for blasphemy; because you, being a man, make yourself God", the point is that the Jews do not realize, as do the readers, that "the man" really *is* God or the *heavenly* Man. The same applies to 19: 5, "Behold, the man".[1]

Otherwise the Fourth Gospel, like the others, uses the expression Son of man, and on the lips of Jesus himself. In this respect the gospel stands in the same line of tradition as the synoptic sources. But frequently the Johannine Son of man is invested with elements belonging to the heavenly Man. How far is the resultant figure transformed, and how far does it still retain elements from old tradition? Does it contribute anything to the understanding of the problem of Jesus and the Son of man?

It is not very easy to classify the Son of man sayings in John. The work of S. Schulz[2] is not, as the title might suggest, devoted to the Son of man as such or alone, but is concerned to bring out the connections between the four themes Son of man, Son, Paraclete, and "return" (14: 3, "I will come again"), all of which, it is claimed, are derived from the apocalyptic Son of man. Schulz's method of *Themageschichte* has been adversely criticized.[3] But his findings on the Son of man sayings are important. He assigns to pre-Johannine tradition the following passages: 1: 51; 3: 13–15; 5: 27–29; 6: 27, 53; 13: 31f. In the remainder (6: 62; 8: 28; 12: 23, 34) only splinters ("Traditionssplitter") of the Son of man tradition are present. These the evangelist has taken from the other passages, and used in other connections.[4]

If, however, the sayings are classified in the same way as the synoptic ones, we get the following results.

A. Earthly activity of the Son of man: none.

B. Sufferings of the Son of man: 3: 14f.*; 6: 53; 8: 28*; 12: 23*; 12: 34*; 13: 31f.*.

C. Glory of the Son of man: 1: 51; 3: 13; 3: 14f.*; 5: 27; 6: 27; 6: 62; 8: 28*; 12: 23*; 12: 34*; 13: 31f.*.

---

[1] Barrett, *John* 450, sees here a clear trace of the myth of the heavenly Man behind the Johannine Son of man.

[2] *Untersuchungen zur Menschensohn-Christologie im Johannesevangelium* (1957), subsequently cited as Schulz.

[3] J. M. Robinson, JBL 78 (1959), 247–52.

[4] ἀναβαίνειν 6: 62 (3: 13); ὑψοῦν 8: 28; 12: 34 (3: 14); δοξάζειν 12: 23 (13: 31f.), Schulz 122f.

One saying, 9: 35, stands outside these categories.[1] Jesus finds the man born blind whom he had healed, and asks him, "Do you believe in the Son of man?"[2] Here the church is speaking through the earthly Jesus who, in accordance with Johannine anachronism, is at the same time the Christ of glory, the exalted and vindicated Son of man, the Lord. The question of Jesus and the man's reply, "Lord, I believe" (verse 38), reflect the primitive Christian confession, "Jesus is Lord".[3] This points to the Son of man as the evangelist's fundamental and principal Christology, an impression which is strengthened by the fact that in John the main statements of the kerygma concerning Jesus are given in terms of the Son of man. The incarnation is described as a descent of the Son of man (3: 13), his death as his being lifted up (ὑψοῦν 3: 14; 8: 28; 12: 34) or glorified (δοξάζειν 12: 23; 13: 31f.), the ascension as his return or ascent to heaven (3: 13; 6: 62), for which the verbs ὑψοῦν and δοξάζειν, used to denote the passion, do double duty;[4] he exercises judgement in his capacity as Son of man (5: 27).

The absence of any saying about the Son of man's activity on earth in his status of humility as a man among men is remarkable, but corresponds to the absence of any such saying in the synoptic traditions which can be accepted quite unhesitatingly as genuine in its present form as a Son of man saying.

Sayings relating to the sufferings, death, and resurrection of the Son of man are virtually confined to Mark. They are not connected with those which refer to the exalted Son of man's future activity or to his parousia. The passion is separated from the glory in two different categories of sayings. The Fourth Gospel, however, has no Son of man sayings at all which are

[1] "The Son of man" is a variant reading in 5: 19 (D f13 2145 d, for the first ὁ υἱός), and 5: 25 (KS 28 al), but too weakly supported to be genuine. Also 6: 56 is followed by a Western addition in D (a ff[2]): καθὼς ἐν ἐμοὶ ὁ πατὴρ κἀγὼ ἐν τῷ πατρί. αμην αμην λέγω ὑμῖν, ἐὰν μὴ λάβητε τὸ σῶμα τοῦ υἱοῦ τοῦ ἀνθρώπου ὡς τὸν ἄρτον τῆς ζωῆς, οὐκ ἔχετε ζωὴν ἐν αὐτῷ. This appears to be based on 6:53.

[2] This reading is so strongly attested (P[66] P[75] אBDW pc sys sa ac[2] fam) as to be almost certainly correct, over against "the Son of God" in the textus receptus, for which it is very unlikely to be a substitute. It is therefore incorrect to deny that "Son of man" is ever a "Bekenntnis-Titel" (H. Conzelmann in RGG[3] 3 (1959), 631: "Als Menschensohn wird J. nicht angerufen, sondern erwartet").

[3] Acts 2: 36; Rom. 10: 9; 1 Cor. 12: 3; Phil. 2: 11.

[4] In the asterisked passages in B and C above.

simply and solely passion sayings.[1] The passion and glorification of the Son of man are one and the same thing or, one might say, the passion is subsumed under the glory. The preponderance of sayings having to do, in one way or another, with the glory of the Son of man corresponds to the fact that all the main synoptic sources (Mark, Q, L, M) agree in having sayings of this type, which is not the case with the other groups. Moreover, although ὑψοῦν is given a double meaning, that of death, the starting point and underlying emphasis is the idea of exaltation. The same thing applies to δοξάζειν. Otherwise more straightforward words would have been chosen to describe the passion. Finally, it is not too much to say that there is not a single one of these sayings which does not refer to the future status and activity of the glorified Son of man. Even 6: 53 is no real exception, for the flesh which is to be eaten and the blood which is to be drunk are those of the heavenly Son of man, although he is retrospectively represented as speaking in the person of the historical Jesus.

Up to this point there is both a striking confirmation of the synoptic data, and also an advance upon it determined by theological considerations. Even the lack of explicit identification of the Son of man with Jesus (the hall-mark of an authentic synoptic saying) is possibly represented (1: 51; 6: 27). But, as 9: 35 shows, this identification is otherwise assumed as an article of faith. Jesus and the Son of man exalted to Lordship are one and the same. The main feature which is absent is the parousia of the Son of man. Such a conception lies outside the Fourth Gospel's terms of reference. The Son of man has descended to earth and has ascended again to where he was before, or has been lifted up or glorified. There can be no "second" coming.[2]

It is also possible to divide the sayings into two main groups according as they contain what may be called "synoptic

---

[1] Except perhaps by implication 6: 53, but even here it is really the glorified Son of man who is speaking. John never speaks of the "resurrection" of the Son of man.

[2] There is, however, a Johannine equivalent (πάλιν ἔρχομαι 14: 3; ἔρχομαι πρὸς ὑμᾶς 14: 18, 28; ἕως ἔρχομαι 21: 22f.), but it is divorced from the Son of man concept because the evangelist is not using his Son of man source. The obverse is ὄψεσθέ με (16: 16, 17, 19). Cf. Heb. 9: 28, ὁ Χριστὸς . . . ἐκ δευτέρου χωρὶς ἁμαρτίας ὀφθήσεται.

traits" or features foreign to the synoptic Son of man. These may be styled respectively "sayings of synoptic type" and "sayings of non-synoptic type". This method of classification is the best fitted to our purpose. We shall note the degree of encroachment of non-synoptic ideas on the synoptic ones.[1]

(1) *Sayings of synoptic type:* 1: 51; 3: 14f.; 5: 27; 8: 28; 12: 34.

(2) *Sayings of non-synoptic type:* 3: 13; 6: 27; 6: 53; 6: 62; 12: 23; 13: 31f.

(1) Sayings of synoptic type

John 1: 51. "Truly, truly, I say to you, you will see heaven opened, and the angels of God ascending and descending upon the Son of man."[2]

We may first enumerate the resemblances to synoptic sayings.

(a) In the saying itself, whatever its present connection with the context may be, there is no explicit identification of the Son of man with Jesus.

(b) Of the twenty-five Johannine sayings introduced by "amen, amen",[3] only this one and 6: 53 are also Son of man sayings. There are only three synoptic Son of man sayings introduced by "amen", and they are all in Matthew. Of these Matt. 10: 23 and 16: 28[4] refer to the coming of the Son of man, and 19: 28 speaks of him sitting on his throne of glory. That is, they all look to the future glory of the Son of man, as does John 1: 51, and are eschatological in outlook.

(c) The mention of the heaven opened is reminiscent of Stephen's vision of the heavens opened, revealing the Son of man standing in the presence of God, and less directly of Mark 14: 62, "You will see the Son of man sitting at the right hand of power".

---

[1] The term "synoptic" naturally denotes not *all* the synoptic data about the Son of man, but those particular data which contribute to the understanding of the problem of Jesus and the Son of man.

[2] See H. Windisch, "Angelophanien um den Menschensohn auf Erden", ZNW 30 (1931), 215–33: an interpolated fragment of Son of man mythology inconsistent with the Logos Christology; N. A. Dahl in *Current Issues in New Testament Interpretation: Essays in honor of Otto A. Piper*, ed. W. Klassen and G. F. Snyder (1962), 136f.: the central thought is the future vision of the glorified Son of man.

[3] Cf. B. Noack, *Zur johanneischen Tradition* (1954), 65f.

[4] Matthaean editorial modification of Mark 9: 1.

(d) The Son of man is associated with angels, as in a number of synoptic passages (Mark 8: 38 (parr. Matt. 16: 27; Luke 9: 26); Mark 13: 27 (par. Matt. 24: 31); Matt. 13: 41; 25: 31).[1]

But only the Fourth Gospel (3: 13; 6: 62) speaks of the Son of man ascending or descending. Whatever meaning is to be attached to this use of the verbs in these passages, here the notion of the ascending and descending angels of God seems to have some sort of connection with the thought of the Son of man sitting at the right hand of power and coming with the clouds of heaven. It is surely not without significance that this is the sole non-synoptic feature of the saying.

It is recognized that the problem of this saying is the conception of the angels ascending and descending. It is also widely held that there is some connection with the exegesis of Gen. 28: 12[2] found in *Genesis Rabbah* 68: 18,[3] quoted by C. F. Burney[4] and by others after him.[5] The exegesis in question is attributed to R. Yannai, one of the Amoraim of the first generation, who thought that the Hebrew *bô* in the passage in Genesis referred not to the ladder, but to Jacob. The midrash goes on to refer to the "image" of Jacob in heaven, so that the angels "were ascending on high and looking at his image (אִיקוֹנִין = ἐικόνιον), and then descending below and finding him sleeping". Thus there is a continuous traffic between the earthly Jacob and his heavenly counterpart. The meaning of this is obscure, especially as "ascending and descending upon Jacob" is interpreted as meaning "they were taking up and bringing down upon him"—but what? It has been suggested that it is Jacob's image, the heavenly man.[6] If John is thinking on similar lines, we might suppose that what is meant is that the Son of man, replacing Jacob, is both in heaven and on earth, and that there is a combination of the

---

[1] In Luke 12: 8f. "the angels of God" is a periphrasis for God.

[2] The language of John 1: 51 closely resembles the LXX, οἱ ἄγγελοι τοῦ θεοῦ ἀνέβαινον καὶ κατέβαινον ἐπ᾽ αὐτῆς (i.e. the κλίμαξ).

[3] English translation by H. Freedman, *Midrash Rabbah, Genesis II* (1939), p. 626 (68: 12).

[4] *The Aramaic Origin of the Fourth Gospel* (1922), 116f.

[5] H. Odeberg, *The Fourth Gospel* (1929), 33f.; Dodd, *Interpretation* 245; cf. Barrett, *John* 156.

[6] Burney, op. cit., 116f.

idea of the heavenly man with that of the incarnation.[1] There is much in this view which corresponds to Johannine thought, but it is not central in this passage. While there is some allusion to the story of Jacob and the ladder in Gen. 28, there are objections to the view of Burney and others that this is the main thought in John 1: 51.

R. Yannai lived in the third century, so that direct knowledge of his interpretation of the passage on the part of the evangelist is ruled out. Such an interpretation could, of course, have been known much earlier, even to the evangelist, but this is by no means necessary to the understanding of John 1: 51.

In the synoptics the angels are associated with the Son of man as a retinue of attendants or servants,[2] and the Son of man is the centre and focus of attention. Further, M. Black has expressed doubts as to whether the picture of angels ascending and descending upon the Son of man "is one that the Semitic mind would entertain". The picture rather is that "of the heavens opened and angels from above and beneath converging on the Son of Man, the central Figure".[3] That this is correct is proved by the sequence of events. It is only after the opening of the heavens that the vision can be seen, as in the case of Stephen. It is a *heavenly* vision of the Son of man in glory, attended by the angels.[4] In other words, John refers to the exaltation of the Son of man in heavenly glory,

---

[1] Cf. Barrett, *John* 156. Odeberg, op. cit., 40, who gives an inclusive sense to all the Johannine instances of the Son of man, explains John 1: 51 as implying a promise to believers of a spiritual experience of communion with the heavenly world expressed in the symbolism of the ascending and descending angels. I do not think that this mystical interpretation is correct, nor that the Son of man in John, any more than in the synoptics, has a collective sense; cf. R. Bultmann, *Das Evangelium des Johannes* (1950), 74.

[2] C. C. Torrey, *The Four Gospels* 186, 318, renders John 1: 51 "in the service of the Son of Man".

[3] Black, *Aramaic Approach* 85, where evidence is adduced for the Aramaic 'al (rendered by ἐπί in John 1: 51) meaning "towards", as the equivalent of the Hebrew 'el. But even ἐπί itself can mean "towards" as well as "upon".

[4] So it is not the *earthly* Son of man, replacing Jacob-Israel, who is in mind, as Schweizer holds (*Menschensohn* 203, n. 63); but he admits that the Son of man, being united with the Father, "gewissermassen schon inthronisiert ist". G. Quispel, "Nathanael und der Menschensohn (Joh. 1.51)", ZNW 47 (1956), 281–83, suggests Christian adaptation of esoteric Jewish speculation on Ezek. 1: 26.

and employs basically the same features as the synoptic traditions.[1]

It is a mistake to import into John 1:51 the third-century midrashic interpretation of Gen. 28:12, so as to give centrality to the Jacob-Israel-Son of man motif. The use of the passage in Genesis is secondary both in importance and chronologically.[2] The sole use made of this passage concerns the ascending and descending angels, and while this may be based on the LXX, an Aramaic stage is not excluded. The purpose of the borrowing is to emphasize the central figure, the Son of man. The present form of the saying is due to the context to which it is attached. It is difficult to decide whether verse 50 is the evangelist's addition to the account of Nathanael's confession, originally concluding with the emphatic declaration, "You are the king of Israel", and is intended to provide the link between it and verse 51. As has often been observed, ὄψεσθε does not follow well after μείζω τούτων ὄψῃ. Furthermore, καὶ λέγει αὐτῷ at the beginning of verse 51 seems quite unnecessary, since Nathanael is still being addressed. These difficulties disappear if it is supposed that verse 51 is a completely separate saying, which has been adapted to the context to which the evangelist has appended it.[3] It is introduced, apparently superfluously, by the words, "and he says to him", precisely because it is an utterance of special importance, for it is prefaced by "amen, amen". The sole non-synoptic trait, the ascending and descending angels, is only an oblique reference to the story in Genesis, and its inclusion is the main detail of adaptation of an earlier form of the saying to fit the context, and in particular the climactic conclusion of Nathanael's confession, "You are the king of Israel". Israel (Jacob) is now replaced by the new head

[1] Note the use of ὄψεσθαι here and in Mark 13:26 (parr. Matt. 24:30; Luke 21:27); 14:62 (par. Matt. 26:64); Luke 17:22.

[2] W. Michaelis, "Joh. 1, 51, Gen. 28, 12 und das Menschensohn-Problem", TLZ 85 (1960), 561–78, tries to show that the passage in Genesis has not influenced John 1:51 at all. Schweizer (TLZ 86 (1961), 169) accepts this, maintaining that the passage probably reflects in a fragmentary form a special tradition identifying Jesus the Son of man with the new Jacob-Israel.

[3] The plural ὑμῖν instead of σοί which would be more appropriate in this place, along with ὄψεσθε, may be due to incomplete adaptation to the present context of the saying from a separate source; cf. E. C. Broome, "The Sources of the Fourth Gospel", JBL 63 (1944), 109f. But this is less probable than the originality of the plural in the saying.

of a new Israel, by the Son of man. Behind this saying, therefore, there lies a Johannine equivalent to Mark 14: 62, where Jesus admits that he is the Messiah, the Son of the Blessed, but continues, "And you will see the *Son of man* sitting at the right hand of Power, and coming with the clouds of heaven". So in John, Jesus hears Nathanael's confession that he is the Son of God, the king of Israel. But he and the rest will see ("you (plural) will see", as in Mark 14: 62, in address to the high priest) a greater phenomenon still, that of the *Son of man*.

John 3: 14f. "And as Moses lifted up the serpent in the wilderness, so must the Son of man be lifted up, that whoever believes may in him have eternal life."

As finally arranged by the evangelist, the whole section 3: 13–15 forms a unit, verse 13 implying that it is only the one who has ascended into heaven whence he descended, who is able to declare the heavenly things, and verse 15 with its reference to eternal life as possible only for the believer, anticipating the almost identical language of verse 16, to which it is joined by the logical conjunction γάρ.[1] But both sayings (verses 13 and 14) are fully intelligible in isolation both from their present context and from one another. What has brought them together is the fact that they both relate to the Son of man, and the apparent similarity in meaning of ἀναβαίνειν and ὑψωθῆναι. But the application to the Son of man of the verbs ἀναβαίνειν and καταβαίνειν marks the saying in verse 13 as non-synoptic, whereas verse 14 possesses two features which justify its classification as synoptic in character.

δεῖ is used in the synoptics to express the divine scriptural necessity of the passion and resurrection of the Son of man.[2] The fourth evangelist is quite familiar with this meaning of the word.[3] Here it is connected with the idea that in some way the story of Moses and the brazen serpent is prophetic of the lifting up of the Son of man.

---

[1] In verse 15 the words ἐν αὐτῷ ἔχῃ belong together, because John does not use πιστεύειν with ἐν. T. W. Manson, JTS 46 (1945), 130, recommended the adoption of the sub-Akhmimic version as the correct text. This presupposes πιστεύων εἰς αὐτὸν ἐν αὐτῷ ἔχῃ ζωὴν αἰώνιον.

[2] Mark 8: 31; Luke 17: 25; Matt. 26: 54; John 20: 9, οὐδέπω γὰρ ᾔδεισαν τὴν γραφήν, ὅτι δεῖ αὐτὸν ἐκ νεκρῶν ἀναστῆναι.

[3] Cf. 12: 34; W. Grundmann, TWNT ii. 24f.

The word ὑψοῦν is not used in Num. 21: 8f.[1] It might therefore be supposed that the evangelist has introduced it himself,
especially as he has brought "believe" and "eternal life" from
the following verse into verse 15, both these verses, of course,
being his own composition. This, however, cannot be the
case.

ὑψοῦν is only used in the Fourth Gospel in connection with the
Son of man (8: 28; 12: 34). 12: 32 is a special case. Both 8: 28
and 12: 34 are among the passages in which Schulz sees only
fragments of the Son of man theme. In 8: 28 ("When you have
lifted up the Son of man, then you will know that I am he") the
primary meaning must be crucifixion, since the verb is used
in the active in reference to human agents. 12: 34 repeats the
expression in 3: 14, δεῖ ὑψωθῆναι τὸν υἱὸν τοῦ ἀνθρώπου, and
the reference back to 12: 32 ("And I, if I am lifted up from the
earth, will draw all men to myself") and the meaning given to
this utterance of Jesus ("He said this to show by what death he
was to die"), show the primary meaning again to be crucifixion.
But 3: 14 is the decisive text for the association of ὑψοῦν with
the Son of man. This association is not the work of the evangelist, but was already present in his source.[2] This is proved not
only by his failure to use the verb except in reference to the
Son of man, but also by the early kerygmatic use of it in non-
Johannine circles to describe the exaltation of Jesus.

Acts 2: 33, "Being therefore exalted (ὑψωθείς) at the right
hand of God"; Acts 5: 31, "God exalted (ὕψωσεν) him at his
right hand as Leader and Saviour". It is possible that this
meaning of the word in these passages depends on the Aramaic
verb *zkph* in the primitive preaching. In any case Phil. 2: 9,
"therefore God highly exalted him" (ὑπερύψωσεν) belongs here.
If Paul has adapted an earlier Aramaic Christological hymn,

---

[1] LXX has ἔστησεν αὐτὸν ἐπὶ σημείου. T. F. Glasson, *Moses in the Fourth
Gospel* (1963), 36–39, on the basis of the familiar Johannine allusiveness,
tries to import into John 3: 14f. the idea of the σημεῖον in the sense of ensign
or standard, as in Num. 21: 8f. "And the Lord said to Moses, Make a fiery
serpent, and set it on a standard (ἐπὶ σημείου) ... And Moses made a
serpent of bronze, and set it on the standard" (ἐπὶ σημείου). But σημεῖον is
such a favourite word with the fourth evangelist that it is inconceivable
that he would not actually have used it here if he had intended it at all.
See also above, p. 114, n. 1, on Glasson's earlier suggestion that the σημεῖον
of the Son of man in Matt. 24: 30 is not a sign but an ensign or standard.
[2] Schulz 107, n. 6, 108.

and if, as Lohmeyer suggested,[1] ὡς ἄνθρωπος in verse 7 represents the Aramaic *k*e*bhar nāšā'*, it would be a remarkable parallel to John 3: 14. It is to be expected that, if the meaning of ὑψοῦν in John 3: 14 corresponds to early kerygmatic usage, it must denote primarily exaltation to the right hand of God.[2] But our passage has complications which do not exist in the others mentioned, and other factors must be considered.

There can be no doubt that in John 3: 14 ὑψωθῆναι, although meaning primarily exaltation, also means "to be crucified".[3] The use of δεῖ points to this.

It is widely held that ὑψωθῆναι derives its double meaning from the Palestinian Aramaic verb *'izd*e*kēph*, which is supposed to have stood in an Aramaic source used by the evangelist.[4] Since, however, any presumed Aramaic *Vorlage* of the non-Johannine examples of the use of ὑψωθῆναι already cited could not possibly have borne the meaning of crucifixion as well as of exaltation, this source or tradition must have been of a special kind and must have been moulded by special motives.[5] The influence of Num. 21: 8f. on the formation of John 3: 14f. is chronologically secondary. The point of resemblance between the setting up of the brazen serpent on a pole and the fastening of Jesus to the cross in the mind of the evangelist or a predecessor is not that the serpent is a type of Christ,[6] but that the

---

[1] *Der Brief an die Philipper*[10] (1954), 95; see also above, p. 151, n. 1.

[2] Cf. Dodd, *Interpretation* 375f. It is thought that a factor in the choice of the word may have been Isa. 52: 13, which refers to the exaltation and glorification of the Servant (ὑψωθήσεται καὶ δοξασθήσεται). δοξάζειν is used of the Son of man in John 12: 23 and 13: 31f., and like δόξα is a favourite Johannine word but is not, like ὑψοῦν, restricted to the Son of man. Elsewhere in the New Testament it is surprisingly scarce in references to Jesus (Acts 3: 13; Heb. 5: 5). I do not think that Isa. 52: 13 was as influential in this respect as is urged most recently by Thüsing 36.

[3] But it is incorrect to restrict it to this meaning, as does J. H. Bernard, *The Gospel according to St. John* i (1928), 112ff.

[4] G. Kittel, ZNW 35 (1936), 282–85; Black, *Aramaic Approach* 103; Barrett, *John* 9. Thüsing 36 doubts the validity of this suggestion. J. Dupont, *Essais sur la christologie de saint Jean* (1951), 259f., n. 6, sees no double meaning in any of the Johannine occurrences, but only that of crucifixion.

[5] The examples cited from the purely Greek side by Bernard, op. cit., ii. 708, Dodd, *Interpretation* 377, n. 4, and Thüsing 37, from the second-century writer Artemidorus (e.g., *Onirocritica* 1. 76, κακοῦργος δὲ ὢν σταυρωθήσεται διὰ τὸ ὕψος καὶ τὴν τῶν χειρῶν ἔκτασιν [cf. John 21: 18, ἐκτενεῖς τὰς χεῖράς σου]), are not very helpful because the verb ὑψοῦν is not actually used.

[6] As in later Christian writers, e.g. Barn. 12. 5; Justin Martyr, *Apol.*

elevation of the serpent and the recovery given to those who gazed upon it, as a sort of antidote to the serpent-bites, are prophetic of the lifting up of the Son of man and the bestowal of eternal life on those who have faith in him. This exegesis may be based on an earlier preacher's application of the story of Moses and the serpent to the exaltation of Christ in the Aramaic stage, and ὑψωθῆναι derives its twofold meaning from the Aramaic verb *'izdᵉkēph*. But the choice of this word in this particular connection and with this twofold meaning was already determined by a still earlier stage of the tradition which contained a saying, "the Son of man must be lifted up", in the sense both of being exalted and of being crucified. The pre-Johannine association of the Son of man with the primitive use of the word ὑψοῦν for the exaltation of Jesus in itself gave the verb its double meaning. "The Son of man must be lifted up" is thus also a Johannine parallel to the synoptic predictions of the passion and resurrection of the Son of man. The passive form ὑψωθῆναι corresponds to primitive usage (Acts 2: 33), in meaning primarily "the Son of man must be exalted" by God (God is the subject in Acts 5: 31; Phil. 2: 9). But the thought of the passion and death of the Son of man is also incorporated in the same word.

The logion is thus a Johannine or rather a pre-Johannine version of the expression both of the early Christian belief in the exaltation of Jesus to the right hand of God, and of the belief that this was accomplished, in accordance with divine decree and scriptural necessity, by the suffering of death on the cross. In the latter sense ὑψωθῆναι is the exact equivalent of σταυρωθῆναι in Luke 24: 7.[1] Of course, the mention of crucifixion is a later tendency. But it is quite possible that σταυρωθῆναι and ὑψωθῆναι are ultimately translation variants of the same Aramaic verb. If so, Luke's rendering, although correct, is a later departure from the meaning of *'izdᵉkēph* in the primitive preaching, where it denoted the exaltation of Jesus,

---

I. 60; *Trypho* 94, 112; Tert., *Adv. Marc.* iii. 18. The story was a favourite one also among Jewish exegetes, cf. H. Odeberg, *The Fourth Gospel* (1929), 98–113. The Fourth Gospel preserves the earliest extant Christian exegesis; on its antiquity and Palestinian origin and rival Jewish exegesis, cf. T. W. Manson, JTS 46 (1945), 129ff.

[1] Cf. Matt. 26: 2, εἰς τὸ σταυρωθῆναι (editorial); 20: 19, σταυρῶσαι (par. Mark 10: 34, ἀποκτενοῦσιν).

while the Johannine form has preserved both this original connotation and the second meaning the word acquired in Aramaic-speaking circles, where more developed theological reflection had brought it into conjunction with the title Son of man.

John 5: 27. ". . . and has given him authority to execute judgement, because he is the Son of man".

It might be thought that the section 5: 27-9 formed a unity before its incorporation by the evangelist.[1] It is marked off from what precedes, where the subject is the Son, and from verse 30, where Jesus speaks in the first person.[2] But whereas verse 27 has only one Johannine feature, ἐξουσίαν ἔδωκεν,[3] the other two components of the verse (κρίσιν ποιεῖν[4] and υἱὸς ἀνθρώπου) not occurring elsewhere in John, verses 28f. possess several Johannine stylistic characteristics,[5] and are not reminiscent, like verse 27, of Dan. 7: 13f., but of Dan. 12: 2.[6] The last two verses of the section give the impression of being the evangelist's own composition. The words "all who are in the tombs will hear his voice" are modelled on verse 25, "the dead will hear the voice of the Son of God"; and the words "to the resurrection of life" are reminiscent of "will live" in that same verse. The two verses are an expansion of verse 27, which alone is to be regarded as derived from a tradition or source.

This saying about the Son of man differs from all the others in this gospel in having an anarthrous form of the Greek for Son of man—υἱὸς ἀνθρώπου. Schulz's explanation is that it is not a technical term such as is found in the Similitudes of Enoch, but is directly dependent on Dan. 7: 13f., where the "one like a son of man" is contrasted with the beasts. This, he urges, points to the antiquity of the saying in that the name Son

---

[1] So Schulz 114.
[2] The sentence οὐ δύναμαι ἐγὼ ποιεῖν ἀπ᾽ ἐμαυτοῦ οὐδέν is modelled exactly on verse 19.
[3] 1: 12; 17: 2.
[4] E.g. Gen. 18: 19, 25; Deut. 10: 18; Isa. 1: 24; 1 Macc. 6: 22; examples from non-biblical Greek in W. Bauer–W. F. Arndt–F. W. Gingrich, *A Greek-English Lexicon of the New Testament*, etc. (1957), 453.
[5] μὴ θαυμάζετε (cf. 3: 7), 1 John 3: 13; ἔρχεται ὥρα 4: 21, 23; 12: 23; 16: 2, 25, 32; ὥρα ἐν 4: 52f., cf. 5: 25; ποιεῖν and πράσσειν, cf. 3: 20f.; E. Ruckstuhl, *Die literarische Einheit des Johannesevangeliums* (1951), 161.
[6] Cf. Schulz 113.

of man is not yet a designation of Jesus, and lies somewhere between the late Jewish and the Christian Son of man traditions.[1]

It is doubtful, however, whether in this particular respect[2] John 5: 27 is directly dependent on Dan. 7: 13, where it is ὡς υἱὸς ἀνθρώπου (LXX, Θ), "one like a son of man", which means "a human-like figure", a figure who appears to be human, but is in fact divine. If the absence of the article in our passage is given full weight, the meaning might conceivably be "a son of man", "a human being". But this is improbable.

The expression υἱὸς ἀνθρώπου is unique not only in the Fourth Gospel, but in the rest of the New Testament. Heb. 2: 6 is no real exception. The author has a Son of man Christology, but in this connection he does not use Dan. 7, but Ps. 8, and the phrase υἱὸς ἀνθρώπου only in quoting the psalm. His object in borrowing the term is not so much to express the humanity of Jesus in itself, as to illustrate the theme of humiliation and exaltation.

There is no reason why the phrase in John 5: 27 should not mean *the* Son of man, in accordance with the rule that definite predicate nouns preceding a verb usually lack the article,[3] just as θεοῦ υἱός in Matt. 27: 54 may actually mean "*the* Son of God". Further, there is a strong probability that υἱὸς ἀνθρώπου is not to be explained only from the Greek side. It may well represent the Hebraic construct state such as is used in the Aramaic of Dan. 7: 13 (*kᵉbhar 'ᵉnāš*), and is sometimes reproduced in translations like πνεῦμα κυρίου (Luke 4: 18) and ἄγγελος κυρίου (Luke 1: 11).[4] In this case the term in John would translate an Aramaic *bar nāšâ*, "the Son of man".

We have earlier noted the possibility that in the Christological hymn "like a man" (ὡς ἄνθρωπος) at Phil. 2: 7 renders the Aramaic expression in Dan. 7: 13, and that this is the source of Paul's application to Christ of the title ἄνθρωπος, which is to

[1] Schulz 111–113.
[2] Despite the similarity of language (Dan. 7: 14 LXX, καὶ ἐδόθη αὐτῷ ἐξουσία), ἐξουσίαν ἔδωκεν is Johannine, see above p. 165, n. 3.
[3] Cf. C. F. D. Moule, *An Idiom-Book of New Testament Greek*[2] (1959), 115f. Analogy with the anarthrous use of θεός and κύριος as proper names (R. Bultmann, *Das Evangelium des Johannes* (1950) 196, n. 3) is less likely, for this would be the sole example.
[4] Cf. Moule, op. cit., 117, 177.

THE SON OF MAN IN THE FOURTH GOSPEL

be regarded as replacing the older form, "the Son of man", familiar in the gospel traditions. The expression in John 5: 27 may be viewed as analogous to the Pauline word, but as more ancient both than this and the normal expression for "the Son of man" in the gospels, because it is an absolutely exact rendering of the Hebraic construct state. Thus:

Dan. 7: 13 k^ebhar '$^en\bar{a}\check{s}$: ὡς υἱὸς ἀνθρώπου—υἱὸς ἀνθρώπου (John 5: 27) —ὁ υἱὸς τοῦ ἀνθρώπου; ὡς ἄνθρωπος—(ὁ) ἄνθρωπος (Paul).

In John 5: 27 the title Son of man is even more definite than in its more usual form. The Son of man is to judge precisely because he *is* the Son of man. This rules out the notion that Jesus judges as a man.[1]

In this respect the saying is of synoptic type, for in the synoptics also the Son of man is judge.[2] But nowhere in them do we find a categorical statement like that in John, that it is precisely as Son of man that he is to act as judge. This is in agreement with Jewish apocalyptic,[3] but it only makes explicit what is implicit in the synoptics.[4]

But if the conception of the Son of man as judge corresponds to synoptic ideas, its mode of expression does not. The phrase κρίσιν ποιεῖν in John 5: 27 only occurs elsewhere in the New Testament in Jude 15, ("Behold, the Lord came with his holy myriads), to execute judgement on all" (ποιῆσαι κρίσιν κατὰ πάντων). It is significant that this same expression should only appear again in the New Testament in a passage which is a

---

[1] It is, therefore, not true that "contrary to current opinion, the meaning of John 5: 27 is that Jesus judges by virtue of his manhood", E. M. Sidebottom, *The Christ of the Fourth Gospel* (1961), 93; cf. also B. F. Westcott, *The Gospel according to St John* (1882), 87f.; G. H. C. MacGregor, *The Gospel of John* (1936), 179; M.-J. Lagrange, *Évangile selon saint Jean*[8] (1948), 148; A. Schlatter, *Der Evangelist Johannes* (1948), 152. Barrett, *John* 218, remarks: "it seems [also] wholly improbable that precisely at this place, where judgement—the characteristic function of the apocalyptic Son of man—is in mind, John would turn his back on the common Christian (and his own) usage".

[2] Possibly the idea of the Son of man/judge may be implied also in Acts 10: 42 and 17: 31, cf. A. M. Hunter, *Paul and his Predecessors*[2] (1961), 86, n. 3. H. Dieckmann, "'Der Sohn des Menschen' im Johannesevangelium", *Scholastik* 2 (1927), 229–47 (243f.) sees a parallel to the present passage in Mark 2: 10 (parr. Matt. 9: 6; Luke 5: 24).

[3] "The sum of judgement was given to the Son of man", 1 En. 69: 27; cf. also 61: 8–63. 12, where the Elect One or the Son of man is judge. Elsewhere in Jewish thought God himself is the judge.

[4] Cf. Cullmann, *Christology* 158.

quotation from 1 En. 1: 9, in the section describing Enoch's vision of the last judgement. Moreover, 1 Enoch is of Semitic origin, chapters 1–5 having probably been written in Hebrew.[1] This tends to support the suggestion that the form of the title Son of man in John 5: 27 is of Semitic origin, and that the saying as a whole is of considerable antiquity.

The conclusion I should draw is, therefore, that it is an isolated pre-Johannine saying from a tradition about the Son of man. But the evangelist has so adapted it to the context to which he has attached it that it is the Son who is the subject, while the Son of man is the predicate. To him the Father has given all judgement (verse 22) because he is also the Son of man.

John 8: 28. "When you have lifted up the Son of man, then you will know that I am he."

John 12: 34. "How do you say that the Son of man must be lifted up? Who is this Son of man?"[2]

Although these two sayings, like 3: 14, associate the Son of man with the verb ὑψοῦν, they do not appear to have been taken from a special tradition.

8: 28. Since the verb "lift up" is here active (ὅταν ὑψώσητε), and the agents are the enemies of Jesus, the primary meaning must be "crucify". But the following words, "then you will know that I am he", suggest that there is also present the idea of exaltation, the primary meaning of the verb in 3: 14 which in this respect, as we have seen, follows the use of ὑψοῦν (and its Aramaic original) in the early preaching. 8: 28 is the evangelist's own composition.

The rest of the saying, "then you will know that I am he", appears to mean that this knowledge of who Jesus is will be given as a result of their lifting him up on the cross, an act of which they are indeed the agents, but an act also with a far deeper significance than its perpetrators realize. Thüsing[3] has shown that the words "you will know" cannot mean "you will know to your cost (or too late)", but must imply a promise of

---

[1] R. H. Charles, *The Book of Enoch translated*, etc.[2] (1912), lviif.

[2] The omission of the words τίς ἐστιν οὗτος ὁ υἱὸς τοῦ ἀνθρώπου in P[75] is probably the result of haplography rather than a genuine textual variant. P[75] also omits ὅτι before δεῖ in this verse.

[3] See the full discussion of the text by Thüsing, 15–22.

salvation to those of the Jews who *will* believe as a consequence of the lifting up of the Son of man, because γινώσκειν in the Fourth Gospel has only the positive sense. The opposite is expressed in verse 24, "for unless you believe that I am he, you will die in your sins". But does "I am he" mean the same thing in both verses? If so, ἐγώ εἰμι, as often in John, is a "theophanic formula" corresponding to '*ⁿî hû*', the formula of divine self-affirmation in the Old Testament.[1] But it may equally well mean "I am the Son of man", and answer the question "Who are you?" in verse 25. This has some support in the mention of judging (a function of the Son of man) in verse 26. Such an interpretation corresponds closely to 3: 14f., where the Son of man must be lifted up in order to evoke belief. In 8: 28 the effect of the lifting up is knowledge of his true status as the exalted Son of man. The saying is modelled by the evangelist on the pattern of the traditional saying in 3: 14 concerning the necessity of the lifting up of the Son of man. Both the addition to the latter saying in verse 15 and 8: 28 spring from the evangelist's predilection for the Son of man Christology, and from his emphasis on the necessity of belief in Jesus as the Son of man.[2]

12: 34. Jesus has not said in this context that the Son of man must be lifted up. In fact, he has not mentioned the Son of man at all. For this reason it has been proposed to transpose the verse so as to follow 8: 28f.[3] where, although Jesus has not actually said "the Son of man must be lifted up", he has spoken of him. This is unnecessary. The statement that the Son of man must be lifted up is taken by the evangelist from the saying from the source he has incorporated in 3: 14,[4] for the present passage, like 8: 28, belongs to the secondary group of sayings. The statement of Jesus in verse 32, "if I am lifted up", is suggested by the use of the verb in verse 34, and anticipates it. Its primary meaning in both places is crucifixion, as in 8: 28. This is clear from verse 33, "He said this to show by what

---

[1] E. Stauffer, *Jesus and His Story* (1960), 142ff. (154, 156); Barrett, *John* 282f.

[2] John 9: 35.

[3] Bultmann, op. cit., 269, n. 7.

[4] Dieckmann, op. cit., 241, suggests that the title "Son of man" is taken from verse 23, "oder [aus] einem späteren, von Johannes nicht berichteten Ausspruch Jesu".

death he was to die". This is taken by the hearers as a sheer contradiction of scriptural teaching, that the Messiah is to remain for ever.[1] They therefore ask uncomprehendingly, "Who is this Son of man?" What sort of a Son of man is this? Son of man and Messiah are equivalent terms. The crucifixion of the Son of man is a stumbling-block.[2]

As in 8: 28, however, the lifting up of the Son of man includes the idea of exaltation. When the evangelist comments that Jesus spoke thus in order to show "by what death he was to die", the deeper meaning his readers are meant to grasp is that, as they knew, that death was the saving death on the cross,[3] for by it Jesus would draw to himself all (who believed). Thus the basic meaning is the same, although rather differently expressed, as in 8: 28, "When you have lifted up the Son of man, then you will know that I am he". There the emphasis is on his enemies' lifting up of the Son of man on the cross, which will bring them (not only to believe but) to know that he *is* the Son of man. Here the emphasis lies rather on his being lifted up *from the earth*,[4] whereby in drawing to himself on the cross all (who believe), he draws them also to his glory. The "all" in 12: 32 is restrictive, "all who believe", and means fundamentally the same thing as "then you will know" in 8: 28. Both statements are to be read in the light of the evangelist's addition, "that whoever believes", etc. (3: 15), to the saying from the Son of man source, "the Son of man must be lifted up".[5]

In this group of sayings there are comparatively few non-synoptic ideas. 1: 51, 3: 14, and 5: 27 enshrine very old traditions, going back to the Aramaic-speaking church. This is

[1] Cf. Ezek. 37: 25; C. F. Burney, *The Aramaic Origin of the Fourth Gospel* (1922), 120.

[2] Cf. 1 Cor. 1: 23.

[3] Thüsing 24, "von welcher Heilsbedeutung sein Tod sein werde".

[4] Cf. Thüsing 24–26. "Dadurch, dass der Gekreuzigte ἐκ τῆς γῆς erhöht ist, ist der Einheitspunkt gegeben, der das Ziehen ans Kreuz und in die Herrlichkeit zusammenschauen lässt" (26).

[5] It may also be observed that the judgement of the Son of man (5: 27, 29f.) is associated with all three passages about his being lifted up. The principle of judgement depends on belief or unbelief (3: 17–19); there is the mention of judging before 8: 28; and Jesus says, "Now is the judgement of this world" (12: 31) immediately before speaking of his being lifted up.

especially clear in the latter two. By contrast, 8: 28 and
12: 34 have only a secondary importance, because they are not
drawn directly from a tradition, but have been built up by the
evangelist round the kernel-saying in 3: 14, "the Son of man
must be lifted up". We may assume that the first three sayings
in this group are Johannine parallels to the synoptic traditions
in regard to the passion, exaltation, glory, and judgement of
the Son of man. In turning to the second category, clearer
signs of non-synoptic ideas are evident, and it will be necessary
to ask how far their presence points to inferior tradition or to
the creativity of the evangelist.

(2) Sayings of non-synoptic type

John 3: 13. "And no one has ascended into heaven but he
who descended from heaven, the Son of man."

This saying is treated separately because, unlike the one in
the next verse, it is not of the synoptic type. Although it is
true that the Son of man in the Fourth Gospel has features
resembling the heavenly Man in Hellenistic thought of various
kinds,[1] the main source, as with the synoptics, is early Christian
usage. What is said of the descent and ascent of the Son of man
in this passage does not sound like anything in the synoptics.
The use of καταβαίνειν to denote the incarnation is found in
John elsewhere only in the sixth chapter (verses 33, 38, 41,
42, 50, 51, 58). But it is not confined to this gospel.

There is this passage (Eph. 4: 8–10). "Therefore it says,
When he ascended on high he led captivity captive, and gave
gifts to men. In saying, He ascended, what does it mean but
that he had also descended into the lower parts of the earth?
He who descended is he who also ascended far above all the
heavens, that he might fill all things." It is uncertain whether
the descent to the lower parts of the earth is descent into the
lower regions or simply to the earth itself. But in any case the
emphasis is on Christ's ascent into heaven which enabled him
to dispense gifts to men. In John 3: 13 also the emphasis is on
the ascent of the Son of man into heaven. In both passages the
one who ascends can only be he who descended. But in John

---

[1] Particularly in Philo and the *Hermetica*. Dodd, *Interpretation* discusses
these similarities in detail and stresses especially the archetypal Man in
Poimandres.

3: 13 the Son of man's ascent is also the primary thought, for the simple reason that otherwise he would have been unable to reveal the heavenly things. That Christ has ascended into heaven is also implied in Rom. 10: 6. "Do not say in your heart, Who will ascend into heaven? (that is, to bring Christ down) or Who will descend into the abyss? (that is, to bring Christ up from the dead)."

But positive proof that ἀναβαίνειν, the word in John, was used in the early preaching in connection with the ascent of Jesus to heavenly glory is provided by Acts 2: 34f. "For David did not ascend into the heavens (ἀνέβη εἰς τοὺς οὐρανούς); but he himself says, The Lord said to my Lord, Sit at my right hand, till I make thy enemies the footstool of thy feet." It was not David who ascended into the heavens but, it is implied, Jesus, the one who was exalted (ὑψωθείς) to the right hand of God (verse 33), to be made Lord and Christ (verse 36). We have seen before that ὑψοῦν in John 3: 14 is derived from primitive usage, of which Acts 2: 33 is an example. In the preceding saying (John 3: 13) ἀναβαίνειν is also derived from primitive usage, of which Acts 2: 34 is an example. But only in the Fourth Gospel (see later on 6: 62) is it said that the Son of man ascends. In one place (John 20: 17) the word is used twice, with Jesus speaking in the first person. The analogy with the use of ὑψοῦν is strikingly close. Only once does it occur in words of Jesus in the first person (John 12: 32), and there it is suggested by its use shortly afterwards (verse 34). It is the risen but not yet ascended Jesus who says, "I have not yet ascended to the Father" (John 20: 17). This, it is urged, depends on the association of the word "ascend" with the Son of man in the other two passages. Of these, 3: 13 is taken directly from a source, for the idea is of the Son of man who has already ascended into heaven. We see signs, then, that like ὑψοῦν, another term in kerygmatic use, ἀναβαίνειν, was coupled with the Son of man in a tradition used only by the fourth evangelist. This Johannine tradition, however, does not speak of the *ascension* (Himmelfahrt) as an event (cf. Acts 1: 9–11) but of *ascent* (Aufsteigen) into heavenly glory as a theological fact.[1]

[1] Cf. Thüsing 274: " 'Den Menschensohn aufsteigen sehen' [6: 62] ist wohl ... gleichbedeutend einem 'an seine Thronbesteigung glauben'." On the correspondence between θεωρεῖν and belief (6: 62, cf. 64; 6: 40;

But it is quite unsynoptic,[1] unlike ὑψοῦν which is used in 3: 14 and 12: 34 ("the Son of man must be lifted up") in what may also be regarded as a Johannine parallel to the synoptic predictions of the passion and resurrection of the Son of man. Special attention was called to Luke 24: 7, "the Son of man must be crucified".

John 6: 27. "Do not labour for the food which perishes, but for the food which endures to eternal life, which the Son of man will give to you."

John 6: 53. "Truly, truly, I say to you, unless you eat the flesh of the Son of man and drink his blood, you have no life in yourselves."

Both sayings are taken from a tradition, but one of a special kind, in that the idea of the Son of man as both the dispenser of food and as that food himself (flesh and blood) is unexampled. Possibly the former idea was suggested by the familiar Jewish belief that in the messianic age the manna would be brought down again (2 Baruch 29: 8), or that the Messiah would bring it down, as Moses did,[2] for the promise of imperishable food leads on to the allusions to manna (verses 31, 49).

At first sight 1 En. 62: 14 seems to offer a striking parallel.

"And the Lord of spirits will abide over them,
And with that Son of man shall they eat
And lie down and rise up for ever and ever."

But the parallel is at best only partial. The Son of man is not the dispenser of the food, much less is he that food himself. The thought in the two sayings we are considering arises out of the Johannine Christology. But by this is meant not only the Christology of the evangelist, but that which is implicit in the source at his disposal. If the Son of man is the basic Johannine Christology, it is to be expected that Jesus as the dispenser

---

12: 44f.) see Michaelis, TWNT v. 362. Relevant here, although differently expressed, is Heb. 4: 14, about Jesus as the great high priest who has "passed through the heavens", and 9: 11f.; cf. Schweizer, *Lordship* 74f.

[1] There is no synoptic reference to the ascension except Luke 24: 51, καὶ ἀνεφέρετο εἰς τὸν οὐρανόν (omitted by ℵ* D a b e ff² j l sys), and Mark 16: 19.

[2] SB ii. 481; H. Odeberg, *The Fourth Gospel* (1929), 242f.; E. C. Hoskyns, *The Fourth Gospel*² (1950), 293f.; Dodd, *Interpretation* 335ff.

of the food of eternal life should perform this function as the Son of man. As in other directions, however, the evangelist is dependent on an already existing tradition about the Son of man. This must have been a special branch of tradition connected with the eucharist. This applies to both the sayings in John 6. At first sight, however, they seem so different that it is hard to see how they can have belonged to the same source. It is well known that this difficulty has led many scholars to regard verses 51c ("and the bread which I shall give for the life of the world is my flesh")—58 as a redactional eucharistic addition[1] to the discourse on the bread of life which, from its beginning in verse 26 to verse 51b, understands the words of Jesus about himself as the bread of life (verses 35, 48) to refer to his teaching.

In fact, so far from being inconsistent and incompatible with one another, the two sayings together form the framework of the whole discourse, and the transition made by the evangelist in his construction of it is quite clear. The identification of Jesus himself with the bread of life (verse 35, repeated in verse 48) follows from the "oracular ambiguity"[2] of verse 33,[3] which can mean either "the bread of God is that bread which descends from heaven" or "the bread of God is he who descends from heaven". Further, as Dodd points out,[4] the phrase ὁ καταβαίνων is reminiscent of 3: 13, "No one has ascended into heaven but he who descended from heaven, the Son of man". By this reference back to another saying he has used about the descent of the Son of man from heaven, a saying drawn from a special tradition, the evangelist is able to provide a transition from 6: 27 to 6: 53.

3: 13, the Son of man descended from heaven;
6: 27, the Son of man gives imperishable food;
6: 53, the Son of man himself is this food.

Of course, Jesus has already called himself the bread of life (verses 35, 48) so some preparation has already been made for

---

[1] Cf. Schulz 115, n. 11. Ruckstuhl, op. cit., 220–71, however, advances convincing arguments for the Johannine style of the section; cf. J. Jeremias, *Die Abendmahlsworte Jesu*[3] (1960), 101, who formerly (in the second edition (1949), 59) held the redactional view.

[2] Dodd, *Interpretation* 337.

[3] ὁ γὰρ ἄρτος τοῦ θεοῦ ἐστιν ὁ καταβαίνων ἐκ τοῦ οὐρανοῦ.

[4] Ibid.

this startling pronouncement. But the immediate preparation for it is the statement, "I am the living bread which came down from heaven" in verse 51, an even closer approximation to 3: 13 (ὁ ἐκ τοῦ οὐρανοῦ καταβάς in both). It is probable that both the sayings (6: 27 and 6: 53), and not only the second one, come from a pre-Johannine eucharistic discourse,[1] and consequently that this earlier homily is not to be confined to verses 53–8,[2] but that these two sayings occupied approximately its beginning and its climax respectively, as they do in the discourse constructed by the evangelist.[3] Verse 51c ("and the bread which I shall give for the life of the world is my flesh") is a Johannine paraphrase of the first word of institution,[4] but it was suggested by the saying about the flesh and blood of the Son of man in verse 53.

Of all the Johannine Son of man sayings these two are the most un-synoptic. The intrusion of the Son of man concept into a eucharistic context in the homiletical tradition reflected in them is a radical departure. But it is explained by the importance attached by the evangelist to the Son of man Christology he found in his tradition, an importance further emphasized by his introduction of the second saying (6: 53) with the solemn asseveration of Jesus, "Verily, verily, I say to you". In this tradition, familiar in the community to which the evangelist belonged, the main articles of the kerygma about Jesus were expressed in terms of the Son of man.[5] Further, if it is unambiguously clear in 6: 53 that the Son of man is Jesus, this is because the hearers of the homily are reminded of the question they were asked before being baptized, "Do you believe in the Son of man?" (9: 35). Jesus is the object of belief as the Son of man. The two closely related sayings in 6: 27 and 6: 53 express

[1] Cf. Schulz 116, n. 3.
[2] As by Jeremias, op. cit. [1960], 101, 102, 130.
[3] B. Gärtner, *John 6 and the Jewish Passover, Coniectanea Neotestamentica* xvii (1959), 24n., 26–29, has emphasized the close connection between verses 51c–58 and the preceding section of the discourse by pointing out resemblances between the whole discourse and the Jewish Passover Haggadah, and especially the occurrence of the four questions (verses 28, 30f., 42, 52), the last of which comes in the disputed section (verses 51c–58), corresponding to questions of a similar type in the Haggadah.
[4] Cf. Bernard, op. cit. (above, p. 163, n. 3), clxxff.; Dodd, *Interpretation* 338; Jeremias, op. cit. (1960), 101f.
[5] See above, p. 155.

the eucharistic faith of the church as it speaks through the words of the crucified, exalted, and glorified Son of man.

John 6: 62. "Then what if you were to see the Son of man ascending where he was before?"

Jesus now addresses some among the disciples. The "hard saying" (verse 60) to which they object refers especially, but not quite exclusively,[1] to the climactic portion (verses 51c, 53–8) of the discourse, to the initial statement of which (verse 51c) the Jews have already objected (verse 52). The two statements that follow, first about the ascent of the Son of man, and then about the Spirit ("It is the spirit that gives life, the flesh is of no avail; the words that I have spoken to you are spirit and life. But there are some of you that do not believe"), explain how his words are to be understood. It is a spiritual eating that is meant, and correspondingly the Son of man is not Jesus of Nazareth, but the Son of man who came down from heaven and has returned there.

The following considerations show the secondary character of this saying as compared with 3: 13.

(a) In 3: 13 ἀναβαίνειν means only the ascent of the Son of man, whereas here it must be implied that this ascent to heavenly glory, which will cause offence, takes place through his death (which is also his exaltation). This meaning is strictly secondary, however, and is derived from ὑψωθῆναι in 3: 14, originally a saying independent of the preceding one to which the evangelist has attached it. This is supported by the sole remaining instance of ἀναβαίνειν in a theological sense in the Fourth Gospel, namely 20: 17, where the crucified and risen Jesus says, "I have not yet ascended to the Father".

(b) The words "where he was before" allude to the descent of the Son of man *from heaven* (3: 13).

(c) The prospective outlook is secondary to the retrospective viewpoint of the earlier passage from the evangelist's tradition. Here he is writing himself and utilizing the idea of ascent in the tradition, just as the viewpoint is prospective also in 20: 17.

(d) The close parallelism with 7: 38f. "He who believes in me, as the scripture has said, Out of his heart shall flow rivers of living water. And this he said about the Spirit, which those

---

[1] Cf. Thüsing 261f.

who believed in him were to receive; for the Spirit was not yet given, because Jesus was not yet glorified."

6: 62, the ascent is still in the future; cf. 20: 17, οὔπω γὰρ ἀναβέβηκα;	7: 39, οὐδέπω ἐδοξάσθη;
6: 63, the operation of the Spirit comes after the ascent of the Son of man; 6: 64a;	7: 39, the gift of the Spirit is still in the future, to come after the glorification of Jesus; 7: 38, the necessity of faith.

It is hardly too much to say that 6: 62–64a is another version, in terms of the Son of man, of the section in the seventh chapter. We have noted the influence of 3: 13 ("No one has ascended into heaven but he who descended from heaven, the Son of man") in the eucharistic discourse (verses 33, 51). We now see it also in the explanation of the meaning of the discourse.

John 12: 23. "The hour has come for the Son of man to be glorified."

The word "glorify" (δοξάζειν)[1] is thoroughly Johannine. In contrast to the word "exalt" (ὑψοῦν), which he confines to the Son of man, the evangelist uses it in other connections as well. Jesus says that the Father is glorified (14: 13; 15: 8); that the Father (8: 54) or the Spirit of truth (16: 14) glorifies him; and that the Son of God is glorified through the sickness of Lazarus (11: 4). Elsewhere, however, the word includes the meaning of death, with Jesus as the subject, both in comments by the evangelist (7: 39; 12: 16), and in words attributed to Jesus (17: 1). So closely knit has become the idea of the death of Jesus as glorification (of himself and of the Father, 17: 1), that even his prophecy that Peter would be crucified is described by the evangelist in the same way. "This he said to show by what death he was to glorify God" (21: 19).[2] In both the passages (12: 23; 13: 31f.) where the Son of man is glorified, δοξάζειν has this twofold meaning. It therefore resembles ὑψοῦν. But there is also a notable difference. The former word does not

---

[1] On the idea of glorification see W. Grossouw, "La glorification du Christ dans le quatrième évangile", *L'Évangile de Jean* (*Recherches Bibliques* iii, 1958), 131–45.

[2] τοῦτο δὲ εἶπεν σημαίνων ποίῳ θανάτῳ δοξάσει τὸν θεόν; cf. 12: 33, τοῦτο δὲ ἔλεγον σημαίνων ποίῳ θανάτῳ ἤμελλεν ἀποθνήσκειν.

specify the mode of death, but the latter does. This is because ὑψοῦν is a translation of the Aramaic word denoting both exaltation and crucifixion. But δοξάζειν has no such background. This difference makes it likely that the use of "glorify" in the Fourth Gospel is secondary.

Like ὑψοῦν, however, δοξάζειν seems to have belonged to the language of the kerygma. "The God of Abraham and of Isaac and of Jacob, the God of our fathers, glorified his servant Jesus" (Acts 3: 13). "So also Christ did not glorify himself to be made a high priest, but he who said to him, Thou art my Son, today I have begotten thee; as he says also in another place, Thou art a priest for ever, after the order of Melchizedek" (Heb. 5: 5f.). It is true that δόξα was used of the glorious office of the high priesthood,[1] but here it is not limited in this way. There is also Luke 24: 26, "Was it not necessary that the Christ should suffer these things and enter into his glory?" This is a somewhat Lukanized form of the idea of glorification.[2]

In the discussion of John 3: 14 it was suggested that that pre-Johannine saying already referred in its Aramaic form both to the exaltation, as in the early preaching about Jesus, and to the death of the Son of man by crucifixion. This dual sense of ὑψοῦν is, therefore, not the invention of the evangelist, but he has developed it in the other passages where he uses the term. But δοξάζειν cannot have had the same history nor a second meaning in its pre-Johannine use. The resemblance between John 3: 14 and Luke 24: 26, both referring to divinely ordained necessity, is balanced by the no less important distinction that in John 3: 14 a single verb embraces the two conceptions of suffering (death) and of glorification in the Lukan passage.

John 12: 23 is thoroughly Johannine.[3] The following verse, introduced by the double amen, refers back to it and explains it as an allusion to death. Possibly the two Johannine passages which associate δοξάζειν with the Son of man are based on a

---

[1] Ecclus. 45: 23, καὶ Φινεὲς υἱὸς Ἐλεαζὰρ τρίτος εἰς δόξαν; 2 Macc. 14: 7, τὴν προγονικὴν δόξαν, λέγων δὲ τὴν ἀρχιερωσύνην. Cf. J. Héring, *L'épître aux Hébreux* (1954), 52.

[2] H. Conzelmann, *The Theology of Saint Luke* (1960), 203, n. 2, decides that the glory is already the possession of the risen, but not yet ascended and exalted, Christ; cf. John 3: 14.

[3] The first four words, "glorify", and cf. p. 165, n. 5 above.

separate stratum of a Son of man tradition. But it is much more likely that the evangelist has adopted the earlier use of this word for the glorification of Jesus, and has himself given it the second meaning of death, in reference to the Son of man, on the analogy of ὑψοῦν. His use of it in non-Son of man contexts supports this view.[1]

Finally, in contrast to John 3: 14, the present saying cannot be classed as of the synoptic type, for no synoptic passage refers to the glorification of the Son of man.

John 13: 31f. "Now is the Son of man glorified, and God is glorified in him; if God is glorified in him, God will also glorify him in himself, and immediately he will glorify him."

The omission of these verses (from 31, νῦν ἐδοξάσθη) would cause no break in the sense, and they may therefore be an intrusion. It has even been suggested that they are a pre-Johannine hymn about the Son of man.[2] Their rhythmical structure has often been noted, but this can be exaggerated and is greatly reduced if the words "if God is glorified in him" (verse 32a) do not belong to the original text. Comparison of the ideas in this passage with others in the gospel is no more favourable than in the case of the preceding one to a pre-Johannine origin. There the evangelist has borrowed the earlier use of δοξάζειν for the glorification of Jesus, and has given it a second meaning on the analogy of ὑψοῦν. In 13: 31f., however, this double meaning only comes in the first occurrence of the word, "Now is the Son of man glorified". Here lies the importance of the "now" (νῦν).[3] In 12: 23, "the hour has come" is not quite the same as "now". In 13: 31 not only has the hour drawn near and become imminent, it is *now*, and the

---

[1] As with ὑψοῦν (see above, p. 163, n. 2) the Johannine use of δοξάζειν is not likely to have been suggested by Isa. 52: 13 (LXX). This holds good despite the allusion to Isa. 52: 13 in Acts 3: 13, ἐδόξασεν τὸν παῖδα αὐτοῦ Ἰησοῦν. But the analogy would have been facilitated by the fact that the two verbs are practically synonymous: Isa. 52: 13; *Test. Joseph* 10. 3, ὑψοῖ καὶ δοξάζει; cf. also Ps. 36 (37): 20; Isa. 4: 2. The corresponding nouns may also be synonymous, Isa. 35: 2, καὶ ὁ λαός μου ὄψεται τὴν δόξαν κυρίου καὶ τὸ ὕψος τοῦ θεοῦ (kindly pointed out to me by the Bishop of St. Davids, Dr. J. R. Richards).

[2] Schulz 121f., sees a Jewish Christian adaptation of the glorification of the Elect One (= the Son of man) by the Lord of spirits in 1 En. 51: 3.

[3] Contrast οὔπω, 7: 39.

Son of man is already glorified. Jesus as the Son of man speaks retrospectively of his death which is his glorification. Not only is he glorified, but God is glorified in him. This is exactly the same thought as in 17: 1, "Father, the hour has come; glorify thy Son that the Son may glorify thee", only now the word of Jesus is prospective. "The hour has come" (cf. 12: 23) for the glorification of the Son. The future tenses in 13: 32[1] must denote an aspect of the glorification of the Son of man not included in the past tense in the preceding verse. Glorification is something more even than the death of the Son of man in obedience to the end. Here again we must compare chapter 17. "I glorified thee on earth, having accomplished the work which thou gavest me to do" (17: 4). While this work includes the whole ministry of Jesus, it is completed in the passion.[2] This is equivalent to 13: 31, "and God is glorified in him". Similarly, 17: 5, "And now, Father, glorify thou me in thy own presence with the glory which I had with thee before the world was", is parallel to 13: 32, "God will glorify him in himself, and immediately he will glorify him".[3] The only new feature, as compared with 17: 1, 4f., is the statement, "and immediately he will glorify him". But this emphatic "and immediately" is necessitated by the νῦν ἐδοξάσθη (13: 31). If that is *now*, what remains to complete the glorification cannot be long delayed, but must take place at once.[4] This is the resurrection, not only in itself, but as exaltation to incomparable glory in the presence of God.[5] All this is in entire accord with the expression of early belief that "God glorified his servant Jesus" (Acts 3: 13).[6]

What is said of the Son in chapter 17, therefore, is said of

---

[1] The first clause of 13: 32 (εἰ ὁ θεὸς ἐδοξάσθη ἐν αὐτῷ) is omitted by P⁶⁶ ℵBDW it sys, probably correctly (cf. Barrett, *John* 376). Lagrange, op. cit. (above, p. 167, n. 1), 365f., admits the strength of the case for omission, but decides that it is due to homoioteleuton, since there seems to be no reason why the words should have been added; cf. also Thüsing 235. The addition, if such it is, could be an attempt to provide a link between the two groups of aorist and future tenses.

[2] With 17: 4, ἐπὶ τῆς γῆς, cf. 12: 32, ἐκ τῆς γῆς.

[3] That ἐν αὐτῷ is intended is certain; for the sense cf. 17: 5, παρὰ σεαυτῷ.

[4] εὐθύς therefore is the same as νῦν in 17: 5.

[5] Cf. Lagrange, op. cit., 367; H. Strathmann, *Das Evangelium nach Johannes* (1955), 204f.

[6] The fourth evangelist agrees that this glorification does not await a parousia. Also the Servant Christology in John is subsumed under that of the Son of man, cf. Dodd, *Scriptures* 92f.

the Son of man in our passage. In both the Son (or the Son of man) is not only glorified himself, but his glorification involves that also of the Father (or God). In 13: 31f. we have a composition of the evangelist in which the thought of glorification is associated with the Son of man, and is expressed in a quasi-poetical form as a solemn introduction to the farewell discourses. Jesus speaks for the last time in this gospel as the Son of man. In this way the evangelist seeks to convey to his readers the central meaning of the passion he is about to record.

This second group of sayings stands out quite clearly from the other, although this is not to say that there are no resemblances between them. Although the idea of ascent and descent in 3: 13 appears to be reminiscent of the ascending and descending angels in 1: 51, it seems rather to be a matter of different kinds of association of the Son of man with this idea in two separate strands of the pre-Johannine tradition. But the passages are alike in that both concern the heavenly glory of the Son of man. 6: 27 and 6: 53, however, express ideas which are totally absent from the synoptic group. Of the remaining passages, 6: 62 is based by the evangelist on the older saying in 3: 13, and is not traditional material. Neither are the two sayings about the glorification of the Son of man (12: 23; 13: 31f.). These are constructions of the evangelist, who has given the word δοξάζειν its double meaning on the analogy of ὑψοῦν.

The encroachment of non-synoptic conceptions on synoptic ones does not amount to very much. In the category of synoptic-type sayings the non-synoptic features, namely, the ascent and descent of the angels (1: 51) and the association of the idea of exaltation with the Son of man (3: 14), are an enhancement of the Son of man rather than an intrinsically different picture. In the second category the divergence from synoptic tradition is greater. But this does not mean that this branch of tradition is necessarily inferior. In both groups the hand of the evangelist has been at work, even to the extent of composing sayings, whether on the pattern of those in his tradition (8: 28; 12: 34 based on 3: 14; 6: 62 based on 3: 13), or as analogies to a saying in different terminology (12: 23; 13: 31f.). Not only Jewish apocalyptic, but Hellenistic thought has been operative in the milieu from which the sayings came. This is clearest in 3: 13, where the Son of man who came down from heaven strongly resembles "the man from heaven" in 1 Cor. 15: 47. Nevertheless, the main background of thought even here is more probably early Christian usage than imported Hellenistic ideas. Again, the fact that the two sayings which bring together the Son of man and the eucharist are quite unparalleled, does not imply the inferiority of the category to which they belong, but only that the "Johannine" colouring is more prominent.[1]

In some cases (1: 51; 3: 14) a saying is preserved in a form expanded from its original kernel in order to fit the context. The sayings are isolated units, scattered about in an apparently haphazard fashion, and then only in the first part of the gospel (chapters 1–13). But the manner of their distribution is less important than the fact that taken together, and exclusive of the evangelist's own compositions (6: 62; 8: 28; 12: 23; 12: 34; 13: 31f.), they cover the incarnation (3: 13), death (3: 14), ascent into heaven (3: 13), exaltation (3: 14), and judicial functions (5: 27) of the Son of man. One can only conjecture as to the extent of the source of which we have only these fragmentary extracts.

It cannot be claimed that the tradition used in the Fourth Gospel sheds any fresh light on the problem of Jesus and the Son of man. But it does support the view that the Son of man was the basic Christology of the early church, and perhaps it was nowhere valued so highly as in the Johannine communities which introduced it into eucharistic worship. Also, as nowhere in the synoptics, the Son of man is pre-existent,[2] like the Logos

---

[1] These conclusions are the consequence of findings concerning the structure of the sayings which differ at some important points from those of Schulz. Schulz 123 assigns the sayings from the evangelist's tradition to three literary *Gattungen*; midrash (1: 51; 3: 13–15; 5: 27–29), homily (6: 27, 53), and hymn (13: 31f.). But of these only the homily is to be accepted. The so-called hymn I have ascribed to the evangelist himself. In 1: 51 the place of Gen. 28: 12 is at the most secondary, perhaps even non-existent. The reference to the story of Moses and the serpent (Num. 21: 8f.) in 3: 14 only came in at a secondary stage in the formation of the present form of the saying; and in 5: 27–29 only the first verse is derived from the tradition.

[2] John 3: 13; 6: 62; cf. Mowinckel 447f.

of the prologue and Jesus in Pauline thought (Phil. 2: 6f.). Moreover, the Johannine tradition, although failing to make any positive contribution to the problem of Jesus and the Son of man, agrees with the other gospel traditions in providing no sure evidence that Jesus spoke of himself as the Son of man, either in his involvement in his earthly ministry, or in regard to his approaching passion. The traditional Johannine Son of man sayings have as their subject, in varying terminology, the exalted and glorified Son of man. This aspect has its roots in the teaching of Jesus himself, alongside the conception of the parousia which, while less prominent in his teaching than is often supposed, cannot be dismissed entirely as the expression of an early Christian belief with no basis in that teaching. The difference from the synoptics is that the glory *of the Son of man* is nowhere connected with the parousia, but only with his exaltation to the right hand of God,[1] as in the early preaching, with the further important distinctions, however, that this exaltation is not only the consequence of his passion, but a part of it, and that his glory is the pre-existent glory of the pre-existent Son of man, which he now resumes on his return from earth to heaven (John 17: 5, cf. 12: 41).

It seems clear that the Johannine Son of man tradition is of Palestinian origin. This agrees with other features of the Fourth Gospel which suggest that the evangelist had access to reliable historical traditions.[2] The Son of man tradition used and adapted by the evangelist is a remarkable phenomenon. The circles in which it arose had so developed the Son of man Christology as to have bridged the gap which, as is evident in the synoptics, existed in Jesus' own teaching between his

---

[1] Cf. Dieckmann, op. cit., 247: "Die Erhöhung und Verherrlichung, von der Johannes spricht, schildern die Synoptiker konkret in den Parusiereden Jesu."

[2] See my book, *The Historicity of the Fourth Gospel* (1960). It may be added that the Son of man sayings all occur, with two exceptions, in the Aramaizing sections of the gospel as distinguished by C. F. Burney (see the discussion by T. W. Manson in *Studies in the Gospels and Epistles* (1962), 115ff.). Aramaic features are to be expected in the sayings derived directly from the evangelist's tradition (3: 13f.; 5: 27; 6: 27, 53; 9: 35), and also in those members of the secondary group (6: 62; 8: 28; 12: 34) based on them. The use of the verb "glorify" itself in 12: 23 in this group is, as we have seen, not an Aramaism. Of the exceptions, 1: 51 can hardly be excluded from the sections with Aramaisms. The absence of Aramaisms from 13: 31f. corresponds to our findings on the composition of these verses.

references to his passion and resurrection and his allusions to the Son of man as the heavenly witness and eschatological judge. In the synoptics also, of course, the *church* believes in Jesus as himself the vindicated and exalted Son of man. But the Johannine form of the tradition represents Jesus as, so to speak, himself bridging this gap by speaking of his own exaltation as the Son of man. In this way the Johannine Jesus expresses the church's faith in him as the Son of man in whom alone salvation is to be found.

Chapter 8

JESUS AND THE SON OF MAN

1. *The sources tabulated*

No reference is made here to the Fourth Gospel because, as we have seen, it makes no positive contribution to the problem of Jesus and the Son of man. The references to probably authentic sayings or those directly derived from such are printed in italics, and an asterisk indicates a saying probably based on an I-word. References in square brackets are to editorial formulations.

A. *Earthly activity of the Son of man*

MARK	Q	LUKE	MATTHEW
2: 10	Luke 6: 22 (par. Matt. 5: 11)	19: 10	[13: 37]
2: 27f.	Luke 7: 34*=Matt. 11: 19*		[16: 13]
	Luke 9: 58=Matt. 8: 20		
	Luke 12: 10=Matt. 12: 32		

. *Sufferings of the Son of man*

MARK	Q	LUKE	MATTHEW
8: 31		[17: 25]	[26: 2]
9: 12		22: 48	
9: 31		24: 7	
10: 33f.			
10: 45*			
14: 21*			
14: 41			

C. *Glory of the Son of man*

MARK	Q	LUKE	MATTHEW
8: 38	Luke *11: 30* (par. Matt. 12: 40)	*17: 22*	10: 23
9: 9	Luke *12: 8* (par. Matt. 10: 32)	[17: 30]	[13: 41]
13: 26	Luke 12: 40=Matt. 24: 44	18: 8b	[16: 27]
14: 62	Luke *17: 24* (par. Matt. 24: 27)	21: 36	[16: 28]
	Luke *17: 26* (par. Matt. 24: 37)		19: 28
			24: 30
			[24: 39b]
			25: 31

2. *Consideration of results*

There is not a single saying in A which can be claimed as an authentic utterance of Jesus, and only one (Luke 7: 34 = Matt. 11: 19) which may be presumed to have a direct dominical basis. Group B has two sayings built upon words of Jesus (Mark 10: 45; 14: 21). Sayings of this group are mostly in Mark, and the two (both in Luke) which are not merely editorial reflect the Markan theme of the betrayal or delivering up of the Son of man. Q has no sayings of this category at all, but has four important sayings of group A. These characteristics of Q are of great importance. Equally significant is the presence in Q of several sayings of group C with a very strong claim to authenticity. It has been remarked earlier[1] that the complete absence from Q (a sayings-collection) of sayings about the passion and resurrection of the Son of man is evidence of the unauthenticity of such sayings in Mark (and Luke), in addition to the results of examination of each of them in turn. The phenomena of Q really constitute the key to the problem of the complete absence from all the sources of genuine Son of man sayings of groups A and B along with the presence of authentic words, in Mark and Luke as well as in Q, of group C.

In Mark 8: 38 the Son of man is counsel for the prosecution, but in 14: 62 the judge. Q presents a different atmosphere, for it has nothing about the Son of man coming in glory with the angels or with the clouds of heaven, features which understandably prevent many critics from adopting a positive attitude to these two sayings. Despite their importance, however, and the interpretations of them suggested earlier, it is the Q sayings which are of decisive significance. Even if the suggestion that in Mark the Son of man is portrayed now as witness, now as judge is considered improbable, it is difficult to avoid such an interpretation of the Q sayings.

Apart from the probability that in Luke 11: 30, a notoriously difficult passage, the Son of man is the eschatological judge, there is Luke 17: 24, where the idea of the day of the Son of man[2] is bound to include that of judgement. In Luke 12: 8, however, it is equally plain that the Son of man is an advocate

[1] Above, p. 133.
[2] Which also stood originally in verses 22 and 26; see above, pp. 82ff.

Luke 19: 10, they are confined to Mark and Q, for both the examples in Matthew (13: 37; 16: 13) are editorial. The clue to the relationship between the Q sayings of group A and those in group C is provided by Mark 2: 10 and 2: 28. Both of these are Christological affirmations intended to justify church practice—absolution of sins and reduced emphasis on the Jewish sabbath—by appeal to the authority of Jesus during his earthly ministry who now, as the risen, glorified, and exalted Lord, the Son man, has received from the Father full authority over his church. The passages show how the church early came in retrospect to interpret the ministry of Jesus as in fact, for those who knew the truth, the activity of the Son of man. For outsiders, however, this divine activity of the heavenly Son of man in the life and ministry of Jesus of Nazareth was veiled, and to the post-resurrection generation of Jews it was incomprehensible. At the same time, the somewhat meagre Markan material shows how the church was able simulta- neously to preserve Jesus' own distinction between himself and the Son of man (Mark 8: 38; 14: 62). The Q material, how- ever, is both more extensive and more valuable. There, as we have seen, the Son of man is again either witness or judge, and in Luke 12: 8 the distinction between Jesus and the Son of man is at its clearest. Such a distinction could not possibly have been invented by Christians, but must stem from Jesus himself. Here we find virtual proof that the Q sayings of group A, like Mark 2: 10 and 2: 28, cannot be the words of Jesus, but like them are expressions of faith in the exalted Jesus Christ the Lord as the Son of man to whom he alluded. Both the Markan sayings are solemn pronouncements on the status and authority of the Son of man. The Q sayings of group A must be understood in the light of these, and also in comparison with the sayings of group C.

Luke 6: 22: persecution not only for the sake of the man Jesus, but for the sake of the risen Christ exalted to the status of Lord of the church and Son of man. It is precisely because Jesus Christ as the Son of man is the Lord of the church that Christians can expect persecution. The hope of blessedness is guaranteed by the promise of eschatological reward made by Jesus himself, for in the belief of the church the one who made this promise is the same one who will see to its fulfilment, the Son of man who now in heaven acknowledges those who accepted him on earth.

Luke 7: 34 = Matt. 11: 19. Although based on an utterance of Jesus, this saying in its present form has become a Christological expression of faith in Jesus, the Son of man. This generation in rejecting Jesus has done something far more serious than that. In rejecting him it has rejected the Son of man himself, whose activity on earth it failed to discern in the ministry of Jesus.

Luke 9: 58 = Matt. 8: 20: a Christological affirmation of faith in the risen Christ as glorified and exalted to the status of Son of man. The outcome of Jesus' ministry was rejection, but rejection not only of Jesus of Nazareth, but of the Son of man. The thought is not far distant from that in the prologue of the Fourth Gospel, where he who was not received by his own countrymen (John 1: 11) was the Logos.

Luke 12: 10 = Matt. 12: 32 characterizes Jewish opposition to the church and its faith as blasphemy against the Lord of the church, the Son of man.

All four sayings are closely related variations on a common theme—Jewish opposition to the church, and therefore to its Lord, the exalted Son of man. Briefly stated, they concern persecution for the sake of the Son of man (Luke 6: 22), rejection of the Son of man (Luke 7: 34 par.; 9: 58 par.), blasphemy against the Son of man (Luke 12: 10 par.). The two Markan sayings also reflect the same Jewish opposition as it was directed against specific aspects of the church's life, namely, the claim to forgive sins and the claim that the sabbath was now subordinate in importance to the Lord's day. The answers to both criticisms take the form of appeal to the authority of the Son of man.

The church, however, did not import into the A sayings the features of the Son of man in those of group C.[1] They contain no references to the Son of man as the heavenly advocate or judge, nor to the day of the Son of man, nor to his parousia, because their setting is the earthly ministry of Jesus. Nevertheless the same Son of man is meant. This constitutes the essential unity of the conception of the Son of man in Q. This also

[1] Cf. Tödt 249: "Die transzendenten Eigenschaften des kommenden Menschensohnes wurden nicht auf Jesu irdisches Tun übertragen."

applies, of course, to Mark, but less satisfactorily, because Mark 8: 38 is less valuable than Q (Luke 12: 8f.), and Q, unlike Mark, is not complicated by predictions of the passion and resurrection of the Son of man. The earthly activity of Jesus in the A category of sayings relating to the conviction of the unique status and authority of the Lord Jesus Christ as the glorified and exalted Son of man, which inevitably aroused Jewish opposition, as Jesus' own attitude to aspects of Jewish religion had provoked hostility to his ministry, is viewed as transcending past historical events. It is seen *sub specie aeternitatis*. Post-resurrection faith identified the Son of man, to whom Jesus appeared to refer as the eschatological advocate or judge, with Jesus of Nazareth himself. The ministry of Jesus among men was felt to be nothing less than the veiled activity of the Son of man, on whose present and future activity the church based its claims to authority and its hopes for the future.

There remains the total absence of any predictions of the passion and resurrection of the Son of man which can be attributed to Jesus. If our detailed analysis of the sayings in group B and its conclusions need any corroboration, it is to be sought in two directions. Firstly, in the study of Q it was urged[1] that the complete lack of any sayings of this type in Q, primarily a collection of sayings of the Lord, is *prima facie* evidence of the unauthenticity of such sayings elsewhere. Secondly, if the conclusion is correct that Jesus referred to the Son of man as if to another figure and then only in connection with the future, and did not call himself the Son of man in any allusion to the circumstances of his ministry on earth, it is impossible to believe that he could have spoken of his death and resurrection in terms of the Son of man.

At this point we may summarize the relationship between the three categories of sayings and their probable chronological order of development.

The starting point is to be found in genuine references by Jesus to the future activity of the Son of man. Of major importance are those in Q in their Lukan form. That the line of demarcation leading to more and more interpretation is the resurrection of Jesus appears in the replacement of the "day" of

[1] Above, p. 133.

the Son of man in Luke 17: 24, 26 by his "parousia" in Matt. 24: 27, 37. Matthew combines with the Son of man concept the idea of the parousia of the Lord which must have arisen very early, since Paul uses it in 1 Thess. 4: 15.

The coexistence within the same sources (especially in Q) of sayings of this type and sayings describing the earthly activity of the Son of man presents no difficulty, because the latter are Christological statements about the exalted Son of man, and they could well have developed side by side with the secondary sayings of group C in Q and Mark. Since Matthew displays a particular interest in the apocalyptic aspects of the Son of man, we have to reckon with degrees of development varying at different times and with the interests of different Christian communities.

It is generally agreed that the recorded predictions of the passion and resurrection of the Son of man are a secondary development because they first appear in Mark and are rarely found in Luke and Matthew. But it would be a mistake to place all the Markan sayings of group B on the same level. Two of them, 10:45 and 14:21, have strong claims to a dominical basis.

I made some reference at the *end* of chapter 1 to the connection between the Son of man tradition and the passion narrative. I doubt whether the latter as such was a very powerful factor in the development of the passion predictions in group B, save in regard to some details. Certainly the Son of man tradition has not entered the actual passion narrative in any of its forms. Jesus speaks as the Son of man for the last time on the *threshold* of the passion story. In John 13: 31f. this is after the departure of Judas from the supper; in Mark 14: 41 it is immediately before the arrival of Judas and the arrest; in Luke 22: 48 Jesus addresses Judas himself after his kiss of betrayal. The sayings of group B are all, broadly speaking, *prophetic* of the passion. They *point to* the passion, right up to the actual opening of the final drama. But they do not enter it. The sayings, therefore, are the fruit of reflection on the significance of Jesus' death and resurrection as the experience of him who had been exalted to the dignity of the Son of man.

3. *The implications of these results*

The implications are both negative and positive.

I. Negative implications

If the conclusions reached are correct, that Jesus called himself the Son of man neither in his earthly ministry nor in predictions of his death and resurrection, but only alluded to the Son of man as if to a heavenly advocate, witness, or judge, it follows that a vast amount of speculation on this important topic has been conducted on incorrect lines. If, as I am inclined to believe, this is in fact the case, the root cause has often been an insufficiently critical appraisal of the relevant texts, resulting in a bewilderingly wide variety of views, most of which, it is suggested, come to grief through failure to take seriously the possibility that Jesus never used the title Son of man as a self-designation. It is with understandable reluctance that I venture to differ from eminent predecessors in this field, and am impelled by what I take to be the evidence of the texts to abandon widely accepted assumptions. The outcome, however, is by no means all loss. On the contrary. As I shall try to show in section II, the conclusions actually provide the material for a positive and valuable assessment of Jesus' consciousness of his own status and his mission. In the present section it will be sufficient to indicate briefly the deficiencies of the current main solutions of the Son of man problem in the gospels.[1]

The following theories, then, are rendered untenable if these studies are on the right lines.

(a) If Jesus did not identify himself as the Son of man, he could neither have himself imported into the conception features derived from the figure of the Suffering Servant and so have regarded himself as a suffering Son of man nor, alternatively, could he have applied to himself already current notions of a suffering and dying Son of man, even if such notions existed in pre-Christian Judaism.

(b) Similarly, it becomes impossible to attribute to Jesus a collective or corporate understanding of the Son of man concept. It has been suggested, to be sure, that such an interpretation may be saved by finding it in parousia sayings which originally may have applied to the elect community as the Son of man, and were only later applied to Christ's second coming.[2]

[1] See also in chapter 1.
[2] V. Taylor, "The 'Son of Man' Sayings relating to the Parousia", ET 58 (1946), 12–15; *The Interpreter's Bible* vii (1951), 118f.; *Mark* 383f.;

But I agree with the verdict of most scholars that there is no really compelling evidence that the undoubted communal element in the teaching of Jesus is anywhere associated with the Son of man concept—and this despite Dan. 7.

(c) Our findings, if correct, would also involve the rejection of the various attempts to account for the supposed application by Jesus to himself of the eschatological concept of the Son of man in relation to his ministry among men. These attempts may be classified in three main categories; but despite differences in detail they are all alike in trying to find an association between the Son of man, which is a messianic figure belonging to the *Endzeit*, and the work of Jesus on earth.

(i) Just as the kingdom of God has still to come in fullness of power, so Jesus, it has been suggested, has still to be the Son of man. In his work on earth, viewed as the kingdom operating in advance of its full coming, he performs proleptically the functions of the eschatological Son of man. In other words, Jesus is the Son of man designate. "The Kingdom and the Son of Man 'spill over' or 'jut out', as it were, on to this side of the cross, yet the cross itself remains the decisive event which sets both in motion."[1] But this theory entails accepting as authentic utterances of Jesus the sayings about the ministry on earth and the passion of the Son of man. The true explanation of the apparent "spilling over" or "jutting out" of the Son of man on to this side of the cross is rather to be found in the retrospective thought of the church as it looked back to the earthly ministry of Jesus, and saw him there in the light of its faith in him as the exalted Son of man to whom he had apparently pointed, as himself that Son of man *already* in his life, ministry, passion and resurrection.

(ii) From another point of view the problem is the coming of Jesus as Son of man before the *Endzeit*. Cullmann[2] finds the solution in the thought of Jesus himself and in his transference of Jewish eschatological ideas into the present. Since the *Endzeit* has already arrived, the eschatological Son of man has also come in Jesus' own person. The validity of this approach

---

The Names of Jesus (1953), 33f.; *The Life and Ministry of Jesus* (1954), 73f.; cf. H. H. Rowley, *The Servant of the Lord* (1952), 81, n. 4; *The Unity of the Bible* (1953), 125, n. 1; *The Relevance of Apocalyptic*³ (1963), 136.
[1] Fuller 107f.   [2] *Christology* 159.

must obviously depend on the acceptance of "Son of man" as Jesus' self-designation, and therefore is subject to the same objections as the preceding view.

(iii) The third variation on this theme connects Jesus' use of the title with the idea of the messianic secret. Since he appeared before the *Endzeit*, the time of the Son of man, he must have regarded himself as the *hidden* Son of man.[1] But this cannot stand if Jesus did not employ the expression except in regard to the future Son of man in all his authority and glory.

(d) Reasons have been advanced in chapter 1 for the rejection of the derivation of the Son of man in the gospels from Ezekiel. To these must now be added the insuperable objection that Jesus' use of the title, so far from being devoid of eschatological associations and being mainly prophetic in content, was wholly directed to the future and was never applied by him to his ministry on earth.[2]

II. Positive implications

In chapter 1 reasons were advanced for the intrinsic improbability that Jesus called himself the Son of man. Subsequent examination of the actual texts confirms this view. Nevertheless the Son of man Christology is of vital importance in the New Testament church because it stems *ultimately* from the use of the term and concept by Jesus himself. Comparison of what he meant by it with the wealth of meaning attached to it by the early church is an excellent illustration of the complex origins of Christology, in the sense that from one point of view the source is certainly Jesus himself, from another it is the primitive church. Thus the *complete* answer here is obviously that the source is not to be sought exclusively either in the one or the other, but in both.[3] The same is true basically of the

---

[1] Théo Preiss, *Le fils de l'homme* (1951), 44f.; Sjöberg 218f.; J. Schniewind, *Das Evangelium nach Markus*⁸ (1958), 55, 120, 174.

[2] At the other extreme, our studies would exclude the possibility that Jesus never used the term Son of man at all, even as if referring to another figure, as held by Vielhauer (see chapter I). Cf. S. J. Case, "The Alleged Messianic Consciousness of Jesus", JBL 46 (1927), 1–19: Jesus did not speak of the Son of man either in reference to himself or, in the third person, to an "already enthroned messianic official", with whom the disciples later would have found it very difficult to identify him.

[3] On the problem of Christological origins see W. Marxsen, *Anfangsprobleme der Christologie* (1960).

Son of God Christology,[1] with the difference that here the Christology in its outward expression originated not in Jesus' own use of a title[2] but in his filial consciousness reflected in the baptism and temptation narratives, and expressed in his customary address to God as Father,[3] not to mention the whole tenor of his teaching which leaves on every reader the impression that he believed he enjoyed a uniquely close relationship to God as Father.

(a) The Servant Ideal

It has become almost axiomatic that Jesus thought of himself as combining in his person and work the ideals of the Suffering Servant in Deutero-Isaiah and the Son of man who appears as a corporate figure in Dan. 7.[4] But if he did not employ the title Son of man as a self-designation and therefore did not believe himself to be a "suffering Son of man", it does not follow that he did not feel himself to be in a very real sense the fulfilment of the Servant ideal in the Servant poems and especially in Isa. 53. If this was so, he could not have thought merely of his sufferings as such and in themselves, but must have applied a redemptive significance to them, because the Servant suffers for others. If Mark 1: 11 is a trustworthy record of his experience at his baptism, he was already conscious of his mission as the Servant (Isa. 42: 1), although it is unlikely that at this early stage he foresaw his passion, especially as the first Servant poem does not depict the Servant as suffering. But basically authentic

[1] On which see now B. M. F. van Iersel, "Der Sohn" in den synoptischen Jesusworten (1961).

[2] Neither the sole synoptic reference (Matt. 27: 43) nor those in John (5: 25; 9: 35 v.l.; 10: 36; 11: 4) are evidence of Son of God as Jesus' self-designation. The title "the Son" is attributed to Jesus especially in the Fourth Gospel, but also in Mark 13: 32 (par. Matt. 24: 36) and in Q (Luke 10: 22, par. Matt. 11: 27); but the form of these synoptic sayings has been influenced by the pre-Johannine Son Christology or something parallel to it; see CJT 202ff.

[3] On Abba see Manson, Sayings 168; V. Taylor, The Person of Christ in New Testament Teaching (1958), 176–80; J. Jeremias in Synoptische Studien [A. Wikenhauser Festschrift] (1953), 86–89; van Iersel, op. cit., 93ff. The remarks of E. Schweizer (in Church Order in the New Testament (1961), 2c, n. 55), are fully justified, in my opinion. ". . . he avoided it [the title Son of God] entirely. All this is not to say that Jesus did not regard himself as Christ, servant of God, and Son of God; but it probably does mean that he consciously refused to have his activity classified under the usual titles."

[4] Cf. e.g. Manson, Son of Man 144.

sayings in the first person represent him as referring meta-
phorically to suffering (Mark 10: 38; Luke 12: 50; 13: 32f.),
and it is in the light of these that the genuine kernels of the
sayings in Mark 10: 45 and 14: 21 should be understood. In
the earlier discussion of these passages it was suggested that
Jesus said respectively something like, "I shall (or "I came to")
give my life as a ransom for many" (cf. Isa. 53: 12), and "I
go (to death)". The full content of his meaning is revealed in
his words over the bread and the cup at the Last Supper.
Therefore the evidence, although not extensive, clearly points
to his having regarded his death as including the fulfilment of
the prophetic ideal of the Suffering Servant, and as possessing
redemptive significance for all who united themselves with him.
But this has nothing to do with the Son of man as a figure of
suffering. Jesus never called himself the Son of man in this or
any other connection.

On earth Jesus believed himself to be God's Son acting as
the Servant of God foretold in prophecy. Only in the heavenly
realm, again as the Son of God, will he perform functions
associated in current Jewish belief with the Son of man. In this
sense alone can it be said that Jesus applied to himself the idea
of the Son of man.[1] So far, therefore, from combining the ideas
of the Servant of God and the Son of man in a unitary conception, he held them separate and distinct.

(b) *Jesus' knowledge of the Son of man belief*

At this point we may perhaps pause and ask, After all, what
proof exists that Jesus knew anything at all about the Son of
man concept in the form assumed throughout this book to
have existed in certain Jewish circles? If I had entertained any
serious doubts on the matter they would have been dealt with
in chapter 1. I only raise the matter here for the sake of com-
pleteness, but more importantly by way of transition to final
conclusions concerning Jesus' estimate of his status and mission.

The only possible literary sources are Dan. 7 and the Similitudes of Enoch. An obvious answer to the question, To which
of them was Jesus indebted? is that it was the former because
his sole explicit allusion in a Son of man saying (Mark 14: 62)
is to Dan. 7: 13, and "we have no good reason to suppose that

---

[1] See further below, section (c).

he was aware of any other Son of Man than the Danielic".[1] But this view is deprived of most of its cogency if the collective interpretation of the synoptic Son of man is abandoned. It is easy to attach too much importance to Mark 14: 62, and consequently to find in the gospels the societary conception present in Dan. 7.

Doubts have been expressed as to the Similitudes as the source of Jesus' usage. They or the Son of man passages within them have sometimes been regarded as Christian interpolations into the Jewish work,[2] and in any case a pre-Christian date has been called in question.[3] It is certainly a curious fact that the extant portions of the Greek text of 1 Enoch contain nothing from chapters 37–71. These hesitations about the Similitudes have been encouraged by the fact that although Aramaic fragments of 1 Enoch have been found among the Qumran writings, once again, as in the case of the Greek, nothing has turned up from this portion of the work. This has been regarded as due not to chance but to the post-Christian date of the Similitudes.[4] The position may be somewhat analogous to the relationship between the Christian[ized] Testaments of

---

[1] Manson, *Son of Man* 143.

[2] The old view of the Christian origin of the Similitudes (A. Hilgenfeld, G. Volkmar; scholars like J. C. K. von Hofmann, H. Weisse, and F. Philippi extended this view to 1 Enoch as a whole; see M.-J. Lagrange, *Le judaïsme avant Jésus-Christ*[3] (1931), 242; E. Sjöberg, *Der Menschensohn im äthiopischen Henochbuch* (1946), 3ff.) is reappearing in some quarters; cf. Fuller 98; J. T. Milik, *Ten Years of Discovery in the Wilderness of Judaea* (1959), 33. Among representatives of the view that the Son of man pericopae are Christian insertions are Lagrange, op. cit., 242ff., and J. Y. Campbell, JTS 48 (1947), 145ff. N. Messel, *Der Menschensohn in den Bilderreden des Henoch* (1922), 4ff., regarded all the Son of man passages either as Christian insertions (chapters 62f.) or as parts of later additions to the Similitudes (69: 26–71: 17), except for 46: 2–4 and 48: 2 where (as Manson, *Teaching* 229, n. 2, concluded independently for the Similitudes as a whole) the Son of man is a corporate symbol for Israel, as in Dan. 7.

[3] Cf. V. H. Stanton, *The Jewish and the Christian Messiah* (1886), 63; G. Dalman, *The Words of Jesus* (1902), 242f.; T. F. Glasson, *The Second Advent* (1945), 60f.; J. Y. Campbell, JTS 48 (1947), 145ff.; Dodd, *Scriptures* 116; *Interpretation* 242f.; Fuller 98. Arguments against this tendency have been brought forward by G. H. P. Thompson ("The Son of Man—Some Further Considerations", JTS n.s. 12 (1961), 203–9), on the ground that Mark 2: 10 and John 12: 32–34 are evidence of first-century belief in the heavenly Son of man as depicted in the Similitudes. But Thompson underestimates the primarily Christological significance of these passages.

[4] Cf. Milik, op. cit., 33: they are a Jewish or Jewish-Christian production of the first or second century.

the Twelve Patriarchs[1] and the portions of the Testaments of Levi and Naphtali, in Aramaic and Hebrew respectively, discovered at Qumran. But it would be premature to accept this view of the Similitudes as proven. Their absence from the Qumran literature may be purely accidental, or perhaps the type of apocalyptic they present did not appeal to the sect.[2] Even if the date of the Similitudes remains uncertain, beliefs about the Son of man resembling those of the book could have been current before and in the time of Jesus, and so could have been known to him.[3] But whatever ideas were known to him were radically transformed in his own employment of the conception. In the Similitudes, broadly speaking, the Son of man is a celestial figure who will judge the wicked, and deliver the righteous. But the conception in Jesus' teaching is characterized by the quite new idea that the attitude of the Son of man in the presence of God depends on a man's acceptance or rejection of Jesus. Further, in Jesus' teaching the Son of man is as much an advocate as a judge.

In any case the importance of Dan. 7 for Jesus' ideas seems to have been exaggerated, because only one passage (Mark 14: 62) alluding to it can be regarded as containing a genuine utterance. Certainly the pre-Christian date of Dan. 7 is, unlike that of the Similitudes, not in doubt; but its real significance is that it is itself evidence of belief in an individual Son of man about 200 B.C., but interpreted in a corporate sense.[4]

The upshot is that if Jesus was acquainted with a belief of this kind he could hardly have regarded himself, a man on earth, as the Son of man and have been sane. His references to the Son of man must all have been directed as if to another than himself. And this is precisely the result to which study of the texts has brought us. Jesus said nothing whatever about

[1] M. de Jonge, *The Testaments of the Twelve Patriarchs* (1953); "Christian Influence in the Testaments of the Twelve Patriarchs", *Novum Testamentum* 4 (1960), 182–235; and *Novum Testamentum* 5 (1962), 311–19.

[2] Cf. Schweizer, *Menschensohn* 194, n. 32, and in JBL 79 (1960), 122, n. 8.

[3] Direct literary dependence on the Similitudes is probable in some unauthentic Matthaean sayings: Matt. 16: 27, the Son of man as judge, cf. 1 En. 62: 5; 69: 27, 29; Matt. 19: 28; 25: 31, "the throne of his glory", cf. 1 En. 45: 3; 55: 4; 61: 8; 62: 2, 3, 5; 69: 27; and for the Son of man's throne see 1 En. 62: 5; 69: 27, 29. John 5: 27 also belongs here.

[4] Mowinckel 352.

himself as the Son of man. He referred to him as if to a future advocate, witness, or judge. He also spoke of his own mission to men and of how it would culminate in his death, to be followed almost immediately by his resurrection. But in his teaching on these matters the idea of the Son of man played no part.

(c) *Jesus and the Son of man*

The problem with which we have been concerned is that of Jesus *and* the Son of man. I do not think that any of the attempts to demonstrate that Jesus thought of himself as the Son of man or as destined to become the Son of man or to be identified with him in the future can be sustained. The problem can only be understood correctly when his *non-identification* with the Son of man is brought into the centre. The crucial passage is Luke 12: 8f.:

"Everyone who acknowledges me before men, the Son of man also will acknowledge before the angels of God; but he who denies me before men will be denied before the angels of God."[1]

Nothing could be clearer than the distinction between Jesus now and the Son of man then.[2] Yet is it possible to speak meaningfully even of Jesus' expectation of a *future* identity with the Son of man,[3] unless he believed in the actual objective existence of such a figure? What is the evidence that he did?

According to Otto, Jesus was so influenced by the ideas in 1 Enoch and current in Galilee, especially concerning Enoch who "would be exalted to become the one whom he had proclaimed",[4] that he viewed his own mission in similar terms as that of the one destined to become the Son of man. Again, E. Sjöberg[5] thinks that 1 En. 70f. portray the elevation of Enoch

---

[1] Cf. Mark 8: 38. In Matt. 10: 32f. (par. to Luke) the Son of man title has been removed through the influence of later equation of Jesus and the Son of man.

[2] T. W. Manson appreciated this, but tried to find support for his societary interpretation of the Son of man as "the Remnant, the true Israel of which Jesus is the head" in the variant "me and mine" (om. λόγους with W k* sa) at Mark 8: 38 (*Sayings* 109). But this text is in any case secondary to Luke 12: 8f., which mentions neither "mine" nor "my words". Moreover, Luke (9: 26) knew the phrase "me and my words" in Mark 8: 38. In Luke λόγους is omitted by D a d e l syc Or.

[3] Cf. J. Héring, *Le royaume de Dieu et sa venue*[2] (1959), 96ff.

[4] R. Otto, *The Kingdom of God and the Son of Man*[2] (1943), 213.

[5] *Der Menschensohn im äthiopischen Henochbuch* (1946), 171, 185f.

to heaven and his identification there with the pre-existent
Son of man. The difficulty of such a process, however, is well-
nigh insuperable, as Sjöberg himself admits.[1] Mowinckel calls
it "inconceivable",[2] and holds rather that in 70f. (originally not
a unity) Enoch is translated *to be with* the Son of man, not *to
be* the Son of man.[3] The fact that both Otto and Sjöberg
regard the Similitudes as a unity certainly increases the difficulty of the idea that Enoch somehow becomes the one he had
proclaimed, or the Son of man he had seen in the earlier
visions. But Mowinckel's own solution is not free from objections. M. Black has suggested[4] that 70f. represent an older tradition in which Enoch *is* the Son of man. Thus he does not
have to *become* the Son of man, much less *be with* him. But if
Jesus was acquainted with this presumed older tradition, there
is not the slightest hint of it in the gospels nor the smallest
suggestion that he identified himself in any way with this
Enoch-Son of man. Moreover, since Enoch in the Similitudes is
probably not to be understood as *becoming* the Son of man, they
provide no pattern for Jesus' supposed expectation that he
would *become* (united with) the Son of man. In short, Jesus
thought neither that he was nor that he would become in some
way the Son of man, in the usually accepted sense of a heavenly
person. His ideas about the Son of man are virtually confined
to his judicial functions. This rules out theories about the "pre-
existent" Son of man so far as the thought of Jesus is concerned.
How could he, with his unexampled consciousness of filial
relationship to God, have believed in the existence of a divine
being with the privileged status of the Son of man alongside
God, and how could he have envisaged his becoming fused or
united with that being? It is not always sufficiently realized,

[1] Op. cit., 187.
[2] Mowinckel 444.
[3] Op. cit., 441.
[4] "The Eschatology of the Similitudes of Enoch", JTS n.s. 3 (1952),
1–10. Three of the Ethiopic manuscripts at 70: 1 explicitly apply the title
Son of man to Enoch, ibid., 4, n. 2. Partly because no trace of the Similitudes has been found among the Qumran literature, whereas all other
chapters of 1 Enoch 1–101 are represented by fragments, Black now allows the
possibility that they are post-Christian, and that the identification of the
Son of man with Enoch may be "post-Christian and derivative" (the new
Peake's Commentary on the Bible (1962), 608d.). I am indebted to Professor
Black for a written statement of his present views on this question.

strange as it may be, that after all the Son of man was never an objective reality, but an idea in the minds of certain Jews.[1]

We return to the paradox that the Son of God Christology arose despite the absence of explicit statements by Jesus that he was God's Son, and that the Son of man Christology arose despite the absence of any claim by Jesus to be the Son of man either now or in the future. The genesis of both Christologies, however, is undoubtedly to be found in the thought of Jesus, only the result is further from that thought in the case of the latter than in that of the former, for Jesus certainly believed God to be his Father in a unique and special sense. The roots of the Son of man Christology are to be found in the crucial passage, Luke 12: 8f. Men's attitude to Jesus here and now on earth determines the attitude of the Son of man to them on the day of reckoning. But the Son of man is neither another figure than Jesus nor a figure with which he is somehow to become identified. In Jesus' thought the Son of man is none other than the Son of God. *The Son of man idea was adapted by Jesus to denote himself as the Son of God he already believed himself to be, reinstalled in his heavenly seat.*[2] *The Son of man is the Son of God exercising his intercessory or judicial functions.* This is tantamount to speaking of "the Son of man" in inverted commas. This thought, it may be observed, is correctly preserved in the Fourth Gospel, where it is the Son who exercises judgement in his capacity as also, in this respect, the Son of man (John 5: 22, 27).[3]

The stages in the growth of the Son of man Christology from this beginning are readily explicable. The first stage, direct identification of the risen and exalted Christ the Lord with the Son of man, was inevitable. If it is objected that this hypothesis involves the attribution to Jesus of easily misunderstood

[1] See the pertinent remarks on this point by J. Knox, *The Death of Christ* (1959), 71f.

[2] It is an over-simplification to say that Rom. 1: 4, echoing a primitive creed, means that "the sonship of Jesus started with his resurrection" (Schweizer, JBL 79 (1960), 123), and to equate sonship too closely with the Lordship to which the primitive church believed Jesus to have been exalted (Acts 2: 36; Rom. 10: 9; 1 Cor. 12: 3; 16: 22, μαρανα). Even the earliest belief seems to have included only a *superficial* adoptionist attitude to Jesus' sonship (cf. C. K. Barrett, *The Epistle to the Romans* (1957), 20), and did not exclude Jesus' possession of sonship already. This becomes more certain if the Christological hymn in Phil. 2: 6–11 is pre-Pauline. In any case this does not affect Jesus' own thought about his sonship.

[3] Cf. above, pp. 165ff.

language which he could have avoided if he had not used the term Son of man, the reply is that this objection is much less weighty than when it is supposed that he used the title more frequently, in referring also to his earthly ministry or to his death and resurrection, or to both. Jesus' use of the Son of man title is in any case one of the most baffling of New Testament problems. But the present suggestions tend to ease the problem. In their favour is the fact that the first stage in the development of this Christology does not go in essentials so very far beyond the thought of Jesus himself. It is only a short step from speaking, as I suggest that Jesus did, of performing Son of man functions in the future to thinking of him, the exalted Lord, as the church soon came to do, as actually the Son of man. It is a matter of transition from his employment of the term Son of man in a functional sense to the church's use of it as a title. Once this step had been taken, it needs no stretch of the imagination to understand how the early church in the course of preaching and teaching came to attribute to Jesus not only other sayings of a similar kind, but also Son of man sayings relating both to his ministry on earth and to his passion and resurrection, in which the Son of man is devoid of his traditional functions, and is the subject and object respectively of actions quite foreign to the Son of man in Jewish thought. Since to Christian faith Jesus had himself become the Son of man in heavenly glory and power through his resurrection from the dead, it was natural in retrospect to describe his death and resurrection as that of the Son of man he had subsequently become and, a stage still further back, to view him in his life and ministry as already the Son of man. The remarkable thing is the reserve of the early church in this respect. This is clearly discernible in the remarkable restriction of the use of the Son of man title in the gospels to Jesus himself, where although it becomes a self-designation in all three categories of sayings, the tradition is preserved that it was Jesus, and Jesus alone, who spoke of the coming and the judicial or intercessory functions of the Son of man. It is seen also in the actual *Christological* content of the sayings in both the categories A and B.

(d) *Jesus and his mission*

The gospels are valuable historical sources for the life of

Jesus. Nevertheless, they must be handled with care. It is asking too much to expect a rigid consistency in the reported words of Jesus, both because of the different and deficient strands of tradition in which they have been handed down, and because he may not have given a complete and self-consistent exposition of the purpose of his mission; at any rate the gospels do not present us with one. In the absence of a systematic *apologia pro vita sua* (if the expression may be allowed), we have to do the best we can with the incomplete and frequently indirect information in the gospels.

Until recently it has been held as almost axiomatic that Jesus combined the concepts of the Suffering Servant of the Lord and the Son of man in such a way that, while never outwardly claiming to be or calling himself the Servant, he infused into the Son of man title and concept the idea of vicarious suffering associated with the Servant. Thus Cullmann writes: "Here again [in Mark 8: 31] he combines the Son of Man title with the idea of the Suffering Servant of God."[1] But analysis of the predictions of the Son of man's passion shows that they are not the words of Jesus, but community creations.

It does not follow from this that the place of the Servant ideal in Jesus' thought must be minimized to the point of extinction. For in place of what I believe to be the discredited attempt to see in his teaching a combination of Suffering Servant and Son of man resulting in a "suffering and dying Son of man", a new orthodoxy is gaining ground according to which the story of Jesus is now to be understood after the pattern of "the humiliation, suffering, and exaltation of the righteous one". I submit that this approach, admittedly justified up to a point, tends to imply a diluted Christology unsupported by the biblical material.

Miss Morna D. Hooker sees no connection between Mark 10: 45[2] and Mark 14: 24[3] and Isa. 53. Yet in fact these two sayings are the very ones which give the strongest evidence for

---

[1] *Christology* 160.
[2] *Jesus and the Servant* (1959), 74–79. C. K. Barrett thinks the saying applies to Jesus as Son of man the theme, familiar in post-Maccabaean Judaism, of the atoning sufferings of the righteous martyrs; see my discussion of the text above, pp. 36ff.
[3] Ibid., 80–83.

the idea of atoning sacrifice in the teaching of Jesus, and both are dependent on Isa. 53.[1] But it is also significant that "the Son of man" is not part of the original word of Jesus in Mark 10: 45.[2] On a wider plane Miss Hooker develops the thesis that neither Jesus nor his followers regarded him as the Suffering Servant of Deutero-Isaiah, and that the primitive church attached much less importance to the Servant passages than is customarily thought. Curiously enough, however, as Jeremias has pointed out in a trenchant review of Miss Hooker's book,[3] the total result "is not so revolutionary as it may seem at first sight", because the emphasis "is only shifted from the 'Servant' to the Son of Man". For she finds the background in the apocalyptic movement and the sufferings of the righteous, culminating in those of Jesus as the Son of man. But here we must call a halt. Referring to Dan. 7, Miss Hooker admits that the Son of man himself does not suffer, and continues: ". . . he is the symbol of the righteous Remnant, the restored people of God, who are at present enduring afflictions: the Son of Man thus represents those who have passed through persecution; the righteous community which is suffering today will tomorrow be the glorified Son of Man." "[But] Jesus realized that the Son of Man himself must suffer with his people, since he alone was the perfectly righteous man; in Jesus we find the consummation of the sufferings of the martyrs."[4] Having got rid of the Servant theme, Miss Hooker without justification attaches to the Son of man concept the quite alien thought of suffering—an association of ideas which we have also found not to be an element in Jesus' own thought.

Two further points may be added.

It is quite true that, even if they were substantially authentic, the Son of man passion predictions in Mark 8: 31; 9: 12; 9: 31; 10: 33f. would be inadequate evidence for the presence of the Servant idea.[5] Our analyses have shown that this is an understatement of the case, for these sayings are not dominical at all.

On the other hand, it is untrue that this "radical" estimate

---

[1] See especially E. Lohse, *Märtyrer und Gottesknecht* (1955), 117ff.
[2] See above, pp. 48f.
[3] JTS n. s. 11 (1960), 140–44.
[4] Op. cit., 160, 162.
[5] Hooker, op. cit., 92ff.

of these sayings means that we must "reject at the same time the idea that Jesus spoke about the meaning of his death at all".[1] The much more important and indeed crucial texts at Mark 10: 45 and 14: 24 are sufficient answer.

Some reference has already been made in chapter 1 to the important contributions of E. Schweizer to the debate. I wish to add here only a few observations.[2]

It is, of course, indisputable that the theme of the humiliated and exalted righteous one is prominent both in later Judaism and in early Christianity.[3] But whether Jesus himself interpreted his mission merely on these lines is another question. Schweizer remarks that the one vital objection to his view is that "the Synoptists speak of the resurrection of Jesus, but very rarely, if at all, of his exaltation".[4] I do not think that he allows sufficient weight to this objection; nor do I believe that the implications of his reasoning (if I understand it correctly) are convincing, namely, that since the early Christian texts outside the synoptics testify to belief in the exaltation of Jesus to Lordship, therefore he did not allude to resurrection from death, but thought of his exaltation from humiliation and degradation. This looks like viewing the thought of Jesus in the light of early beliefs about him.

Jesus foresaw his resurrection.[5] The evidence, though slight, is reinforced by genuine predictions of his passion and death. To a Jew death must be followed by resurrection. Of exaltation as such Jesus said nothing.[6] Rather, what we get is a hiatus. He spoke in metaphorical language of his death (Mark 10: 38; Luke 12: 50; 13: 32f.) as of redemptive significance (Mark 10: 45; 14: 24), and of his resurrection (Mark 14: 28). He also spoke of the activity of the Son of man in heavenly glory as an advocate, and as judge in his "day". This hiatus can be closed (see below); but the link cannot be as Schweizer suggests. He writes:[7] "the verb *paradidosthai* is used so often of the Son of

---

[1] Hooker 93.

[2] For the sake of brevity I here confine my references to Schweizer's more summary treatment in his article "The Son of Man", JBL 79 (1960), 119ff.

[3] On the atoning death of the martyrs and the righteous in late Judaism, see Lohse, op. cit.

[4] Op. cit., 123.　　　　　[5] Mark 14. 28; see above, pp. 56f.

[6] Not even in Mark 14: 62.　　　　　[7] Op. cit., 120f.

man that he must have been said to have been 'handed over' at a very early stage of the tradition. Thus it is probable that Jesus spoke of himself as the Son of man who was to be humiliated and rejected by men, yet exalted by God." I confess my inability to appreciate this argument. Schweizer passes on to the sayings of group A describing the Son of man's humble life on earth, some of which he accepts as dominical. But if they are not, nothing remains in support of the view that Jesus thought of himself in the way Schweizer suggests.

Jesus enjoyed a unique consciousness of sonship to the Father, although he did not call himself the Son or the Son of God, as the church came to do. Believing himself to be God's Son, in his humble life on earth he fulfilled consciously the role of the Suffering Servant, and especially in his death "for many" (Mark 10: 45; 14: 24). He proclaimed the active presence of the kingdom in his words and works, and also its near approach in full power. The lack of association of kingdom and Son of man[1] is not due to his non-use of the title Son of man (Vielhauer), nor to his not directly connecting his mission as Son of man with the coming of the kingdom (Schweizer). He did not think of his mission as that of the Son of man at all.

In his life and ministry he was the Son of God filling the role and actualizing the ideal of the Servant. Response to or rejection of his preaching of the kingdom and confession in or rejection of himself are two aspects of the same thing—acceptance or rejection of the will of God. Acceptance involves incorporation in what came to be known as the body of Christ, but which Jesus must have regarded as but an interim community which would last for the comparatively short time leading up to the end of the present world order. Without ever speaking of his own exaltation Jesus presupposed it in his allusions to the Son of man in heaven confessing or denying those who had confessed or denied himself on earth, or acting as judge. So it is here that the hiatus is closed. The real connection with the kingdom is seen here, for this confessing or

---

[1] Luke 17: 20–22 is only an apparent exception, because at verse 22 there is a change of audience. The saying about the kingdom, if authentic, probably belongs to another context. Mark 9: 1 also does not stand in its original setting following 8: 38.

denying is equivalent to accepting or rejecting the message of the kingdom. As Son of God once again in his rightful place in the presence of God, he performs the functions of the "Son of man", not only as counsel or witness, but also as judge. For if Luke 17: 22–27 has been correctly interpreted,[1] Jesus spoke of the Day (of judgement) of the Son of man as the end and climax of a period—what Matthew in the parallel passage terms the parousia of the Son of man. We are thus not confined to the disputed saying in Mark 14: 62. The apparent inconsistency of the two ideas of witness or advocate and judge has already been noted.[2] This cannot perhaps be fully resolved. Both are described in future tenses. But the day of the Son of man perhaps emphasizes the *climax* of his activity in the presence of God, which will be wound up as a preliminary to the full coming of the kingdom. And Jesus seems to have believed that this consummation was not far distant, and would occur in his own generation (Luke 11: 29f.). Also Luke 12: 8f. seems to imply the same thought as is expressed in the reference to this generation in the less original form of the logion in Mark 8: 38, along with Mark 9: 1, "some of those who stand here".

Jesus' fundamental understanding of his mission thus went far beyond (though it may have included it as a secondary element) the thought of the humiliation and exaltation of the righteous in contemporary Judaism. It was conditioned by a much more profound consideration—the consciousness of his sonship to the Father, Abba. The early church naturally came to explain all that had happened to its Master as the humiliation, death, and exaltation of "Jesus Christ the righteous" (1 John 2: 1). In the authentic synoptic sayings (see the beginning of this chapter), reinforced by the valuable early tradition preserved in Acts 7: 56, the Son of man is portrayed *as already in a state of exaltation* in the presence of God, and as exercising the functions of the supreme witness, or of the judge. We therefore ought not to speak of Jesus as pointing to the eschatological Son of man as to an objective figure distinct from himself, nor as foreseeing his future identity or fusion in some way with that figure, nor as referring to his own exaltation as Son of man from humility and suffering to heavenly glory, but rather as showing the vital soteriological connection between

[1] See above, pp. 82ff. [2] Above, pp. 186f.

his humble life on earth ending in death and subsequent resurrection, and his future activity characterized by the dignity and authority, delegated by God, of the "Son of man".

The Palestinian Johannine tradition concerning the exaltation of Jesus the Son of man is of special importance here as the link in the chain of thought from Jesus' own references in the synoptics to the "Son of man" functions he would perform, to the unanimous New Testament faith in the crucified and risen Jesus as "both Lord and Christ".[1]

[1] Acts 2: 36.

ADDENDA

1. My article in CJT has now appeared in a revised form in *Promise and Fulfilment: Essays Presented to Professor S. H. Hooke*, ed. F. F. Bruce (1963), 128–41.

2. The English translation of Bultmann, *Tradition*, by John Marsh (*The History of the Synoptic Tradition*, 1963), appeared after my manuscript had been sent to the press. Page references (in parentheses) to this translation are as follows: p. 33, n. 2 (152), p. 37 (93, 144), p. 55, n. 2 (259–61, 427f.), p. 84, n. 1 (117), p. 91, n. 2 (175), p. 93, n. 1 (119), p. 124, n. 1 (28, 98), p. 127, n. 1 (131), p. 135, n. 1 (118), p. 136 n. (112), p. 137, n. 1 (113), p. 138, n. 3 (118).

3. J. Jeremias's *The Parables of Jesus*, translated by S. H. Hooke (1954), has appeared in a revised and enlarged form (1963) based on the sixth German edition (1962). Below are given page references (in parentheses) to this new English version.

P. 91, n. 4 (155, now, however, accepting Luke 18: 8b as "an early Son of Man saying"), p. 92, n. 2 (155, abandoning this earlier interpretation of "faith"), p. 93, n. 1 (78, n. 28), p. 97, n. 2 (23, 81, 224ff.), p. 97, n. 3 (81–5), p. 98, n. 3 (79), p. 116, n. 3 (109, n. 82), p. 117, n. 2 (206), p. 122, n. 4 (160, n. 37), p. 122, n. 6 (160, n. 37), p. 135, n. 5 (108), p. 140, n. 4 (50), p. 140, n. 5 (49–51).

4. *Add to chapter 1*, p. 24, n. 5: See now P. Vielhauer in *Zeitschrift für Theologie und Kirche* 60 (1963), 133–77 ("Jesus und der Menschensohn: zur Diskussion mit Heinz Eduard Tödt und Eduard Schweizer").

5. *Add to chapter 4*, p. 97, n. 3: English translation, "End-expectation and Church in Matthew", in *Tradition and Interpretation in Matthew* (1963, translated by Percy Scott from *Uberlieferung und Auslegung im Matthäusevangelium* (1960)), 44.

6. *Add to chapter 6*, p. 144, n. 1: Cf. my paper in NTE, 132, n. 3. N. Perrin, *The Kingdom of God in the Teaching of Jesus* (1963), 99f., finds "evidence that a collective interpretation of 'Son of Man' was to be found in Judaism at the time of Christ" in 1QS 8. 5–8, in which the words "to render the wicked their desert" from Ps. 94: 2, where the reference is to God, are said to be strongly reminiscent of the thought of Dan. 7: 14, where the son of man figure receives "dominion, and glory and a kingdom", and to describe the community as the agent of "the eschatological visitation". Perrin is the most recent writer to attempt a defence of T. W. Manson's collective interpretation of the Son of man in the teaching of Jesus (90–100), but this aspect of the defence would be more convincing if the actual term Son of man were to be found in the Qumran writings.

7. *Add to chapter 8*, p. 201, n. 4: See also his article, "The Son of Man Problem in Recent Research and Debate", *Bulletin of the John Rylands Library* 45 (1963), 305–18.

INDEX OF MODERN AUTHORS

INDEX OF MODERN AUTHORS

213

INDEX OF REFERENCES
OLD TESTAMENT

OTHER SOURCES